Women's Costume
of the Near and Middle East

Women's Costume
of the Near and Middle East

Jennifer Scarce

Unwin Hyman
London Sydney

First published in Great Britain by Unwin Hyman, an imprint
of Unwin Hyman Limited, 1987.

UNWIN HYMAN LIMITED
Denmark House, 37–39 Queen Elizabeth Street, London SE1 2QB
and
40 Museum Street, London WC1A 1LU

Allen & Unwin Australia Pty Ltd
8 Napier Street, North Sydney, NSW 2060, Australia

Allen & Unwin New Zealand Ltd with the Port Nicholson Press
60 Cambridge Terrace, Wellington, New Zealand

British Library Cataloguing in Publication Data

Scarce, Jennifer M.
  Women's costume of the Near and Middle East.
1. Costume —— Middle East —— History
I. Title
391'.2'0956   GT1380
ISBN 0–04–391011–4

Designed by Harold Bartram

Set in 11 on 13 point Palatino by Nene Phototypesetters Ltd
and printed in Great Britain by The Bath Press, Avon

Contents

List of Illustrations

List of Diagrams

Acknowledgements

During the years in which I have been studying costume I have received help and encouragement from both colleagues and institutions. I should like to take the opportunity here to thank them.

Great Britain
Edinburgh, Royal Museum of Scotland: Maxine Ross, Naomi Tarrant, Jane Wilkinson.
London, British Museum, Department of Oriental Antiquities: Dr J. Michael Rogers.
London, British Library, Department of Oriental Printed Books and Manuscripts: J. Losty, Norah Titley.
London: Rodney Searight.
London: Dr Ann Saunders, editor of *Costume*, the Journal of the Costume Society.
London, School of Oriental and African Studies, University of London: Dr Margaret Bainbridge, Professor Victor Menage.
London, Victoria and Albert Museum, Department of Textiles: Pauline Johnstone.

Canada
Toronto, The Royal Ontario Museum, Department of Textiles: the late Dr Veronika Gervers, John Vollmer.

Denmark
Copenhagen, Museum of Decorative Arts: Charlotte Paluden.
Copenhagen, National Museum: Dr Inger Wulff, Henry Harald Hansen.

Germany
Berlin, State Museum of Islamic Art: Professor Dr Klaus Brisch, Dr Johanna Zick-Nissen.
Munich, City Museum.

Hungary
Budapest, Hungarian National Museum.
Budapest, Institute of Art History, Hungarian Academy of Sciences: Dr Ida Bobrovsky.
Budapest, Museum of Decorative Art: Szusza Gombos.

Romania
Bucharest, Museum of Art of the Socialist Republic of Romania.
Bucharest, University of Bucharest: the late Corinna Nicolescu.
Bucharest, Village Museum: Natalia Marcu.
Cluj, Ethnographical Museum of Transylvania: Dr Tiberiu Graur, Constanta Simu.
Cluj, Historical Museum of Transylvania.

Switzerland
Berne, Historical Museum, Henri Moser Collection: Ursula Schmidt.

Turkey
Ankara: Emel Aksoy, Audrey Uzmen.
Istanbul, Topkapı Sarayı Müzesi: Dr Filiz Cağman, Dr Zeren Tanındı, Hülya Tezcan.
Istanbul, University of Istanbul, Department of History of Art: Professor Dr Nurhan Atasoy.

I am also grateful to Janet Fleming and Denise Hood for typing my manuscript, and to Antony Kamm for tactful and constant encouragement.

Introduction

The costume tradition under discussion in this book evolved in an area of such historical and cultural diversity that it defies convenient and precise description. The terms indeed by which Western Europe has attempted to define this area admit to defeat as they are either too wide in meaning or simply inaccurate. The term Orient, for example, may be extended to cover China and Japan and also carries emotive overtones of nineteenth-century romanticism about the 'mysterious East'. The apparently more precise geographical terms of Near East and Middle East are equally unsatisfactory, as they are primarily definitions which originated at the beginning of the twentieth century in response to the interests of increasing European strategic and political involvement which the First World War naturally accelerated. The Near East covered the territories bordering the Mediterranean mainly Syria, Palestine and Egypt. The Middle East, however, while originally defining the Arab and Persian Gulf coastal regions so vital to British communications with India was gradually extended to cover Turkey, Iraq, Persia and those same Mediterranean lands included in the Near East. The ensuing confusion was further complicated by the boundary changes which followed the First World War and by the fact that areas such as the Balkans, North Africa, the Caucasus and Afghanistan which were closely linked culturally were not included.

In view of these ambiguities it is perhaps at least clearer to define the area by listing the names of the modern political states whose boundaries fall within it. Beginning at the extreme west, therefore, are the Balkan states consisting of Jugoslavia, Albania, Greece, Bulgaria and Romania, the Republic of Turkey, Iran equally today still known as Persia, Afghanistan, Iraq, the Mediterranean coastal areas of Lebanon, Syria, Israel and Egypt and, to a lesser extent for the purposes of this book, North Africa and the regions of the Arab peninsula. The extremes of terrain and climate encompass the mountainous plateaus of central Turkey and Persia which alternate between the extremes of winter cold and summer heat, the rich agricultural regions of the Mediterranean extending along the western and southern shores of Turkey through Lebanon and Syria, and the harsh deserts of Arabia.

Such geographical and climatic variation was accompanied by an equal diversity of living conditions from sophisticated urban settlement in both inland and coastal regions usually at strategic points along the major communication routes with access to water and other facilities, to widespread villages of agricultural communities and encampments of nomads whose lives were dictated by the need to migrate to maintain adequate pasture for their flocks and herds.

Concurrent with these long established patterns of living was an impressive historical sequence beginning with highly developed neolithic cultures and continuing through the great civilisations of the valleys of the Nile, Tigris and Euphrates, the distinctive settlements of the plateaus of Turkey and Persia, Greek colonial cities, the empires of Rome and Byzantium, and culminating in the successor states to the Muslim Arabs. Naturally, the ethnic, linguistic and religious composition was infinite, but gradually from the seventh century AD onwards as the Arab conquest advanced something approaching a shared cultural identity is discernible in the spread of Islam which became the majority religion although significant communities of Christians and Jews flourished, while its language Arabic functioned not only as a medium of everyday communication but also as a liturgical language among communities whose native tongues were of Persian, Turkish, Berber, or Slav origin.

Naturally enough the traditions of an area of such range and complexity were mirrored visually in the costumes worn. Any of the great cities such as Istanbul, Cairo, Damascus and Isfahan, for example, presented a remarkable procession of these many costumes as officials mingled with local merchants and craftsmen, the ethnic minorities and visiting foreigners to create a colourful and intense crowd which never failed to rouse wondering comment from European travellers. Within such a display it is all too easy to become submerged, and in the resulting confusion fail to see any common influences and underlying themes. Therefore, to achieve any useful study it is necessary to impose definable limits which provide a practical and disciplined framework; this is especially important as the costume traditions of this area have as yet been inadequately studied so some broad guidelines are essential. Criteria could be based on a range of choices – for example, on garment type, geographical region, urban or rural dress. Historical circumstance has, however, already provided a convenient framework – for six centuries from 1299 to 1923 the area was basically under the domination of the Ottoman Turks. After the emergence of their dynasty from the many Turkish groups which inhabited Anatolia in the thirteenth century following the breakdown of Seljuk power and the increasing weakness of the Byzantine Empire, they steadily expanded and consolidated their domination until, at its height in the mid-sixteenth century, from their capital at Istanbul they ruled an empire extending in the west from Hungary through modern Jugoslavia, Albania, Greece, Bulgaria, Romania and the Crimea; and in the east from North-West Persia, Iraq, Syria, Palestine, Egypt, North Africa and parts of the Arab peninsula. Even before the Ottomans established themselves as the major political force in the area the Turkish presence was always important; in the medieval Islamic world Turks were among the palace guards of the Abbasids at Baghdad, the Mamluks of Egypt were descended from Turkish soldiers and the Seljuk rulers of Persia and Anatolia were of Turkish origin. It seems reasonable, therefore, to take as an historical and geographical framework both the period and domain of Ottoman rule. Ottoman influences in methods of government in both civil and military institutions and in culture and language were sufficiently strong to provide a unifying force over indigenous tradition. The imprint of the collective Ottoman personality was enormous and can still be observed today culturally for example, in the number of Turkish words still in the vernacular languages of the successor states, and in the now admittedly declining numbers of elderly Greeks and Jugoslavs who can speak Turkish, and at a more basic level in the shared culinary tradition. Visually the Ottoman presence survives in the distinctive architecture especially in the great urban service complexes of mosque, *medresse* (theological college), *carşi* and *bedesten* (commercial quarters) and *hammam* (public bath).

Another facet of the Ottoman collective personality was costume. Turkish styles were worn throughout the empire's provinces by the Ottoman ruling élite, and emulated in the towns by any of the subject population who had aspirations towards status and wealth and would wish, therefore, to dress in the accepted and fashionable costume of the day. An extraordinary range of costume was to be seen in which Turkish and native traditions existed, both influencing each other to mutual enrichment. With these principles in mind it is possible to explore the origins, background and expansion of the Ottoman Empire through the medium of its sartorial tradition. This involves a discussion of the origins of garment types in Central Asia, an examination of the costume of the Byzantine Empire to see if it contributed significantly to Ottoman fashion after the fall of Constantinople and the documentation of the evolution of clothes in both Turkey itself and in the subject provinces of both Europe and Asia, to include the influence and adaptation of traditions of such close neighbours as Persia. As the subject so defined is vast further limits have been imposed by concentrating the treatment on women's costume of the urban centres as worn by the Muslims who formed the majority of the empire's population, and whose clothes influenced those of the Christian and Jewish minorities. While this is not the place for a detailed discussion of women's role in a predominantly Muslim society, it would be inappropriate and inaccurate to assume that it was uniformly and rigidly circumscribed because private and public behaviours were carefully distinguished; there is at present simply not enough evidence to make general statements. It is even not certain to what degree their lives differed from those of their Christian and Jewish neighbours. In a small provincial town, for example, with a mixed population social manners and practices would tend to be conservative and similar conventions of correct and modest behaviour would be applied regardless of religious affiliation.

Women's costume presents an evolution equally as complex and varied as that of their masculine contemporaries – a fact which has been overlooked because of the lack of officially defined and recognised feminine public roles. Here the aim is to demonstrate the historical development of women's fashion concentrating on the structure of clothes and their combination into distinctive costumes. By discussing the shape, cut and construction of garments and accompanying accessories and evaluating the secondary evidence presented in contemporary illustrative and literary material, it has been possible to document the changes in fashionable image and to indicate the efforts made to achieve it. Such evidence neatly disposes of the tiresomely persistent myth that 'oriental' costume is essentially timeless and can, therefore, be simply dismissed as a few basic items of clothing assembled together to produce a generalised and pleasingly colourful stereotype. Fashion evolved at a gradual pace absorbing new ideas of fabric, shape and ornament, much as it did in Europe before the invention of the sewing machine which meant that clothes could be made quickly and cheaply in factories and discarded after a season's wear. As this study concentrates on the garments in the context of their changing appearance, the composition and decoration of the textiles used inevitably takes second place and is only discussed in relation to their use in costume types. In turn, the costume examples have been mainly drawn from the collections of the Royal Museum of Scotland, Edinburgh which has the advantage of presenting fresh material to the public.

1
The Arrival and Establishment of the Ottomans

The arrival of the Osmanli or Ottoman Turks, as they are more familiarly known, who were to exert an almost limitless impact on Europe and Asia for so many centuries was relatively discreet and modest, as in the simplest terms they were basically just one among the numerous small Türkish principalities which took root in Anatolia from the eleventh century onwards. Their origins lay in Central Asia, and their rise to pre-eminence must be understood against a complex pattern of tribal movements interwoven with the shifting fortunes of the settled kingdoms which dominated the medieval Middle East, namely the Orthodox Christian Byzantine Empire, centred on Constantinople and culturally dominating the Balkans and Anatolia, and the successor states to the dynamic Muslim Arab Empire – principally the Fatimids of Egypt (969–1171), and the Abbasids ruling from Baghdad (750–1258) over territories corresponding to modern Iraq and areas of Persia.

The distant ancestors of the Ottoman Turks were nomadic peoples, who wandered in tribal groups through the Altai mountains east of the Eurasian steppe lands and south of the Yenisei river and Lake Baikal, an area which today forms part of Outer Mongolia. They practised a shamanistic religion which involved the worship of the power of nature through totems and spirits, and a life style dependent on herding animals and plundering the settled communities with which they came into contact, eventually encroaching on Persia, Iraq and Anatolia. Turkish tribal groups already by the sixth to eighth centuries had formed a confederation which expanded territorially from Mongolia to the Black Sea. Here those in the west traded with their neighbours and even entered into a military alliance with Byzantium. As successive waves of immigration continued a pattern of trade based mainly on barter, and a shifting balance between hostility and alliance where the Turks could offer their services as mercenaries was established. Finally, the Turks became a permanent presence in the Muslim world, at times exerting considerable political influence; many a caliph of the Abbasid court at Baghdad owed his position to the support of a Turkish 'praetorian' guard.

With the spread of Islam among the Turks they were becoming

culturally blended into the settled areas. Islam, in any case, was not a new phenomenon to them, as it had already reached Central Asia in the seventh century with the Arab conquest of Persia and Afghanistan but as they became absorbed into the settled territories it spread rapidly among them. Turks who served as mercenaries from the ninth century onwards became converts, while missionary activity among them was carried out among Turkish tribes by members of the mystic Sufi orders from Persia and Iraq rather than by the orthodox Islamic religious establishment. An important element also was the tradition of the *gazi* or 'warrior for the faith' especially prevalent in frontier regions, a tradition which would resurge centuries later in the expansion of the Ottoman Turks. Although the process of conversion was gradual it was steady so that by the end of the tenth century it could be seen that Turks of all ways of life had accepted Islam. With the decline of the Abbasid power Turkish groups set up their own kingdoms – notably those of the Ghaznevids of East Persia and Afghanistan (962–1186) and the Seljuks who dominated Iraq and Persia from the mid-eleventh to early thirteenth century. A consistent shape in the Turkish pattern now developed in which powerful settled Turks inherited and adapted the institutions of their Muslim predecessors, and co-existed with noma-dic tribesmen of Central Asia who were still liable to erupt in waves across the civilised territories. Both sides, however, had a common bond in Islam.

The expansion of the Turks into Anatolia was preceded by their first major settlement as an important military power in the Middle East. The Seljuk Turks had entered Persia and Iraq in the eleventh century under their leader Tuğrul Bey, who by 1055 felt sufficiently confident to compel the Abbasid caliph at Baghdad to recognise him as sultan and as protector of orthodox Islam. Tuğrul Bey and his successors consoli-dated their power by continuing the established system of administra-tion and by creating a regular salaried army, while their patronage of culture and art marked their transition from tribal leaders to sophisti-cated rulers. Parallel to Seljuk settlement in Iraq and Northern Persia was the migration of other Turkish groups into Eastern Anatolia, where they continued their traditional freebooting life style oscillating between raids on neighbouring communities and alliances with local Byzantine and Armenian princes as mercenary troops. This pattern of symbiosis and tension between Byzantine and Turk was further complicated by the invasion of the Seljuks into Eastern Anatolia under Sultan Alp Arslan in 1065 with the intention of controlling these frontier nomads. This had momentous results for the fate of the Turks in Anatolia, as during a series of campaigns Alp Arslan won a great victory in 1071 at the Battle of Manzikert, north of Lake Van over the Byzantine army led by the Emperor Romanus Diogenes. This event effectively ended Byzantine control in Eastern Anatolia, which was then open to the tribes and more significantly to an offshoot of the Seljuks, under the leadership of Süleyman, son of a cousin of Tuğrul

Bey. He and his successors, partly by clever manipulation of the Byzantines, established the dynasty of the Seljuks of Rum based in South-Eastern Anatolia with their capital at Konya which today still preserves the remains of their elegant and colourful architecture. During the eleventh and twelfth centuries, therefore, settled Turks, the Great Seljuks in Iraq and Persia and the Seljuks of Rum in Eastern Anatolia, ruled always against a background of migratory Turkish groups. In Anatolia especially, society was mixed as Muslim Turk co-existed with indigenous Christian Byzantine town and village people. Political and military power was divided between the emirs appointed by the Seljuks of Rum and the beys – commanders of Turkish border tribes.

The pattern was, however, to be abruptly and violently shattered by the Mongol invasions of the early thirteenth century under the leadership of Genghis Khan, who moved relentlessly through Central Asia into Eastern Persia adding nomadic Turks to his vast army as he went, finally overthrowing the last of the Great Seljuks in 1220. By 1242 the Mongols had reached Anatolia and had defeated the Seljuks of Rum, forcing them to recognise Ghengis's son Hulagu Khan as overlord. The Mongols did not, however, establish a permanent base in Anatolia, and after their ultimate withdrawal a pattern emerges of independent Turkish principalities in Eastern Anatolia existing along with the much weakened and shrunk Byzantine Empire in the West. It is among these principalities of the late thirteenth century that the Ottoman Turks must be sought.

Their original territory was advantageously situated to maintain a balanced position between Byzantine and other Turks, as they had settled in Western Anatolia between Eskişehir and Iznik in pasture lands extending from the slopes of the Domanic mountains north-east to Söğüt where the eponymous Osman Bey was born in about 1258. Romantic legends have embellished the arrival of Osman's ancestors in Anatolia; the most familiar and popular story was that a Turkish chieftain Ertuğrul came from the east with 400 followers to help the Seljuks of Rum against the Byzantines and Mongols, and in return for his loyal support was rewarded with lands in Western Anatolia. This version was especially cherished later by official Ottoman historians and hagiographers, who brazenly embellished it by extending Ertuğrul's genealogy beyond the Turks of Central Asia to Noah and finally to Adam. Another more prosaic version may well be nearer the truth – that Osman's ancestors were among the Turkish peoples who entered Anatolia in the eleventh century after the Seljuk victory at Manzikert, and survived by alternating raids with selling their services as mercenaries to the highest bidder. The Ottoman Turks were, however, unique among their contemporaries in their expansion from modest kingdom to mighty cosmopolitan empire. Osman's domain or *beylik* was admirably situated strategically on the Byzantine frontier close to Constantinople, and attracted from the Turkish dominated territories in Eastern Anatolia levies of *gazi* warriors aiming at combining opportunities for plunder with a little pious conversion.

As Byzantine power shrank and the emperors were more preoccupied with the Balkans there was little effective opposition to Ottoman expansion, so that during the fourteenth century they effectively encircled Constantinople. Extending steadily westwards they took Bursa in 1326, which they made their capital, Iznik (Nicaea) and Izmit (Nicomedia) before crossing into Europe where they established a permanent fortified base at Gallipoli (Gelibolu) in 1354. From here they steadily advanced north through Thrace, Northern Greece, Bulgaria and Jugoslavia, significantly transferring their capital from Bursa to Edirne in 1365, and consolidating their presence by the victory at Kossovo in 1389 over the Serbs and at Nicopolis in 1396 over the combined forces of European chivalry, who had united too late in an ineffectual crusade. This impotence of the Christian West was to remain a constant factor in Ottoman expansion, and was only checked temporarily at the beginning of the fifteenth century when Sultan Beyazit I who also campaigned in Anatolia was defeated and taken prisoner by Timerlane at the battle of Ankara in 1402.

The significance of Beyazit's defeat was to set back Ottoman domination in Anatolia so that when the internal crisis of his successor was resolved by the accession of Mehmet I in 1413 their attention was again turned westward to Europe. Mehmet I (1413–21) and his successors Murat II (1421–44, 1446–51) and Mehmet II (1444–46, 1451–81) methodically absorbed areas which had escaped previously, and tightened up control by substituting direct Turkish administration and rule for vassalage. The conquests of Albania, Greece and Jugoslavia were consolidated and Romania was drawn into a tributary status. The final accolade of Ottoman success in Europe was, however, the conquest of Constantinople in 1453 by Mehmet II after a siege of three months. Encircled by Ottoman territories on all sides, the fall of the city was inevitable and had been planned by Mehmet for two years. Though this conquest marks an immediately recognisable turning point in Ottoman fortunes, the late fifteenth and sixteenth centuries witness further expansion. In Europe, Ottoman dominion was carried into Hungary in 1526, while in the Middle East the remaining Turkish beyliks of Anatolia, the Crimea, Syria, Egypt, Iraq, Libya, Tunisia and Algeria, and the coastal areas of Arabia, Aden and Yemen were brought under control. Finally, Cyprus and Crete were taken in 1571 and 1669 respectively. At its height in the sixteenth century, therefore, the empire of the Ottoman Turks encompassed territories representing a bewildering abundance of varied cultural, religious and ethnic traditions. One of the most visible and tangible symbols of Ottoman domination and indeed unity within this vast cosmopolitan area is seen in dress, and here it is essential to separate the various influences which either definitely or allegedly contributed to the evolution and dissemination of an identifiable Ottoman Turkish costume tradition.

2

The Ottoman Inheritance – Byzantium

The taking of Constantinople in 1453 marked a turning point in Ottoman fortunes. Although they had been firmly established as a major power in Anatolia and the Balkans since the fourteenth century, with their capitals at Bursa and Edirne, this was the first time that they had taken so magnificent and important a city, which for centuries had been the wonder of the civilised world. Originally the modest Greek colonial town of Byzantium, it was selected by the Emperor Constantine in 329 to be the capital of the eastern half of the Roman Empire. Its site, at the southern tip of the European shore of the Bosphorus flanked by the Sea of Marmora and the Golden Horn, was of incomparable strategic importance as it was easily defended and commanded the major trade routes from the Black Sea, India and China along which luxury goods of silks, spices, ivory, amber and precious stones passed. Through the centuries successive emperors embellished and beautified it, by the construction of churches, palaces and public structures such as aqueducts and theatres.[1] At its most powerful Constantinople functioned as the capital of a cosmopolitan empire at its widest extent reaching from Italy to the boundaries of Iraq, including Syria, Palestine, Egypt and North Africa. By 1453 because of repeated incursions by Persians, Arabs, Seljuk Turks and Crusaders, the Byzantine Empire had shrunk to little more than Constantinople and its immediate hinterland. The great city itself was in a ruinous state as it had never adequately recovered from the sacking in 1204 by the Fourth Crusade.[2] Contemporary writers of the fifteenth century commented on its desolation, open derelict spaces, poverty-stricken population; even the buildings of the old imperial palace at the south-eastern end of the city were no longer habitable, and the most prosperous quarters were in the hands of such foreigners as the Genoese and Venetian traders based respectively at Pera across the Golden Horn and in the harbour district.

With the conquest of the city the Ottoman Turks inherited both an alternative imperial tradition and a site of great potential. It is important to stress this point as it has been for long assumed that the Ottomans took over almost as a ready-made package, the Byzantine traditions of a hierarchy, administration and social customs. Such a view is naive and based on the assumption that the Ottomans were crude invaders in contrast to the cultured and sophisticated Byzantines. A critical examination of the evidence indicates a complex situation in which it is more accurate to regard both Byzantine and Turkish cultures as societies which in many ways developed along certain parallel lines. The Byzantine Empire had always been cosmopolitan – a great melting pot of different nationalities, languages, religious and social practices, where familiarity with and indeed interest in the affairs of its non-Christian neighbours had always been understood. The presence of Muslims in Constantinople itself was clear; at one time even a mosque was established there, while the ninth-century Arab writer Harun ibn-Yahya gives an eye-witness account of the emperor's procession to divine liturgy and notes among the elders, young men and eunuchs which precede him: '. . . Behind them follow 5000 chosen eunuchs wearing white Khorasanian clothes of half-silk; in their hands they hold golden crosses. Then after them come 10,000 Turkish and Khorasanian pages, wearing striped breast-plates; in their hands they hold spears and shields wholly covered with gold . . .'[3]

At a court level, Byzantine politicians intrigued with their Muslim neighbours when it suited them, which often involved marriage contracts. When, for example, civil war broke out in 1341 between John Cantacuzenos and other regents governing on behalf of the infant Emperor John V, Cantacuzenos sought the support of the Ottoman ruler Orhan, and in 1344 gave him his daughter Theodora in marriage in exchange for 6000 Turkish troops. Sultans Murat I and Beyazit I were the sons of Greek women. On a more popular level this contact is symbolised in the tenth-century hero Digenis Akritas – son of a Christian Greek mother and Muslim Arab father, whose exploits on the frontier between Byzantine and Turkish territory in Anatolia were celebrated in an epic poem.[4]

Parallels between Byzantine and Muslim life appear in a more visual aspect. Among Byzantine imperial buildings the emperor's palace situated at the shore side of the Bosphorus, seemed to be a rambling assemblage of separate apartments, pavilions, kitchen quarters, stables, chapels and reception halls, added at random by successive emperors and their families, and set within a surrounding wall dominated by an enormous gatehouse, rather than a planned uniform structure. This concept of separate buildings within a garden may be paralleled in the Muslim world, and indeed continued into the Topkapi Palace of the Ottoman Turkish rulers. It is known that Byzantine rulers much admired the palaces of their Muslim neighbours. Theophilus (829–842) was so impressed by the palaces of Baghdad that he strove to emulate them, while much later, in the mid-twelfth century, a Seljuk-style hall complete with stalactite decoration, and glazed tiles was constructed in the imperial palace. Furnishing these apartments was imported metalwork, silks and other objects in rock crystal and ivory which influenced Byzantine taste.

In matters of clothing oriental fashions were familiar to the Byzantines, and at times were adopted and adapted by them. Here an interesting example is recorded by the historian Procopius writing in AD 550, who describes the bizarre amalgam of Persian and Hun dress worn by the supporters of the Blues – one of the major teams of charioteers in the Hippodrome races:

> To begin with the partisans changed the style of their hair in quite a novel fashion, having it cut very differently from the other Romans. They did not touch moustache or beard at all, but were always anxious to let them grow as long as possible, like the Persians. But the hair on the front of the head they cut right back to the temples, allowing the growth behind to hang down to its full length in a disorderly mass, like the Massagetae. That is why they sometimes called this the Hunnish style. Then as regards dress, they all thought it necessary to be luxuriously turned out donning attire too ostentatious for their particular station. For they were in a position to obtain such garments at other people's expense. The part of the tunic covering their arms was drawn in very tight at the wrists, while from there to the shoulders it spread out to an enormous width. Whenever they waved their arms as they shouted in the theatre or the hippodrome and encouraged their favourites in the usual way, up in the air went this part of their tunics, giving silly people the notion that their bodies were so splendidly sturdy that they had to be covered with garments of this kind; they did not realise that the transparency and emptiness of their attire rather served to show up their miserable physique. Their cape and breeches too, and most cases their shoes, were classed as Hunnish in name and fashion.[5]

To balance these oriental influences in Byzantium there is evidence that the Ottoman Turks themselves had their own highly developed culture. Sultans such as Mehmet I and Murat II who had many Christian friends, and Mehmet the Conqueror, educated in sciences and philosophy, fluent in Turkish, Greek, Arabic, Latin, Persian and Hebrew, were cultured and well trained. Buildings which still stand today in the early Ottoman capital of Bursa, for example, the mosques of Yildirim Beyazit (1391), the Great Mosque or Ulu Cami (1396), the mosque and mausoleum of Mehmet I (1419–21), show that the Ottomans could well hold their own with the Byzantines in both locating and constructing fine architecture. At Edirne, Mehmet II in 1452 was busy constructing a splendid palace, adorned with fine marbles, sculptures, gold and silver and set in a carefully landscaped garden.[6] Equally, the Cinili Köşk, the oldest part of the Topkapi Palace constructed by Mehmet in 1472, reveals his taste for harmonious and well-proportioned buildings.

Against this historical background of two mutually aware societies and highly developed cultures, Mehmet II's conquest of Constantinople, which he himself recognised as symbolising that he was heir to the Roman Empire, did not result in an adoption of Byzantine ritual and ceremony, as there were sound historical and intellectual reasons against it. The most important and fundamental reason was that the Byzantine Empire had not only inherited the cultural and legal traditions of classical Rome, but was also a Christian realm. Constantinople symbolised not only the New Rome but also the New Jerusalem. A theocratic philosophy justified the Byzantine state in which the emperor functioned as God's divinely appointed representative on earth. Accordingly stages in his life from birth to death were marked by elaborate religious ceremonial.[7] As a prince, the announcement of his birth was received with prayers by the Orthodox patriarch in company with metropolitans and archbishops, and he was given his name three days later at the church entrance. His baptism, marking his formal acceptance into the church, took place after a period of religious instruction, at the baptistry of Aghia Sophia. His coronation was celebrated in a long and splendid ceremony at Aghia Sophia, in which his succession was not recognised as valid until he had been crowned by the patriarch. His death was attended by further ceremony, in which his embalmed and robed body was carried in an open coffin in procession to the Church of the Holy Apostles situated near the Constantine walls for burial.

The Ottoman sultan's position differed fundamentally. While he indeed succeeded to the classical and Christian heritage of the Byzantines by right of conquest, his real inheritance was the traditions of the Islamic world which did not differentiate between religion and state. Constantinople transformed into Istanbul functioned as an Islamic city along with equally venerable competitors such as Cairo and Damascus. It had, indeed, always held some importance in this context as the burial place of the Prophet Mohammad's standard bearer Eyüp Ansari who reputedly fell in battle in the seventh century, and came to be regarded eventually as the heart of the Islamic world after the relics of the prophet were transferred from Cairo to the Topkapi Palace after Sultan Selim I's conquest of Egypt in 1517. The sultan, although he had enormous and wide-ranging powers, was in no way considered as Allah's divinely appointed representative. At most he was the protector of Islam. In contrast to the Byzantine emperor, milestones in his life were not marked by religious ritual, but by secular ceremonies. The birth of an Ottoman prince, since there was no law of primogeniture, was at most heralded by an announcement and public festivity depending on his father's wish since sons were always welcomed. His initiation into manhood, the circumcision, roughly comparable with the Byzantine prince's baptism, again was a secular ceremony, marked by public feasting and processions.[8] The accession of a sultan was quick and businesslike. He simply took up office by seating himself on a throne before the Gate of Felicity, which leads from the second to the third court of the Topkapi Palace, and received notables and important officials who indicated their loyalty by kissing the hem of his robe.[9] This was followed by a ceremonial assembly of the Divan – the imperial council and the main organ of government of the Ottoman Empire. The nearest approach to a religious ceremony was the Girding some days later, when the new sultan travelled to Eyüp Ansari's tomb, and was invested with swords belonging to the prophet which had been brought from the Topkapi Palace in the presence of the Chief Mufti. His funeral, in accordance with Muslim tradition, was equally brisk. His body was washed, wrapped in a shroud and buried without any elaborate procession. Surviving tombs of the sultans are comparatively modest tower-like structures, scattered between certain of the city's large mosques.[10]

Despite the fundamental differences in the nature of their positions and the ceremonies surrounding them, the basic responsibilities however of both Byzantine emperor and Ottoman sultan shared many common duties – such as attendance at divine liturgy in Aghia Sophia, Friday prayers at the city's leading mosques, routine administrative work in council and Divan, reception of officials and ambassadors and leading their armies on regular military campaigns – one as champion of orthodox Christianity, the other as a *gazi* – a Muslim warrior leader committed to fight the infidel in holy war for Islam.

While each court developed an elaborate hierarchy and administration they diverged again on an important aspect – the role and position of women. Here again both religious and legal considerations played their parts. Byzantium as an orthodox Christian state gave great honour to the Blessed Virgin in her role as the Theotokos or mother of God. Early Christianity had indeed always given women full membership of the church where they fulfilled active roles as deaconesses, administering charity. As the emperor was God's representative on earth, so therefore the empress functioned as his feminine counterpart, an image of divine beauty and consolation, balancing his majesty and justice. Great care was exercised in the search for candidates for such exalted office, and all over the empire eligible girls were sought showing the right qualities of dignity, grace and intelligence, which were considered more important than dynastic reasons. The empress's coronation and marriage were consecutive religious ceremonies. She was crowned in the palace at a ceremony in which the patriarch officiated and the emperor invested her with a crown and robes. The marriage ceremony which followed took place at St Stephen's Church within the palace. Within her quarters in the palace the empress had her own court of officials, her own revenues and was able to attend ceremonies with the emperor and give audiences and receptions. Depending on her personality and intelligence and the use she made of her privileges, she could forge a position of great power and influence for herself.[11] Beyond the court and aristocratic circles, women's role and function, though limited normally to a career of arranged marriage and motherhood, was protected by considerable legal rights. Daughters were given dowries which they were allowed to keep, and women could control their inheritance and dispose of it as they wished. Widows were recognised as family heads retaining control of children and family property. Many women found independent careers through the church either by entering convents and rising to high administrative positions, or by donating funds for building churches and founding convents.[12] Paradoxically, however, in view of the reverence given to the Holy Virgin or perhaps because she was held as an unattainable ideal of womanhood from which inevitably most fell short, the church in fact disapproved of women becoming too independent, and sought to keep them out of the public eye.

The position of women within the Ottoman Turkish court and society presented no such contradictions. In Islam there was no tradition comparable to the Christian one of the Holy Virgin, and as the sultan did not function as God's representative on earth, there was certainly no reason why the women of his household should do so and indeed, they occupied no exalted public role. Women entered the sultan's household either as slaves or as gifts and were trained in the various complex levels of service. No external ceremonies marked their progression through the harem hierarchy, and any power and influence they wielded was not publicly acknowledged. The most powerful woman within the harem was the Valide Sultan, the sultan's mother, a position calling for the exercise of considerable administrative skills and abilities.[13] Like their Byzantine Christian counterparts, Ottoman women had a distinct legal status provided by Islam, and were able to own and dispose of property.[14]

Women in Byzantine society were more often seen in public so that it would be logical to expect to be able to reconstruct a reasonably accurate picture of their costume traditions from such sources as contemporary accounts, portrayals of them in paintings, and through surviving textiles, to gain an idea of the texture and shape of their clothes. It should then be possible to see if any elements were absorbed into Ottoman dress. Here the position is disappointing because of the nature of the sources. While Byzantium had a highly developed tradition of pictorial art, expressed in mural painting, mosaic and manuscript illustration, this had severely imposed limitations. Above all it was a religious art, devoted to symbolic representations of Jesus Christ, the Holy Virgin and saints, cycles of the life of Jesus Christ and the seasons of the church. Careful rules governing the subject, composition, conventions of clothing and background and ornament in paintings meant that a stylistic conservatism indeed archaism, prevailed, which limit the use of them as a source accurately documenting fashions in dress. Written accounts are similarly limited, giving little of the detail required to reconstruct the appearance and number of garments in a costume. They give generalised tantalising information, simply hinting at the variety and richness of Byzantine dress.

Byzantine textiles have survived, and were justifiably famous. Silk cultivation was introduced to the West by the Emperor Justinian in about 552, and imperial looms were established in the Great Palace. It has been stated that textiles from the Islamic world were much admired in Byzantium and the influence of their designs, along with a repertoire of motifs of classical Graeco-Roman derivation is found in Byzantine textiles. Surviving pieces, however, exhibit similar conservatism to that found in religious painting, and a series of polychrome silks ranging in date from the late seventh through to the eleventh century are basically designed with repeated circular medallions enclosing complex figure subjects. Several sent as gifts to the West have been preserved in shrines and cathedral treasuries – notably a silk decorated with elephants deposited in the court of Charlemagne *c.* 800, and a magnificent length of gold silk patterned with eagles in purple dating from the tenth or eleventh century in the cathedral treasury of Bressanne. Unfortunately, however, even allowing for the formal conventions of Byzantine painting it is difficult to link these figured silks to specific garments or draperies. These would seem to have been patterned with smaller repeating designs of foliate and floral motif, or neat tendril and interlaced geometrical patterns.

In view of these problems, the material available for Ottoman costume is both more abundant and capable of yielding the type of accurate information which enable changes of fashion to be documented. More examples of textiles and complete costumes have survived, detailed descriptions are more numerous, as European visitors came more frequently to the Ottoman Empire, and the traditions of Ottoman painting, which was a secular art of book illustration recording in meticulous detail the exploits of sultans, court and public festivities, enable the composition and arrangement of costume to be analysed.

Bearing the limitations of Byzantine source material in mind, it is only possible to give a tentative outline of female costume based inevitably on traditions of the court, which may be compared with Ottoman fashions. The earliest useful example is the mosaic composition in the Baptistry of San Vitale in Ravenna executed between 525 and 548, depicting Justinian's empress Theodora among her courtiers (Plate 1). It is a careful static composition in which every figure is frontally posed, with details of drapery folds, colour and pattern of textiles clearly indicated. It is first of all obvious that the costumes are basically derived from the late Graeco-Roman tradition based on simply cut long dresses, cloaks and stoles, folded and amply draped over the shoulders and arms. Theodora wears a long white straight dress with wrist-length tight sleeves. The decoration of a deep band of green and red rosettes within gold borders extending along the hem and vertically to the knee recalls the polychrome tapestry woven insets found as bands or medallions in contemporary garments and fragments from Coptic Egypt.[15] Theodora's ladies wear long dresses in which inset woven

medallions are seen more clearly as circles and squares at knee level. Unlike the Coptic pieces, however, which have plain backgrounds the medallions are set against coloured patterned fabrics, for example, pink with repeated motifs of blue ducks or green leaves. Theodora's costume is distinguished from that of her ladies by her cloak and jewellery. She wears a long purple cloak which is fastened on the right shoulder and falls to her ankles, decorated with a deep gold border at the hem of a procession of human figures in short tunics – a design of Graeco-Roman inspiration. The cloak clearly resembles the classical toga and was probably woven as a semicircular piece rather than cut out from lengths of materials.[16] In contrast, the ladies wear long rectangular shawls either plain or patterned with small repeating designs, thrown across their bodies. Theodora alone wears a heavy collar of pearls inset with plaques of rubies and emeralds. Her hair is piled high and puffed out into an elaborate bouffant frame rising from her forehead and temples to serve as a foundation for the hat-like crown made of a double circlet of pearls from which long pendant strings of pearls frame her face. The ladies simply have their hair confined within gold scarves or nets pulled over their foreheads and knotted at the nape of the neck.

The fashion worn by Theodora changed over the centuries, although the evidence again is sporadic. Portraits of certain empresses of the

Plate 1. The Empress Theodora. Mosaic, San Vitale, Ravenna. AD525–48.

Plate 2. The Empress Zoë. Mosaic, Sancta Sophia, Istanbul, south gallery, *c.*1028.

eleventh to twelfth century give some impression of how Byzantine court costume evolved. These in chronological order are – a mosaic portrait of the Empress Zoë (wife of Constantine IX) in the south gallery of Aghia Sophia *c.* 1028 (Plate 2), a miniature painting of the Empress Maria in a manuscript of the Homilies of John Chrysostom *c.* 1078 (Plate 3),[17] an enamel plaque depicting the Empress Eirene Ducaena *c.* 1100 (Plate 4)[18] and a mosaic portrait of the Empress Eirene the Hungarian again in the south gallery of Aghia Sophia *c.* 1118 (Plate 5). They all show that the tight-sleeved robes with their inset medallions and purple toga-like cloak have given way to a long slender dress with sleeves extending into wide flowing and pointed cuffs, which is wrapped with a sari-like stole, always in a contrasting colour and pattern. This extends in front from the hem of the dress, is swathed around the neck and shoulders, continues down the back and is finally drawn diagonally across the body from the right hip up to the waist where it is tucked into a girdle. The earliest example, a robe in the Empress Zoë's portrait, still retains circular inset medallions on the shoulders and a comparatively straight sleeve indicates its relationship to the robes of Theodora and her ladies. The stole swathed over it is of gold cloth inset with rubies and emeralds. Empress Maria's robe shows the extension of the sleeves into long pointed cuffs, and the expansion of shoulder medallions into contrast bands of deep blue patterned with a neat design of red and gold lozenges decorated with swirling foliage designs which match the deep hem. The stole is in a checked arrangement of rubies and pearls against gold cloth. Eirene Ducaena wears a robe and stole of comparable fabrics and design. The Empress Eirene the Hungarian, however, has a red robe, whose sleeve borders of gold patterned with scrolling foliage in blue and white match the stole wrapped around her.

These somewhat subtle changes – depending on a shift of emphasis in proportion of cuff width and sleeve ornament, were accompanied by changes in accessories and hairstyle. The pearl-ornamented crown of Theodora had evolved into a two-tiered headdress of gold plaques as worn by the Empresses Maria and Eirene the Hungarian, while hair was no longer dressed into a high chignon but worn in coils framing

Left. Plate 3. The Empress Maria. Manuscript illustration. Homilies of John Chrysostom, *c*.1078.

Above. Plate 4. The Empress Eirene Ducaena. Enamel plaque, *c*.1100. Pala d'Oro, St Mark's, Venice.

Plate 5. Empress Eirene the Hungarian. Mosaic, Sancta Sophia, Istanbul, south gallery, *c.*1118.

the face which could extend into heavy braids. An eye-witness account of a fifteenth-century empress by the French traveller Bertrand de la Brocquière writing in 1432, while recording little of her costume apart from her headdress, is valuable for the freshness and immediacy he conveys of the impact her appearance made on him, and gives life to the formalised portraits:

The Empress, daughter to the Emperor of Trebizond, seemed very handsome, but as I was at a distance I wished to have a nearer view; and I was also desirous to see how she mounted her horse, for it was thus she had come to the church, attended only by two ladies, three old men, ministers of state, and three of that species of men to whose guard the Turks entrust their wives . . . At length she appeared. A bench was brought forth and placed near her horse which was superb and had a magnificent saddle. When she had mounted the bench, one of the old men took the long mantle she wore, passed it to the opposite side of the horse, and held it in his hands extended as high as he could; during this, she put her foot in the stirrup, and bestrode the horse like a man. When she was in her seat, the old man cast the mantle over her shoulders; after which, one of those long hats with a point so common in Greece, was given to her; it was ornamented at one of the extremities, with three golden plumes, and was very becoming. I was so near that I was ordered to fall back and, consequently, had a full view of her. She wore in her ears broad and flat rings, set with several precious stones, especially rubies.

She looked young and fair, and handsomer than when in church. In one word, I should not have had a fault to find with her had she not been painted, and assuredly she had not any need of it. The two ladies mounted their horses at the same time that she did; they were both handsome, and wore, like her, mantles and hats. The company returned to the Palace . . .[19]

This necessarily brief and incomplete outline of the main features of Byzantine female costume reveals that garments were mainly simple and geometric in cut, relying on contrasts of fabric texture and pattern, and on the use of swathed stoles and cloaks. Although Eastern dress was well known in the Byzantine world and indeed Islamic textiles were much admired and used, it is difficult however to discern any direct contact between Byzantine and Ottoman dress,[20] as the latter depended for effect on an assemblage of carefully cut and shaped garments. Indeed, in certain details such as the tall pointed hat of de la Brocquière's empress which resembles the headdresses of Turkish women, it might be more acceptable to assume that the Byzantines enjoyed wearing Eastern fashions. Antecedents, therefore, are better sought in regions further east which were in a more direct line to the Ottoman Turkish heritage.

3

The Ottoman Inheritance – Central Asia

Above. Plate 6. Man's shirt. Linen. High Altai, Pazyryk, barrow 2. Early nomadic culture, *c.*5th century BC.

Opposite. Plate 7. Woman's coat and trousers. Red silk and purple wool. North Mongolia, Hsiung-nu, 2nd century BC.

The areas in which the ancestors of the Ottoman Turks had roamed before reaching Persia and ultimately Anatolia were immense, extending from Outer Mongolia to the Black Sea and characterised by a complex racial and cultural mixture constantly enriched by the interaction between existing traditions and those of migratory newcomers. Archaeological, pictorial and literary evidence reveals the working of this process in costume, where the origin of certain methods of cut and construction and shapes of garment preserved in Ottoman Turkish dress can be traced back to Central Asian sources.

The earliest parallels are to be found in the Altai region south of Lake Baikal associated with the original homelands of the Turkish peoples. Here important evidence of the general costume tradition of the region is provided by finds excavated from five great burial mounds at Pazyryk in Western Siberia by the Soviet archaeologist Sergei Rudenko in 1929, and dated to about the fifth century BC.[1] These mounds were burials of nomadic tribal chieftains who were accompanied in death by a retinue of servants and horses and a rich array of equipment including carpets, clothes and personal ornaments. Owing to severe climatic conditions the grave contents have been preserved by the layer of ice which formed over them. Thus a fortuitous combination of burial custom and deep-freeze enable a clear picture of the material culture of the Altai nomads to be reconstructed.

Among the clothes which have survived are examples which show features observed in the much later costumes of Ottoman Turkish women, such as the use of narrow widths of fabric to which shaped pieces are added. A man's linen shirt, for example, made of cream-coloured linen in a close plain weave excavated from Barrow 2[2] shows details of cut and construction which survive in the undershirt or *gömlek* worn by Turkish women (Plate 6). The construction is based on a straight body section made of four rectangular pieces seamed together at the shoulders and at centre back and front. Long narrow sleeves are inserted at right angles and shaping is achieved by adding a triangular section made of two pieces on each side from underarm to hem. All seams and hems are narrow and worked in a neat running stitch – a sewing technique which continued down into Ottoman times. Other garments excavated at Pazyryk continue the parallels. A child's fur coat[3] constructed of separate pieces seamed at shoulders and sides, with a long triangular section added to each centre front to create a wrapover, demonstrates features preserved in the long robe – *anteri* – of Ottoman Turkish fashion. The use of separate pattern pieces in these Pazyryk clothes, however, was dictated by practical reasons; in the linen shirt, narrowness of loom width and a desire to avoid waste of fabric and, in the fur coat, the need to make the best use of irregularly shaped animal skins. A woman's costume in the form of a knee-length long-sleeved jacket with flaring skirt[4] made of squirrel skin and decorated with vertical bands of appliqué leather in stylised leaf patterns may be compared with a type of over garment found in Ottoman times. Apart from these isolated garments a representation of a woman on a gold belt plaque in Peter the Great's Siberian collection gives some idea of the assembled costume.[5] She wears a long-sleeved robe with a crossover front over a round-necked undershirt – again recalling later styles – and a tall cylindrical headdress which also occurs in seventeenth-century Turkish paintings of single female figures[6] and in the costume of Türkmen tribal women, who today inhabit an area corresponding to adjacent parts of North-East Persia, the Soviet Union and Afghanistan.

Contemporary with the Altai nomads were the Scythians, another group of tribes who occupied a territory roughly corresponding to an area extending from the borders of Eastern Turkey and North-West Persia through the Caucasus into South Russia and the Ukraine. Like the Altai nomads they also buried their chiefs with a full complement of servants and equipment. A grave dating from the fifth to the fourth century BC in the Ukraine containing a young woman's burial[7] shows that she was dressed in a long close fitting robe decorated with gold plaques and a tall cylindrical headdress made of successive *repoussé* gold circlets, which again may be compared with the headdress of Ottoman and Türkmen women. Further evidence for the antiquity of garment types is again found in northern Mongolia from a burial dating from the second century BC of the Hsiung-nu tribes. Here again actual garments have survived, notably a woman's coat of red silk trimmed with sable (Plate 7).[8] It is ankle length with a slightly flaring skirt, long straight sleeves and resembles the outer garment – *ferace* – worn by Ottoman women. A pair of voluminous trousers of purple wool gathered at the ankles are comparable with the *şalvar* of Turkish women.[9]

As the Turks extended westwards from the sixth century AD they encountered comparable dress traditions which are recorded in surviving wall paintings, mosaics and sculpture. In the eastern regions corresponding to Chinese Turkestan ninth-century fresco paintings from the sites of Khocho, Yarkhoto and Bezeklik indicate the continuity of cut and construction techniques noted at Pazyryk. Costumes are built up of layers of garments with long dresses and often long-sleeved coats worn over them. In particular the costume worn by two Uighur

Plate 8. Uighur woman. Fresco painting. Bezeklik, Chinese Turkestan, 9th century.

women in the ninth-century fresco from a temple at Bezeklik (Plate 8) shows decided parallels with later Ottoman fashions.[10] Both women wear round-necked red chequered undergarments with sleeves long enough to turn back over the cuffs of their outer garments comparable in form to the Turkish *gömlek*. Other garments are concealed by a long coat of a plain deep yellow fastened at centre front. All seams are bound with a twisted red and yellow cord so it is easy to see that centre back and fronts are made of one piece folded over at the shoulders. A horizontal seam at knee level indicates where extra material was added to make a floor-length garment, while seams at just below shoulder level show that sleeves were set in at right angles. The upper edges of each front are folded back to form a shawl collar. In its essentials this is the form of the ferace worn as an enveloping outer garment by Ottoman Turkish women. Evidence of hairstyles and headdresses is also provided by these paintings from Chinese Turkestan. A painting from the Nestorian temple at Khocho shows a woman with black hair pulled back from the forehead[11] and plaited into numerous braids distributed over the shoulders and the back. This hairstyle was to become widespread with variations throughout Persia and Turkey. The Sogdian paintings of Panjikent and Samarkand which range in date from the fifth to the eighth century depict women in ankle-length *şalvar* trousers and long-sleeved robes with oblique wrapover fronts.[12]

Coming further west the Turks extended into territory which although under Arab control since the mid-seventh century owed its cultural identity to Persian tradition. The evidence for women's dress here is variable, however, since there are no surviving examples of garments and no fresco paintings which depict costume in clear detail. Additionally, in Persian art of the Achaemenid (550–330 BC) and Sassanian (224–642 BC) periods women are rarely portrayed. Among the finds excavated from the frozen burial mounds at Pazyryk, however, were imported fabrics which included a tapestry-woven woollen strip of Persian origin[13] decorated with repeated scenes of women in prayer before an altar. They are shown wearing ankle-length dresses with long sleeves widening at the cuffs and decorated with vertical striped patterns, and long veils hanging from their crowns (Plate 9). The long dress continued into Sassanian times where it is seen most clearly in the mosaics of the palace of Shapur I at Bishapur built in the third century (AD) where girls are shown wearing ankle-length close fitting dresses with long sleeves and round necks (Plate 10) – a style which would have required specially cut pattern pieces.[14] The dresses may be draped with a stole or shawl thrown over the shoulders or wound diagonally over the body. Hairstyles also parallel Eastern styles with side locks hanging on each side of the face over the ears and long hair falling down the back apparently in numerous plaits. A final Sassanian example is to be seen in the female harpists (Plate 11) accompanying the ruler in the carved relief depicting a boar hunt on the left side of the largest rock cut grotto at Taq-i Bostan attributed to the reign of Khusrau Parviz (591–628).[15] Although the figures are damaged it is possible to see that they are wearing a costume assembled from layers of garments, beginning with a round-necked undershirt whose neck and central front borders are edged with a facing followed by a close fitting robe with long sleeves in a richly patterned fabric of quatrefoil flowers and heart shapes – with a deep round neckline which reveals the underwear. Both garments and the manner of wearing them recall the *gömlek* and *anteri* of Ottoman Turkey. These costume traditions continued well into the Islamic period as is shown by a wall painting (Plate 12) from the Jausak palace at Samarra in Iraq dated to *c.* 836–839.[16] Here two dancing girls wear close fitting dresses of plain orange and blue fabrics whose skirts flare out around their ankles and whose long sleeves fit tightly to the wrist. Their long black hair falls in heavy plaits around their shoulders and backs with tendril-like curls framing their faces.

A discussion and comparison of all these examples of pre-Ottoman female dress which cover an enormous range of time and space is not intended to demonstrate any theories of racial unity based on similarity. What does emerge, however, in the territories through which the

Below. Plate 9. Women in prayer before an altar. Wool textile in tapestry weave. High Altai, Pazyryk, barrow 5. Persian, 5th century BC.

Below left. Plate 10. Female harpist. Mosaic. Palace of Shapur I, Bishapur, Persia, 3rd century.

Turks passed on their way to Anatolia is that there was a dress tradition which, although subject to changes of fashion, was based on the concept of close fitting constructed garments worn in varying combinations of layers. The Turks entering Anatolia were, therefore, simply wearing the accepted dress of the day. Paradoxically the evidence for women's costume in Seljuk Persia and Anatolia is more fragmentary than that available for the Pazyryk nomads. Through conversion to Islam the traditions of elaborately equipped burials had disappeared, and in any case the climatic conditions were not favourable to the preservation of organic artefacts such as textile objects. Very little has survived of the Seljuk art of illustrated manuscript painting. At present the most useful information is provided by the somewhat formalised

Plate 11. Female harpists. Stone relief. Taq-i Bostan, Persia, 591–628.

Plate 12. Two dancing girls. Wall painting. Jausak palace, Samarra, Iraq, 836–9.

and stylised figures of women in ceramic and wall tile decoration,[17] which is closely related to the art of painting. Here in various techniques, such as underglaze and lustre painting, they are shown in long close fitting patterned robes with trailing plaited hair. It is perhaps an idealised form of beauty which they represent summed up in a verse from the thirteenth-century book of Dede Korkut which recounts the exploits of the heroes of Turkish epic:

> *My fine-robed one, like a bright leaping flame,*
> *My waving cypress, who walks without pressing the ground,*
> *The red on your cheek like blood on the snow,*
> *Too tiny your mouth to hold twin almonds,*
> *Your black brows are like lines drawn by scribes,*
> *Your black hair is like forty handfuls of smoke.*[18]

4
The Ottomans at Home – Mainly Istanbul

The Ottoman Turks who entered Constantinople 150 years after the beginning of their dynasty were accordingly dressed in fashions which represented a tradition of great antiquity extending over a large area. As their empire evolved and consolidated its institutions throughout the enormous territories which it ruled, costumes also developed which mirrored in their range and sophistication the many levels of its complex society and the cosmopolitan nature of its people. Even a superficial survey reveals a seemingly endless range of costume from luxurious and carefully prescribed robes of the sultan and his court hierarchy, through the dress of the religious and legal professions, trades and craftsmen, to the colourful garments of the many ethnic groups which contributed to the empire's manpower. In this profusion the costume of Ottoman Turkish women, particularly of the court and more affluent urban classes, may be traced from a plentiful array of source material. As always the most important information is to be deduced from the primary sources, the garments themselves and their related textiles. Only after a meticulous study of their shape, cut and construction, the manner in which they fall and are draped can the conventions with which they are depicted in secondary illustrative sources and written accounts be understood.

Collections of costumes have survived and are divided between museums throughout the world and private owners, who are in some cases the descendants of the original wearers. Of museum collections, those of the Topkapi Palace offer the most comprehensive and consecutive historical sequence showing the evolution of women's fashions through the eighteenth and nineteenth centuries with increasing absorption of Western influence until the princesses of the late Ottoman world were dressed in elegant European gowns. These palace collections have been preserved as a result of centuries of occupation uninterrupted by war or natural disasters, and because of the custom of labelling and storing clothes after the royal wearer's death. Other museum collections such as those of the Victoria and Albert Museum, London and the Royal Museum of Scotland, Edinburgh, in addition to women's dress of the eighteenth and nineteenth centuries, share a precious collection of late sixteenth- to early seventeenth-century textiles which from their shape are pieces from garments. Supplementing the costumes are collections of textiles in varied techniques which were made up into garments or functioned as accessories. These include lengths of silk fabric woven in complex weaves often incorporating silver and gold threads and combined with velvet to produce fluent repeating patterns of floral motifs within undulating ogival or oval medallions. There were infinite variations on this type of pattern which was very appropriate for clothes. Other fabrics consisted of lengths of finely woven linen embroidered with striking combinations of floral spray and border motifs in glossy silks and smooth stitches which were used for such articles as girdles, sashes and head covers. Examples have also survived of the needlecrafts used to ornament clothes and accessories such as borders of finely worked needle lace – *iğne oyası* – a distinctive Turkish craft, crochet and beadwork.

The collections of garments and related accessories are supplemented by both pictorial and literary secondary sources. Pictorial sources may be conveniently divided into those of Turkish and of European origin. Here the Turkish sources consist of the miniature paintings which, especially from the sixteenth century onwards, illustrate in meticulous detail histories of the sultans' reigns and important festivities such as the circumcision of royal sons. Recent scholarship is also bringing to light evidence of Ottoman Turkish paintings of the fifteenth century thus extending the range of this type of source material.[1] These fifteenth- and sixteenth-century examples, however, rarely depict women, and it is not until the seventeenth century when single-figure albums of men and women begin to be popular that costumes can be observed in detail. Single-figure albums continued to be fashionable throughout the eighteenth century when Levni who was chief court painter *c.* 1720–30 portrayed series of exquisitely dressed women in both indoor and outdoor costume.[2] A later Turkish painter Abdullah Bukhari *c.* 1735–45, while less gifted as an artist, also produced single-figure studies full of carefully observed costume detail.[3] Following in this tradition was a nineteenth-century painter Osman Hamdi (1842–1910) who combined the advantages of Western technical training with an appreciation of Ottoman culture to create accurate yet sensitively interpreted costume studies of Turkish men and women[4]. Running parallel with these mainstream Turkish paintings were series of albums of single-figure costume studies depicting supposedly typical characters from the many levels and nationalities of Ottoman society. These were probably painted by Levantine artists for a European market to satisfy curiosity about Ottoman life and institutions. They were clearly in production from the sixteenth century, since Rubens in 1597 produced a series of pen and ink drawings of Turkish costume based on a contemporary album.[5] The majority, however, survive from the late eighteenth and early nineteenth century and, since their aim is didactic, are excellent sources of costume detail once their conventions for depicting shape of garment and texture of fabric and decoration are understood.

Turkish paintings are complemented by the paintings, drawings and engravings of European artists which, since they employ formats and conventions different from those of Turkish artists, often clarify ambiguous points. Serious costume studies began as European trade and diplomatic missions to the Ottoman Empire increased from the sixteenth century onwards. Here may be included the engravings of Peter Coeck van Aelst (1533), Nicholas de Nicolay (1551) and Melchior Lorch (1559).[6] By the eighteenth century the careful drawings of the Flemish artist Van Moeur made in 1707–8,[7] and the graceful paintings of the Swiss Jean-Etienne Liotard who lived in Turkey from 1738 to 1742[8] catered to a Turkomania which spread among the aristocracy of eighteenth-century Europe – particularly of France. This was expressed in balls and masquerades costumed à la Turque, while the aristocracy had themselves painted in Turkish dress notably Lady Mary Wortley Montagu who visited Turkey 1717–18[9] and William Ponsonby second Earl of Bessborough who, resplendent in a *pasha's* robes, was painted by Liotard.[10] During the nineteenth century many artists portrayed Istanbul and its varied inhabitants. Among the best for costume studies are Jean Brindisi (mid-nineteenth century), Thomas Allom (1804–72) and Amadeo Preziosi (1816–82). By the late nineteenth century these pictorial sources were supplemented by photography whose technical skills made it easier to record costume objectively. Both European and Turk took to photography with great enthusiasm. The results are seen in the large album of photographs of men and women's costumes from all provinces of the Turkish Empire which were taken for the Vienna exhibition of 1873 by Marie de Launay and Osman Hamdi.[11] Photographs of costume also illustrate contemporary memoirs and travel accounts, while collections of picture postcards from the late nineteenth century onwards often yield valuable information.

Written sources, like illustrations, may be conveniently divided into those of European and of Turkish origin. The majority of the European sources are travel accounts written from the sixteenth century onwards. The most informative descriptions and analyses of costume, however, are found in the accounts of the eighteenth and nineteenth centuries whose authors no longer regarded the Ottoman Empire as an extraordinary and exotic institution and were able to record its customs objectively. Especially valuable accounts here are those of Lady Mary Wortley Montagu (1717–18), Julia Pardoe (1835), Charles White (1844) and Lucy Garnett (1890).[12] Official publications such as that of the Frenchman Vital Cuinet (1890–95)[13] are full of useful facts about the production of textiles, leather and such like materials and their use in costume. Ottoman Turkish sources present more of a problem since there are so many of them and they require specialist skills in order to read and edit them. There are, for example, the court archives of the Topkapi Palace, the later palaces of Dolmabahce and Yildiz, guild registers and the judicial returns of the cadis' courts where wills and inventories were deposited.[14] A more informal Turkish source are the memoirs of court ladies of the late nineteenth and early twentieth centuries which are full of descriptions of receptions and visits including details of the clothes worn. Important sources here are the memoirs of Muzbah Haidar, Emine Foat Tugay and the daughter of Sultan Abdulhamit II (1876–1909) Ayşe Sultan.[15] Another Turkish source valuable for the last years of the Ottoman Empire is oral tradition. Here ladies today in their late seventies and eighties may provide information about the costumes which were gathered together for their *cehiz* – dowries. Where these clothes survive it is possible to see the styles current at the time of their marriages. They are also a source of information about fabrics, and whether they made their clothes themselves or commissioned them from specialist dressmakers and embroideresses.

Although the sources as outlined here are many the records for women's costume are not complete. Ottoman Turkish women played no open role in public life so that there were fewer opportunities to observe their costumes. At home there was a clear division between the *selamlik* – the men's quarters where visitors were received, and the *haremlik* – the private quarters where only members of the family, the women and their female friends spent their time. When women left the house they concealed themselves in all-enveloping cloaks and veils. Inevitably, therefore, there is more information from the eighteenth century onwards when European women came to Turkey and were able to visit households. For the fifteenth to seventeenth centuries the information varies. What does emerge clearly, however, is that the empire could draw on considerable resources in material and manpower to clothe itself in style and elegance. A flourishing textile industry was established in Bursa and supplied silks and velvets to the court. The Bursa looms were later supplemented by those of Istanbul. As a lively trade developed, the textile industry is well documented in both Turkish and Western sources.

Three main groups of silk textile were produced and woven in various sizes; those destined for costume were made in lengths which could be cut and tailored as required. The groups may be classified into *kadife* – velvet, *kemha* – figured brocade silk and *tafta* or *atlas* – a monochrome lightweight silk in satin weave. Examples of these textiles survive both as fragments and as made-up garments. A specially fine type of *kadife* was known as *çatma* – which was a fine tightly-woven lustrous velvet made in Bursa from the late fifteenth century onwards. The example illustrated here (Plate 13) shows the fine red pile characteristic of *çatma*[16] combined with twill weave in gold thread to produce the so-called *çintamani* design based on combinations of three spots and pairs of flickering stripes. This design occurs not only in Ottoman costume but also in ceramic and tile decoration. The *kemha* brocades may also be subdivided. Here the most luxurious category

Plate 13. Length of *çatma*. Crimson silk velvet with design of stripes and spots woven in gold thread. Turkey, late 15th–early 16th century.

was *zerbaft* in which a lot of gold thread was used. A representation of fifteenth-century *zerbaft* valuable because it can be precisely dated is seen on the grave cover of Maria of Mangop second wife of Stefan cel Mare voivode of Moldavia who died in 1477.[17] Turkish textiles were much favoured by the courts of the Romanian principalities, and here Maria wears an all-enveloping cloak made of a gold cloth patterned with large heart-shaped palmettes (Plate 14), in turn containing sprays of tulips and roses reserved against the background. The textile has been well captured by the smooth embroidery technique and shows that bold designs with regularly spaced floral motifs were well established by the late fifteenth century. Another type was known as *seraser* – characterised by the use of silver thread as a dominant element. The example (Plate 15) illustrated here[18] shows how effective this type of textile could be. It is a seventeenth-century piece in which huge gold tulip motifs dominate against the silver background. The colours are given added depth by the technique of winding thin gold and silver threads around yellow and grey silk cores respectively which also produced a more flexible weft. The large design areas are skilfully balanced by outlining motifs in twill weave bands of green and deep pink. A more colourful type of brocaded silk was known as *serenk* seen

Plate 14. Embroidered tomb cover. Portrait of Maria of Mangop. Putna Monastery, Moldavia, Romania, 1477.

Below. Plate 15. Length of *seraser*. Silk brocade woven in gold and silver with large tulip motifs. Turkey, 17th century.

Below right. Plate 16. Length of *serenk*. Blue silk woven with repeated motifs of tulips, cloud scrolls and carnations. Turkey, late 16th century.

Opposite. Plate 17. The entertainment of a prince. Miniature from a manuscript of the *Kulliyat* of Kâtibi, Turkey, c.1460–80.

here as a late sixteenth-century example (Plate 16) in which bold and fluent patterns of tulips and cloud scrolls[19] enlivened with small carnation motifs are woven in silver, crimson and white against an intense blue background worked in warp-faced satin weave. *Atlas* was a much lighter plain fabric in fine weave sometimes stamped with a small repeating pattern such as hexagon motifs. Unlike the heavyweight patterned brocades whose one way designs made them suitable for long robes of simple even severe cut, *atlas* is more usually found as a lining or facing fabric in colours carefully chosen to complement or contrast with the main material. All these fabrics were luxurious. At a more mundane level the wool industry of Salonika produced coarse woollen cloth for the manufacture of the uniforms of the elite infantry corps – the janisseries, while cotton fabrics were manufactured in Merfizon near Amasya which became an important centre of both home and export trade.[20]

Equipped with such a range of textiles Ottoman Turkish women could afford to be well dressed and had in any case a distinguished

Plate 18. Hennin headdress. Embossed metal. Central Asia, 19th century.

tradition from which to develop new fashions. From the evidence available at present it would seem that during the late fifteenth and sixteenth centuries they evolved gradually. In the absence of examples of complete garments, the most reliable documentation is provided by surviving Turkish miniature paintings and comparable European illustrations and accounts. One of the earliest as yet identifiable Turkish paintings in the Topkapi Palace library the Kulliyat or collected works of the poet Katibi may be dated to *c.* 1460–80. One of the miniatures illustrating this work depicts a group of male and female musicians entertaining a prince;[21] it is painted in a clear style in which details of feature and costumes are treated in a somewhat flat schematic way (Plate 17). It is, therefore, possible with a knowledge of how certain weights and types of cloth fall and are draped when made up into garments to interpret their treatment in this painting and to identify their cut and fabric. There are two female musicians, a harpist and a tambourine player. The harpist is wearing a round-necked white undershirt – *gömlek* – which continued to be worn in varying forms right through to the twentieth century. Over this she has a neatly fitting ankle-length robe *anteri* with a V-neck revealing the white *gömlek*, and long sleeves tapering snugly to the wrist. In the use of layers of garments and the shape of the robe the influence of the Eastern tradition of costume construction is evident. The representation of the robe's fabric is interesting as it is painted in a bright clear orange patterned with spaced flickering and swirling gold motifs. At first glance these appear to be closely related to the conventionalised cloud scrolls of Chinese origin which were important motifs in Turkish art, but on closer examination they are more logically a depiction of the pairs of wavy stripes of the *çatma* velvet which in their turn, are perhaps trained and disciplined cloud scrolls. The girl, then, is probably wearing a robe made of *çatma* velvet.

Her headdress also provokes interesting comparisons. It is a tall narrow pointed gold cap with a white scarf wrapped around the brim, in direct line of descent from the high headdresses recorded in Siberia and the Ukraine.[22] This type of headdress in varying proportions of height continued to be worn through to the seventeenth century. A European engraving of Sultan Süleyman the Magnificent's famous wife Hürrem Sultan[23] shows her wearing a version with a veil trailing behind it. Some curious examples in embossed metal from Central Asia of nineteenth-century date (Plate 18) probably retain the original form most faithfully.[24] It is also tempting to speculate whether Eastern fashions influenced those of contemporary Europe, as the tall Turkish headdress is remarkably similar to the exaggerated and pointed hennin of late fifteenth-century Europe (Plate 19).[25] The harpist's companion, the tambourine player, wears a similar robe in *çatma* velvet of the same pattern but with a deep aubergine background. Her costume has variations in a black and white striped sash wound around her waist and a headdress which may indicate that she was of regional origin, since it may be compared with that worn by village women of Eastern Turkey today. A white shawl is folded across her head and then bound with a black scarf twisted to form a bandeau knotted on one side. Both girls have similar hairstyles in which side locks hang down in curly tendrils at the sides of their cheeks and back hair is long again comparable to the fashions observed in Central Asia and Persia.

A second Turkish miniature painting (Plate 20) from a manuscript of Amir Khosrau Dahlavi's long romantic poem the *Khamsa* dated 1498 (903 H) illustrates a variation of this costume.[26] Prince Bahram Gur is seated in a white garden pavilion with the daughter of the emperor of the seventh climate. She is wearing the white undershirt – *gömlek* – with round neck and long close fitting sleeves. Over it she wears a variation

Plate 19. Marriage of King Louis of Naples and Sicily to Princess Yolonde of Aragon. Miniature from Froissart's Chronicle, French, late 15th century.

Above. Plate 20. Bahram Gur in the White Pavilion. Miniature from a manuscript of the Khamsa of Amir Khosrau Dahlavi, Turkey, dated 1498.

Right. Plate 21. Shirin serving wine to Khusrau. Miniature from a manuscript of the Khusrau and Shirin of Sheykhi, Turkey, *c*.1500.

Opposite top. Plate 22. Turkish lady at home. Watercolour painting from a traveller's handbook, Turkey, 1588.

Opposite bottom. Plate 23. Turkish lady in outdoor dress. Watercolour painting from a traveller's handbook, Turkey, 1588.

of the female musicians' robe in plain white – fabric perhaps *atlas* silk with a girdle at the waist. It is long and close fitting with a round neck and centre front fastening. The sleeves, however, are wider and reach only to the elbow. Details of tailoring such as a self-coloured binding at neck and sleeve edges are visible. Her hairstyle continues the fashion for side locks framing the face on each side of a centre parting and long hair falling down the back. Her headdress is simply a long white scarf draped over her head.

Selected sixteenth-century sources indicate that these fashions both continued and developed. A manuscript of *c*. 1500 of the poet Sheykhi's version of the classic Persian love story of *Khusrau and Shirin* includes a miniature of Shirin serving wine to Khusrau.[27] The characters may be legendary but their setting and behaviour could have taken place in any contemporary Turkish household (Plate 21). Khusrau is seated on a chair with Shirin standing before him offering wine. She wears the long-sleeved undershirt now with a low cut square neck over which is a mauve robe. This is close fitting with a V-neck centre front fastening, the wide elbow length sleeves, a neatly folded sash – *kuşak* – is wound round the waist. Her headdress shows a more modest version of the tall pointed cap; here it is a low pillbox in shape with a veil draped over the crown and hanging down her back. Survivals of this type of headdress can still be seen in regional costume of Turkish women today, but the scarf is usually knotted under the chin.

A Levantine painting of 1588 depicting a Turkish lady at home getting dressed (Plate 22) provides more information about certain layers of this type of costume.[28] The illustration is from one of the books

depicting aspects of Turkish life and customs which catered to the curiosity of visitors to the Ottoman Empire. As their aim was to inform, the paintings concentrated on accuracy rather than artistic impression, so that within the limits of his abilities the artist was at pains to depict the texture and volume of garments. All the lady's garments are clearly revealed, especially her underwear. The undershirt – *gömlek* – by now was a long garment reaching to the ankles with long full sleeves which are extremely wide at the wrists and a *décolleté* neckline. Zigzag bands at centre front and along the upper seam of the sleeves indicate where lengths of fabric were joined, as this was a practice seen in similar garments surviving from the nineteenth century. Under the *gömlek* she wears ankle-length white trousers – *şalvar* – which fall in loose horizontal folds. Over the *gömlek* she is fastening a hip-length garment – a short version of the *anteri* – which is close fitting and opens at the front from a round neck. The sleeves are of the wide elbow-length style already seen at the end of the fifteenth century. To complete her costume she could select from a range of long robes to wear over the short *anteri*. Her headdress is as yet unfinished as she is wearing only a pillbox cap with no scarf added, while her long hair trails over her shoulders waiting to be plaited in narrow braids.

Outdoor clothing was different again. As women and men traditionally led separate lives, this segregation was maintained when a woman went out beyond the limits of the home to visit other female friends or on expeditions to the bathhouse or to picnics. Here the woman enveloped herself in all concealing coats and veils. Outdoor fashion, similarly to indoor dress, gradually changed. In the same costume book of 1588 a Turkish woman wearing outdoor costume is depicted.[29] Over her long-sleeved *anteri* she wears a long dark coat – *ferace* with a close fitting round neck, and wide sleeves falling to the elbow (Plate 23). In cut and form it may be compared to the *anteri* but is made on more voluminous lines and is of a discreet black. Her headdress is concealed by two white veils, one draped and secured over the pillbox cap giving the appearance of a pleated toque, the other covering the face from nose to chin and fastened at the back of the head. Collectively the two veils form the *yaşmak*. On her feet are yellow leather boots – which can be pulled on over slippers.

By the seventeenth century the picture of the urban Turkish woman's appearance comes into sharper focus as the documentation improves. There are examples of surviving costume whose forms and textiles can be closely linked to styles depicted in miniature paintings, which in turn give a picture of the total look. The costume pieces which are now divided between the Victoria and Albert Museum, London and the Royal Museum of Scotland, Edinburgh date from the early seventeenth century,[30] and are traditionally reputed to have come from imperial graveyards at Istanbul and Bursa; it was the custom to drape a tomb with the deceased's clothes. All these pieces are small, and as they are from children's garments the pattern shape is preserved complete. The

Plate 24. Child's *anteri*, back. *Serenk* silk brocade in white, blue and silver. Turkey, early 17th century.

fabrics are of the highest quality both velvet and brocade in which technique and design give an effect of subtle richness.

The example illustrated here (Plate 24) is made of *serenk* – with a white silk warp-faced ground woven with repeated eight-pointed star motifs worked in silver wefts.[31] A soft subdued tone of blue in silk is used to outline the stars, and to add life and fluency to the design in an additional pattern level of repeated circles of radiating carnation motifs. The fabric is of a stiff heavy texture and mounted on a lining of coarse white cotton in plain weave. In this case the shape of this piece is of the back and sleeve of an female *anteri* (Diagram 1). The back is cut as one piece on the straight of the fabric with edges turned in to shape the body. The material curves out from the waist to create a bell-shaped skirt, the sleeve is elbow length cut straight to fit to the side of the body and curved at the cuff. To complete the construction of the garment, shoulder and upper arm seams would have joined the back to two fronts. Then sleeves would have been sewn into place and finally the side seams joined. Sewing details show that a narrow seam was used with an allowance of half an inch joined together with a row of running stitches before pressing the edges back to give a neat flat finish. The stiffness of the fabric and its close weave made additional overcasting unnecessary because the raw edge would not run. *Atlas* silk is also found in this *anteri* as a broad strip three inches wide made up of bias-cut pieces or soft grey blue silk stamped with a ridged stripe pattern, which is used as an inner facing surviving on neck and sleeve edges only.

Conclusions to be deduced from a study of this fragmentary garment are that the nature and design of the main fabric were sensibly appreciated and allowed to speak for themselves in a simple cut, and that an appropriate use of lining and facing would have resulted in a neat finish. In shape the garment is to be linked with the robes depicted in the fifteenth- and sixteenth-century paintings, though these do not show so pronounced and curved a skirt. Another fragment from a child's garment (Plate 25) shows the use of *çatma* velvet in a bold yet open pattern of crimson crescents and stars alternating with forked motifs against a gold ground.[32] The shape of the piece (Diagram 2) shows how the front of an *anteri* was cut at this period. It was basically a narrow strip cut obliquely at the front edge with a triangular side section added to give a bell-shaped skirt fanning out from the waist.

Fortunately, from the early seventeenth century onwards there developed a taste in Turkish painting for single-figure studies usually of attractive and stylishly dressed young women. These were painted with precise attention to outline and detail both of main garments and accessories in clear opaque colours so that, equipped with a knowledge

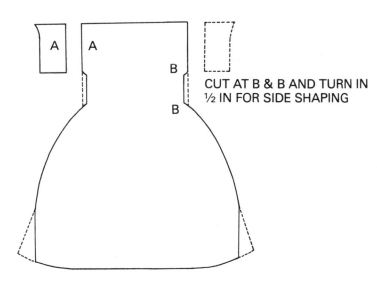

CUT AT B & B AND TURN IN
½ IN FOR SIDE SHAPING

ALL PIECES CUT ON STRAIGHT OF FABRIC
SEAM A-A JOINED USING ½ IN SEAM ALLOWANCE
RUNNING STITCH USED FOR SEAM WHICH IS THEN PRESSED OPEN AND FLAT
DOTTED SECTIONS INDICATE RECONSTRUCTION

Diagram 1. Pattern for child's *anteri*, back. Turkey, 16th–17th century. Scale – 1:12.

CUT AT B-B AND TURN IN ¼ IN FOR SIDE SHAPING

→ CENTRE FRONT

ALL PIECES CUT ON STRAIGHT OF FABRIC

SEAM A-A JOINED USING ¼ IN SEAM ALLOWANCE

RUNNING STITCH USED FOR SEAM WHICH IS THEN
PRESSED OPEN AND FLAT

Above. Plate 25. Child's *anteri*, side. *Çatma* velvet with design of crescents and stars in crimson against gold. Turkey, early 17th century.

Above right. Diagram 2. Child's *anteri*, side. Turkey, 16th–17th century. Scale – 1:11.

of certain basic principles of cut and construction methods favoured by Turkish dressmakers and tailors as revealed in later surviving complete garments, it is possible to visualise accurately the costumes of the seventeenth century and to match them up with the textile fragments already discussed.

Altogether these paintings reveal a handsome and flamboyant style of dressing based on combinations of layers of garments in which contrasts of colour and pattern are skilfully mingled. Two albums dated to *c*. 1618 and 1620[33] contain miniatures which are extremely informative documents of women's costume. One of these albums is a manuscript account of the sojourn of the Englishman Peter Mundy in Istanbul inscribed with the date 1618 and his initials. His text has been illustrated with Turkish miniatures pasted into the pages depicting functionaries, characters and different costumes of the Ottoman Empire. The miniatures are not closely linked to the text but are only added to the relevant sections; for example, those depicting female dress are inserted into the section on women. Some of the miniatures in Peter Mundy's album are very similar – almost identical[34] – to some in the second album, which is simply a book of illustrations – 122 miniatures in all – depicting the range of characters of the Ottoman Empire. It is possible, therefore, that such miniatures were produced in relatively large numbers, and may be compared to the illustrated tourist guide albums already seen in the sixteenth century.

A striking miniature from Peter Mundy's album well illustrates (Plate 26) the total look worn by court and upper class women of the early seventeenth century, and the style of beauty favoured.[35] She is a bold-faced girl with precisely delineated features – plucked arched brows, kohl-outlined almond shaped eyes, a small rouged mouth and a neat but generously proportioned figure well able to carry off the heavy costume. From the miniature it is possible to analyse all the elements of her costume. First the foundation garments are revealed. She wears white ankle-length trousers – *şalvar* – made of a soft textured filmy material which falls in loose horizontal folds. Over this is worn the undershirt – *gömlek* – already observed in fifteenth- and sixteenth-century fashions. Here it is a full-length white garment of fine pleated material which just falls short of the ankles. Details such as a narrow gold picot border at the hem probably representing a gold crotchet or needleworked lace edging have been carefully depicted. The main garments are in bright stiff cloth either plain or patterned. At this level there was considerable scope for the wearer's taste to express itself in combinations of garment and textile.

The girl here wears three layers – two variations of the *anteri* and a sleeveless jacket – *yelek*. The first layer consists of a hip-length *anteri* with long tight sleeves made of a blue and gold brocade patterned in large ogival radiating leaf motifs comparable to the patterns of *serenk*. Her main garment, however, is a full-length *anteri* made from bright orange plain heavy silk. The shape with elbow-length wide sleeves and curved cuffs, centre front opening from a neat collar and bell-shaped skirt was achieved by using a pattern and construction comparable to that of the child's *anteri*. Other construction details are evident which can be paralleled in surviving garments – such as the lining here of a beige pink and the broad facings at the hem made of contrasting emerald green *atlas* silk stamped with a scrolling pattern. The different colours are shown to a good effect by pulling the front skirt border up and looping it through the waist girdle – *kuşak* – whose embroidered ends are tied in a looped bow. The *anteri* is fastened from neck to hem level by a close row of plaited gold thread buttons which slot into corresponding loops and may be left open or closed to suit the wearer's taste. The final garment is a sleeveless jacket which flares out over the hips. It is of a sober dark grey-blue fabric lined with black chosen to harmonise with the *anteri*. It is again made from pieces cut like those of the surviving children's garments with additional details such as short side slits and pockets. The costume is completed by the elaborate headdress consisting of the tall pointed cap – *tarpuş* – made of silver brocade patterned with crimson curved leaves mounted over a stiff frame, and held in place by a white scarf tightly wrapped around the girl's face and chin. A green and gold scarf swathed around the forehead and knotted at the back of the head so that the ends trail over the shoulders completed the headdress. Final details of her costume are soft yellow leather indoor boots – *terlik* – and an embroidered handkerchief – *mendil*.

Other miniatures in the two albums reveal both more details and also

Plate 26. Woman in indoor dress. Miniature from an album of single-figure studies, Turkey, 1618.

variations of individual garments. One (Plate 27) showing a girl clad only in *şalvar*, *gömlek* and short *anteri*[36] is informative about the construction and pattern of the *gömlek* which has features which remained a part of this garment right through to the nineteenth century (Plate 28).[37] The main pattern piece is a centre strip (Diagram 3) folded over at the shoulders and cut to take the neck. A long piece on each side – a single loom width – is folded in two vertically and seamed to the back and front. Beyond the shoulder level the two selvages are seamed together to form a top sleeve seam. The seams may be made into decorative features either by weaving the selvages in different colours or by using lace insertion stitches to join them. The fabric is soft linen

ALL PIECES CUT ON STRAIGHT OF FABRIC
A-A TO C-C JOINED USING ½ IN SEAM ALLOWANCE
ALL SEAMS HAND SEWN, RUN AND FELL TYPE
ALL HEMS ROLLED AND OVERCAST

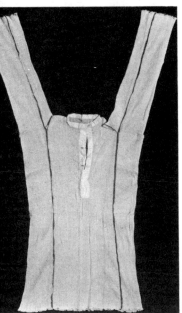

Top. Plate 27. Woman in underclothes. Miniature from an album of single-figure studies. Turkey, *c.*1620.

Above. Plate 28. Pleated linen *gömlek*. Turkey, late 19th century.

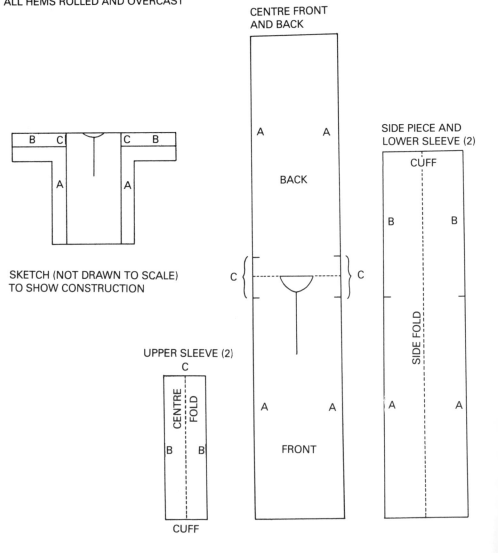

SKETCH (NOT DRAWN TO SCALE) TO SHOW CONSTRUCTION

CENTRE FRONT AND BACK

BACK

FRONT

SIDE PIECE AND LOWER SLEEVE (2)

CUFF

SIDE FOLD

UPPER SLEEVE (2)

CENTRE FOLD

CUFF

permanently pleated. The resulting comfortable loose fitting garment is an appropriate foundation over which to wear stiff brocade, and protects the body from chaffing. Variations are also seen in the style of *şalvar*. Here, in addition to the white pleated type, heavier more tight fitting *şalvar* (Plate 29) are worn made of turquoise brocade patterned with repeating oval foliage medallions.[38] This fashion is a forefunner of later practice when the white flimsy *şalvar* became transformed into undergarments proper.

Further variation is also seen in the shape and use of the different lengths of *anteri*. Here the girl wears a long sleeveless *anteri* (Plate 30) which may perhaps better be regarded as a long version of the waistcoat – *yelek*. Over it she wears a short *anteri* with elbow-length sleeves. Both garments enable her to make a feature of the loose trailing sleeves of the *gömlek*. Her accessories also indicate scope for personal taste. Instead of a fabric *kuşak* loosely swathed around the hips she wears a narrow stiff belt made up of linked metal plaques. Her tall headdress is not swathed in veils and scarves so that the hairstyle is revealed. To match the bold make-up the hair is pulled back severely from a centre parting leaving only a few sidewisps to soften the impression, and bound into plaits which hang down the back. A variation of both stylistic and technical interest is seen in her *terlik* as they are of finely knitted silk in jacquard floral motifs instead of the more usually depicted yellow leather. Outdoor costume (Plate 31) continued the fashions seen in the later sixteenth century of a neat dark *ferace* covering all of women's costume and the two white veils of the *yaşmak* wound and secured over the tall headdress.[39]

Women's fashions did not remain static but continued to evolve at a steady pace through the seventeenth century, but changes are seen more in subtlety of detail rather than in drastic innovation of shape and cut. A late seventeenth-century miniature,[40] for example, shows the continuing taste for brightly coloured fabrics which are carefully contrasted with patterned ones (Plate 32), but there is a tendency towards less multilayered costumes and a softer feeling in the clothes. The addition of the knotted short cloak is an interesting feature for which later parallels may be found in the costume of Kurdish women of Iraq and Persia and in the Caucasus. It is possible that the girl portrayed here is intended to be of Kurdish origin identifiable by her cloak. The headdress is also less severe and shorter with a flaring crown, worn at a more rakish angle. This style is seen in a surviving example in the Topkapi Palace collection of late seventeenth-century date (Plate 33), which neatly documents the type of fabric used and the millinery techniques.[41] The material is brocade woven in a compound silk weave using background wefts of silver metallic thread wrapped around a deep yellow silk core, and pattern wefts of brown silk which are all worked in a repeating design of heartshaped motifs framed in pairs of curved leafy stems. The headdress has a foundation frame made of a circle and length of stiff card for the crown and sides respectively. These

Opposite. Diagram 3. Woman's *gömlek*. Turkey, late 19th century. Scale – 1:14.

Above. Plate 29. Woman in patterned *şalvar*. Miniature from an album of single-figure studies. Turkey, 1618.

pattern pieces are cut out both in the brocade using a bias-cut strip for the side piece, and in dark blue cotton lining material. They are then seamed together, turned right side out and then fitted over the cardboard frames. Finally, the side piece is fitted around the circumference of the circular crown, slip stitched into place and then joined.

The changes in women's fashions noticeable in the tendency towards a softer more relaxed style at the end of the seventeenth century became more pronounced in the eighteenth century. Here it is possible to trace the development more closely as the source materials are more meticulous. Surviving buildings, ceramics and paintings of the eighteenth century reveal a taste for lighter more delicately ornamented creations which is mirrored sensitively in the textiles and costumes. Contacts between Ottoman Turkey and Europe especially France flourished and were manifested visibly in the passion for Turquerie among the French aristocracy – and the textiles of French origin used in Turkish costume. A girl's *anteri* of early eighteenth century date (Plate 34) admirably summarises both the taste for French textiles and innovations in shape and cut.[42] Examples from this period are complete garments so that a detailed and accurate picture including sewing techniques can be reconstructed for comparison with pictorial sources and written descriptions, which in turn provide the information for the total look.

The *anteri* is made of imported French silk in a fine close plain weave. The colours are delicate and understated – a pale cream background with alternating narrow strips of shaded rose pink, and undulating sprays of violets worked a satin ribbon weave using additional silk warp threads. The narrow loom width is neatly finished with corded selvages which are used in the seams to avoid frayed raw edges. A comparison of the shape and pattern to those of the seventeenth century confirms how much change had taken place. To suit the lighter material the form of the *anteri* is more graceful and streamlined and cut along narrower lines. It is ankle length with a close fitting bodice and a flaring skirt with deep side slits which falls gracefully from the hips instead of in a pronounced curve. The sleeves are narrow and tight but are slashed at the cuff and faced with a deep facing to fall back over the wrist, a feature which revealed slim attractive arms in a flattering manner and which could also be used to great effect over a tight cuff or over the flowing sleeves of a *gömlek*. In finishing detail the garment has a neat narrow neck and instead of a row of frogged plaited buttons and loops is edged with a lacy silk border. The pattern draft (Diagram 4) shows that this streamlined effect was achieved by varying the proportions of pattern pieces. In the same way as for the seventeenth century garment, shapes were built up around a central straight section. Here one long rectangular piece is folded in two at the shoulders and cut away at the front for the neck shaping and centre front opening. Narrow slim triangular sections are added at the sides and centre fronts from the waist downwards to create the flaring skirt.

Long shaped sleeves are carefully inserted straight at armhole level. The sewing methods employed are neat and competent, well matched to the fineness of the fabric, a combination is used of run and fell seams where all raw edges are avoided, small running stitches and hem stitch. All hems are turned in twice and sewn down using overcast stitches.

Both Turkish and European illustrative sources witness a change of fashion in the early eighteenth century to more graceful fluid styles, and it is possible, as it was in the seventeenth century, to correlate both textile design and garment shape with them. From these sources two main trends in dress fabric can be documented. The French ambassador to the Ottoman court, de Ferriol, who arrived in Istanbul in 1699 found his interest so stimulated by the life and people around him that he commissioned the Flemish artist J. B. Van Moeur to prepare a set of engravings for him of the different nationalities and levels of society of

Opposite top. Plate 30. Woman in two layers of *anteri, c.*1620.

Opposite bottom. Plate 31. Woman in outdoor dress, 1618.

Top. Plate 32. Woman in short cloak and *tarpuş.*

Above. Plate 33. Woman's *tarpuş.*

Left. Plate 34. Girl's *anteri.*

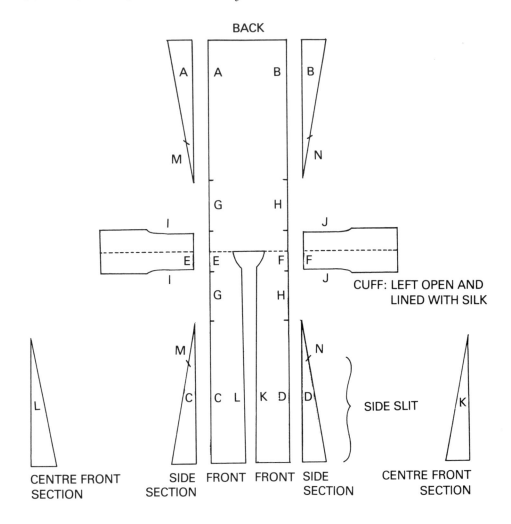

Diagram 4. Girl's *anteri*. Turkey, 18th century. Scale – 1:13.

ALL PIECES CUT ON STRAIGHT OF FABRIC

SEAMS A-A TO N-N JOINED USING RUN AND FELL AND RUNNING STITCH WITH ½ IN SEAM ALLOWANCE

ALL HEMS TURNED IN TWICE AND SEWN DOWN

NECK BINDING – A STRIP OF SILK 1½ IN WIDE FOLDED IN HALF AND HEMMED OVER EDGE

the Ottoman Empire. Van Moeur's engravings based on drawings made during his visit of 1707–8 were a great success, and were much copied by later artists who wished to cash in on this early eighteenth century passion for Turquerie. His studies of women are full of costume details and reveal a fashion for clothes made in plain silk in intense colours – such as deep yellow, crimson and purple. This fabric was embroidered in gold thread with separate floral sprigs forming a repeated pattern. The technique is identifiable as *dıval işi* – the couching of flat gold strip thread backwards and forwards over a stiff card template giving a satin-like effect when completed. This technique may be traced through to the nineteenth century where many fine examples of the finished work have survived.[43] The couching method employed was both economical and practical as it avoided the wastage of expensive gold thread and the distortion of the fine silk that would have resulted by pulling it through to the wrong side of the fabric. One of Van Moeur's engravings 'La Sultane Aşşeki or Sultane Reine' (Plate 35) reveals how such fabric was used and the type of garment accompanying it.[44] As a foundation she wears a white pleated *gömlek* gathered at the neck and the full ankle-length white *şalvar* in fine material patterned with gold stripes. Over a red V-necked *yelek* she wears a close fitting *anteri* in green silk patterned with gold sprigs in

Plate 35. La Sultane Asseki ou Sultane Reine.

dıval işi. It is graceful in shape with a deep V-neck and long sleeves with slashed cuffs, fastened with plaited button and loop fastenings and held in place by a deep jewelled belt. The costume also shows an additional garment worn in winter time but cut along similar lines to the *anteri* – a *kırk* – a type of ankle-length coat with short tight sleeves and lined with fur – which here is white ermine – folded back to form deep facings and borders around neck, front edges and sleeves. The headdress reveals a distinct change from the tall stiff caps of the seventeenth century. Here it consists of two scarfs wound loosely around a flat cap from which long tendrils of black hair twine, thus giving a much softer effect harmonising with the general style of the costume.

A parallel taste for clothes in delicately patterned fabrics in light colours also developed. Imported French silk was used but it is possible that its example stimulated the Turkish textile industry to produce its own versions. A delightful series of single-figure studies of palace girls was painted by the court artist Levni (*c.* 1720–30) and illustrates the type of woman in fashion at that time. Levni painted during the reign of Sultan Ahmet III (1703–1730) popularly known at the Tulip Period because of the Sultan's passion for that flower. He was pleasure loving and artistic admiring light graceful buildings, paintings and indulging in tulip festivals and garden parties. The women of his court strove to match their style and dress to this refined frivolity, and Levni shows how they did it. Fashions in figure and cosmetics corresponded to the style of dress. The face is still precisely and carefully made up but with eyebrows plucked into a more elongated line and sometimes joined over the bridge of the nose by pencilling with kohl to create a continuous sweep. Eyes are outlined with kohl into a shape with extended lines at the outer corners; mouths are still rouged in a neat shape. Figures though streamlined are curvacious with a generous décolletage and curved hips shown to advantage by the new styles of *anteri*.

The miniature here (Plate 36) documents changes in the style of underwear.[45] *Şalvar* are more voluminous falling in loose folds over the feet and are made in a wider range of colours and textures; here they are of a striped red and yellow fabric. The feature of these *şalvar* was the *uçkur* – or waist drawstring – made of a length of cream cotton or linen whose ends were embroidered with silks in graceful floral and foliage designs, provocatively revealed through the open skirts of the *anteri* and the transparent *gömlek*, which still followed the classic pattern but now was fastened at the neck with a jewelled clasp. The fondness for layers of garments in colour combinations which were either a subtle blend of related shades or contrasted ones continued. Here a short hip-length *anteri* is worn first made from lime green silk spotted with gold sprigs. It differs from earlier examples, however, in the curved *décolleté* neckline and the long slashed cuffs which are accentuated by the use of a bright orange lining. Over all is worn an ankle-length *anteri*

of soft grey embroidered silk also with a low neck and tight elbow-length sleeves, encircled by a jewelled clasped belt. The headdress now consists of two loosely swathed scarves – one of a block printed fabric – a *yemeni* – the other plain, tied over long hair which can be worn either in narrow plaits or allowed to hang loose as here.

Other miniatures demonstrate the variation and detail of this costume style. One girl (Plate 37) has chosen to wear two *anteris* in brightly contrasting colours[46] – a red long-sleeved hip-length under-garment over which is worn an ankle-length one with long tight sleeves made from a light blue silk embroidered with flower sprigs. This miniature also shows more construction detail in the side pocket and short slit at the lower side hem. An equally detailed but more solidly visualised interpretation of eighteenth century dress is seen (Plate 38) in one of the paintings of Abdullah Bokhari dating to *c.* 1744.[47] The motifs on the fabrics of the voluminous red *şalvar* and green *anteri* are

Above left. Plate 36. Girl in grey silk *anteri*. Miniature painting signed Levni. Turkey, *c.*1720–30.

Above right. Plate 37. Girl in blue *anteri*. Miniature painting by Levni. Turkey, *c.*1720–30.

Plate 38. Girl in green
anteri. Miniature painting
signed Abdullah Bokhari.
Turkey, *c.*1744.

clearly seen as separate motifs worked in gold thread in the *dıval işi* technique. His painting also documents a new type of accessory – a swathed shawl draped around the hips and waist a fashion which continues throughout the nineteenth century. The scarves of the headdress have also been disciplined into a tightly wound series of coils around a foundation cap. Out of doors the eighteenth century lady continued to discreetly envelope herself in long coats and veils. Levni's charming interpretation (Plate 39) indicates the subtlety of detail which could be used to give this outfit a flavour of provocation without transgressing the required canons of modesty.[48] The *ferace* is neatly cut from a light grey fabric, and all borders are faced with a deep band of blue silk which is worked into a decorative rayed motif at the front hem corners which could be effectively shown and displayed as the wearer picked her way through the streets. The *yaşmak* is represented as two transparent white veils edged with gold.

So far it has been possible to assess in considerable detail the various garments which were needed to clothe a fashionable Turkish woman. Until the eighteenth century, however, the sources have lacked the type of personal account supplied by Lady Mary Wortley Montagu (Plate 40) whose eagerness and curiosity to learn as much about Turkish life as possible, including costume, during her comparatively short stay provides information which infuses life into these clothes. Her letter of 1 April 1717 states:

The first piece of my dresse is a pair of drawers, very full, that reach to my shoes and conceal the legs more modestly than your Petticoats. They are of a thin rose colour damask brocaded with silver flowers, my shoes of white kid Leather embroider'd with Gold. Over this hangs my Smock of a fine white silk Gause edg'd with Embroidery. This smock has wide sleeves hanging halfe way down the Arm and is clos'd at the Neck with a diamond button, but the shape and colour of the bosom very well to be distinguished through it. The Antery is a waistcoat made close to the shape, of white and Gold Damask, with very long sleeves falling back and fring'd with deep Gold Fringe, and should have Diamond or pearl Buttons. My Caftan of the same stuff with my Drawers is a robe fitted exactly to my shape and reaching to my feet, with very long strait falling sleeves. Over this the Girdle of about 4 fingers broad, which all that can afford have entirely of Diamonds or other precious stones. Those that will not be at that expense have it of exquisite Embroidiery on Satin, but it must be fasten'd before with a clasp of Di'monds. The Curdee is a loose Robe they throw off or put on according to the Weather, being of a rich Brocade (mine is green and Gold) either lin'd with Ermine or Sables; the sleeves reach very little below the Shoulders. The Headress is compos'd of a Cap called Talpock, which is in winter of a fine velevet embroidier'd with pearls or Di'monds and in summer of a light shineing silver stuff. This is fix'd on one side of the Head hanging a

Plate 39. Girl in outdoor clothes. Miniature painting signed Levni. Turkey, *c.*1720–30.

Plate 40. Portrait of Lady Mary Wortley Montagu and her son. Attributed to J. P. Van Moeur (1671–1737).

little way down with a Gold Tassel and bound on either with a circle of Di'monds (as I have seen several) or a rich embroider'd Handkerchief. On the other side of the Head the Hair is laid flat, and here the Ladys are at Liberty to show their fancys, some putting Flowers, others a plume of Heron's feathers, and, in short, what they please, but the most general fashion is a large Bouquet of Jewels made like natural flowers, that is, the buds of Pearl, the roses of different colour'd Rubys, the Jess'mines of Di'monds, Jonquila of Topazes etc. so well set and enammell'd try hard to imagine any thing of that kind so beautiful. The Hair hangs at its full length behind, divided into tresses braided with pearl or riband, which is always in great Quantity.

I never saw in my life so many fine heads of hair. I have counted 110 of these tresses of one Ladys, all natural, but it must be own'd that every Beauty is more common here than with us. They have naturally the most beautifull complexions in the world and generally large black Eyes. I can assure you with great Truth that the Court of

England (tho I believe it the fairest in Christendom) cannot show so many Beautys as under our Protection here. They generally shape ther Eyebrows and the Greeks and Turks have a custom of putting round their Eyes, on the inside a black Tincture, that, at a distance or by Candlelight, adds very much to the Blackness of them. I fancy many of our Ladys would be overjoy'd to know this Secret, but try too visible by day. They dye their Nails rose colour, I know I cannot enough accustom my selfe to this fashion to find any Beauty in it.

As to their Morality or good conduct, I can say like Arlequin, 'tis just as 'tis with you, and the Turkish Ladys don't commit one Sin the less for not being Christians. Now I am a little acquainted with their ways I cannot forbear admiring either the exemplary discretion or extreme stupidity of all the writers that have given accounts of 'em. Tis very ease to see they have more Liberty than we have, no Woman of what rank so ever being permitted to go in the streets without 2 muslins, one that covers her face all but her Eyes and another that hides the whole dress of her head and hangs halfe way down her back; and the Shapes are wholly conceal'd by a thing they call a Ferigee, which no Woman of any sort appears without. This has strait sleeves, that reaches to their finger ends and it laps all around 'em, not unlike a riding hood. In Winter 'tis of Cloth and in Summer plain stuff or silk. You may guess how effectually this disguises them, that there is no distinguishing the great Lady from her Slave, and 'tis impossible for the most jealous Husband to know his Wife when he meets her, and no Man dare either touch or follow a Woman in the Street.[49]

Further developments of the fashions so racily described by Lady Mary may be traced by studying the figures portrayed in the albums of types and characters of the Ottoman Empire painted for European patrons. From the many which have survived, one of the finest is the album allegedly painted on the order of Sultan Abdul Hamit I for Friedrich Heinrich von Diez, Prussian ambassador to the Ottoman court 1784–91.[50] A comparative examination of two paintings (Plates 41 & 42) from this series *Sultane en Galla* and *Servante d'une Sultane* or *Dame de Condition Turque* indicates where early eighteenth-century fashions continued and where they changed.[51] Both women wear *şalvar* but of a more voluminous cut which fall over the feet giving more the affect of a bouffant skirt. They also both wear a *gömlek*, finely pleated with a deep V-'neck but tucked into the *şalvar* instead of hanging over them to the ankle as a new fashion which continued through the nineteenth century until European-style dress finally eroded traditional Turkish fashions. Both again wear neat ankle-length *anteris* in light materials of flowered pink and white silks respectively with deep *décolleté* necklines and the sleeves with tight cuffs. Clasped belts and draped shawl sashes are both worn. The garments, however, which each lady wears over her flowered *anteri* differ significantly. The Sultane's fur-decorated *kırk*

Plate 41. Sultane en Galla. Miniature from album of single-figure studies. Turkey, *c*.1790.

continues in the early eighteenth-century tradition, while her companion wears a dark blue *anteri* whose long trailing skirts and slashed cuffs anticipate a style that was to be very popular in the nineteenth century. Construction and cut in their basic principles follow traditional methods; by tracing the gold outlines of the seams it is clear that side sections and sleeves were added to a basic central piece folded over the shoulders and cut to fit at the neck and bosom. Both ladies are encumbered with precarious bulbous headdresses because the artist has not been able to depict them correctly, and also was not willing to sacrifice a single gem of the jewelled ornaments for the sake of accuracy. By comparison with later more carefully depicted examples, the headdresses were based on caps adorned with heavy silk tassels around which a series of scarves were wrapped and secured in place with jewelled pins, pendants and aigrettes depending on the contents of the wearer's jewel casket. The hairstyle accompanying this confection had deep forehead and side fringes while long plaits were brought up from the back and nonchalantly twisted and tucked into the folds of the scarves.

If the sources of the seventeenth and eighteenth centuries have enabled a complete picture of a Turkish woman's costume to be interpreted and reconstructed, those for the nineteenth through to twentieth centuries enable a fascinating wealth of detail to be supplied. First of all they are more plentiful – many garments have survived, and while the art of traditional Turkish painting declined, regarding costume there was more than adequate compensation in the engravings and drawings of European artists. As more Europeans visited the Ottoman Empire and spent long periods in Istanbul so they became familiar with its life, and were, therefore, able to describe and interpret it with objective thoroughness rather than with wonder at its novelty. Accordingly, there are excellent descriptions of costume and its accessories which may be taken together with the illustrations and surviving costumes to create a well-documented survey.

In general, women's fashions evolved during the nineteenth century in a natural way from those of the eighteenth century but exaggerating and developing certain features. An important modifying factor, that of European influence, seen innocuously enough in the eighteenth century in the use of imported French silk for women's anteris, accelerated the pace of change of fashion, however, until by the early twentieth century in upper class urban circles the traditional costumes had given way to smart European dresses. Encouragement of Europeanisation in Ottoman society was a deliberate and indeed mandatory policy coming from the top. Sultan Mahmut II (1808–39), aware that the empire's institutions were no longer coping with its problems, sought a remedy to them by importing European ideas and technology in an attempt at revival. Political and social change was mirrored in costume which proved a sensitive and easily visible barometer of change. Mahmut II himself set the pace by abandoning his traditional Turkish clothes for European inspired frockcoat and trousers. He also moved in 1815 from the old Topkapi Palace to a more modern establishment at Dolmabahce situated on the Bosphorus beyond the Gorden Horn which was furnished with European chairs, tables and beds. His entourage followed suit and hastened to divest themselves of their robes and turbans and put on European-style uniforms which were worn with a fez. These reforms in dress were made law by 1829 for all male citizens, and change was so rapid that traditional costume was retained only by the religious establishment and to a certain extent in the provinces. Mahmut's costume reforms did not find universal approval. Julia Pardoe in 1835 remarks that

> . . . all the admirable reforms wrought by Sultan Mahmoud in his capital overbalanced by the frightful changes that he has made in the national costume, by introducing a more caricature of that worst of all originals – the stiff, starch, angular European dress. The costly turban, that bound the brow like a diadem, and relieved by the richness of its tints, the dark hue of the other garments, has now almost entirely disappeared from the streets; the flowing robe of silk or of woollen has been flung aside for the ill-made and awkward surtout of blue cloth, and the waist which was once girdled with a shawl of cashmere is now compressed by two brass buttons.[52]

Plate 42. Servante d'une Sultane or Dame de condition Turque. Miniature from album of single-figure studies. Turkey, *c.*1790.

Fortunately for Julia Pardoe's peace of mind, women's dress changed more gradually and for a long time a more fluid situation prevailed in which traditional styles and European influences mingled in varying degrees. In 1845, for instance, Thomas Allom was still able to write admiringly:

> The costume of these Orientals is extremely gorgeous; their hair, which, though fine and glossy, is incapable of curling – a peculiarity arising from the effects of the bath – is hidden by the folds of the embroidered handkerchiefs that form their headdress – fastened and decorated with bodkins of diamond and emeralds – jewels they are extremely fond of displaying. They wear an undergarment of silken gauze, or other light material, fringed with narrow ribbon; their robe is generally printed cotton, selected from the gayest and brightest patterns; it is made of one piece, divided on either side from the hip, and girded around the waist by a cashmere shawl. During the cold season, their attire is completed by the addition of a tight vest, lined with fur and most commonly of a gay pink or green colour.[53]

He is also able to differentiate between palace and outside fashions:

> The costume of the Imperial Palaces differs from that displayed in the harems of private individuals in deference to the prevailing fashions introduced by the Sultan, and which are no less admired by his

Sister. The Oriental modes are strangely blended with the European or what is intended to be the European style of attires; but its most indistinctive and least becoming feature is the headdress composed of a printed handkerchief twined around the brow, and at once secured and ornamented by bodkins of costly jewels; the hair is cut square across the forehead, and on each side of the face it is left perfectly straight, and profusely adorned with gems, flowers or the deep fringe of the handkerchief placed so as to form the appearance of a wreath. A number of slender false plaits depend from behind, and some few ladies have adopted the plan of wearing artificial curls, which they arrange in huge clusters beneath their yashmaks; they disfigure with a piece of black sticking-plaster, shaped like a crescent or a star, the space between the eyebrows; and the practice of imparting to the latter a deeper dye, is universally followed by the Turkish women.[54]

His pictorial interpretation (Plate 43) with this exaggerated style of dress may be compared with the more modest version depicted by Jean Brindisi (Plate 44).

Julia Pardoe is more approving of women's fashions than of the men's:

Devlehai Hanoum was dressed in an antery of white silk, embroidered all over with groups of flowers in pale green; her salva, or trousers, were of satin of the Stuart Tartan, and her jacket light blue; the gauze that had composed her chemisette was almost impalpable, and the cashmere about her waist was of a rich crimson. Her hair of which several tresses had been allowed to escape from beneath the embroidered handkerchief, was as black as the plumage of a raven; and her complexion was a clear, transparent brown. But the great charm of the beautiful Georgian was her figure. I never beheld anything more lovely; to the smoothly-moulded graces of eighteen she joined the majesty and stateliness of middle life . . .[55]

An impression of the impact made by such a style of dress is seen in a complete costume – now in the collections in the Royal Museum of Scotland, Edinburgh – (Plate 45) dated to *c.* 1875–85.[56] It is important not only for the information which it provides on style, cut, decoration and sewing methods of Turkish dress but also because it has survived as a total ensemble. Altogether it consists of the following garments and accessories: *gömlek* (chemise), *dislik* (underpants), *şalvar* (trousers), *anteri* (robe) *kuşak* (girdle) *çipşip* (indoor slippers) and *yelpaze* (fan). Individually the garments can be closely correlated with literary and pictorial sources. They are all hand sewn to a high standard of craftsmanship, and employ in their cut and construction the traditional Turkish methods already observed of building up shapes by using narrow widths of cloth joined together with straight seams. The first

garment is the *gömlek*, a garment which was subject to change in style as noted by Charles White in 1844, 'But the fashion has been modified, and the *gömlek* is now fastened at the throat by a diamond, pearl, or coral button, and closed over the chest with two or three similar ornaments. The sleeves are loose, and the whole is edged with satin.'[57] The museum's *gömlek* (Plate 46) conforms to this description in its use of more luxurious material and also shows the influence of Europe in its fabrics. Two are used, a fine machine-woven net of European manufacture for the body and a checkered white silk voile for the sleeves. It has a simple round neck open at the centre front, long slashed sleeves and extends to the knees in a flaring bell shape. The cut (Diagram 5) is based on a central rectangular piece folded in two at the shoulders to which sleeves and side shapings are added. All seams are hand sewn worked in a neat rolled overcasting, and neck and sleeve borders are trimmed with creamy white machine-made lace edging. It is interesting to see the survival of traditional methods of construction based on the use of narrow loom widths which the introduction here of broad widths of European-made net should have rendered obsolete. European stylistic

Above left. Plate 43. Turkish women indoors. Thomas Allom. Character and costume in Turkey and Italy, London, 1845.

Above. Plate 44. La Tasse de Café.

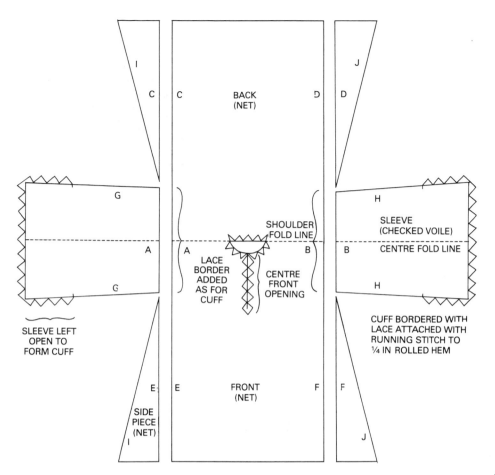

ALL PIECES CUT ON STRAIGHT OF FABRIC

SEAMS A-A TO J-J JOINED USING ¼ IN SEAM ALLOWANCE, ROLLED AND OVERCAST

LOWER HEM ALLOWANCE OF 1 IN FOLDED IN TWICE AND SEWN WITH RUNNING STITCH

ALL OTHER HEMS USE ¼ IN ALLOWANCE WHICH IS ROLLED AND OVERCAST

Opposite. Plate 45. Woman's costume. Turkey, c.1875–85.

Left. Diagram 5. Woman's *gömlek*. Turkey, c.1875–85. Scale – 1:17.

elements had already influenced the construction of the *gömlek* at an earlier date. Thomas Allom's engravings of the 1840s show court women dressed in *gömleks* with deep frothy lace collars and cuffs[58] echoing contemporary European fashions which were to intrude on Turkish dress increasingly as the nineteenth century progressed.

The *gömlek* was worn loose over undergarments known as *dislik*. Again the ever observant Charles White describes them as yet the only author known to do so. He says: 'Dyslik are of calico, very wide, drawn close round the loins with an *outchkoor* and tied at the knee, whence their literal name (knee things).'[59] The fact that *dislik* are not described or illustrated in any earlier source is no reason for supposing that they were a new invention. It would seem probable however that they began to be worn from the eighteenth century onwards because of the changes of fashion already noted in *şalvar* styles. The early

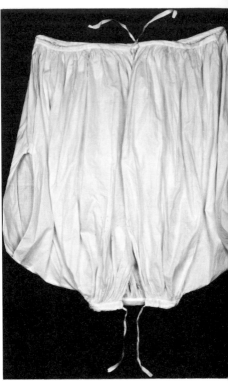

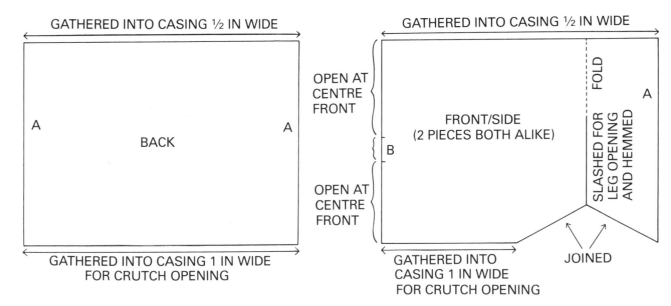

GATHERED INTO CASING ½ IN WIDE

A   BACK   A

GATHERED INTO CASING 1 IN WIDE
FOR CRUTCH OPENING

GATHERED INTO CASING ½ IN WIDE

OPEN AT
CENTRE
FRONT

FRONT/SIDE
(2 PIECES BOTH ALIKE)

B

OPEN AT
CENTRE
FRONT

FOLD

A

SLASHED FOR
LEG OPENING
AND HEMMED

JOINED

GATHERED INTO
CASING 1 IN WIDE
FOR CRUTCH OPENING

ALL PIECES CUT ON STRAIGHT OF FABRIC

SEAMS A ON EACH FRONT/SIDE SECTION JOINED TO
CORRESPONDING A ON BACK SECTION

TWO FRONTS JOINED AT B

SEAM ALLOWANCE ¼ IN & ⅛ IN RESPECTIVELY FOR RUN
AND FELL AND RUNNING STITCH

seventeenth-century women had worn long white *şalvar* of fine cloth. With the introduction of flamboyant ostentatious *şalvar* made from heavy materials often embroidered with gold thread it probably seemed sensible and confortable to wear an undergarment of lighter material. The museum's garment (Plate 47) is certainly to be identified in function as a *dislik* though in shape and construction nothing comparable as yet has been discovered. It is in the shape of a large bag of curious construction (Diagram 6) gathered at the waist with whimsically positioned leg and crutch openings. It is made of fine white cotton hand sewn with neat run and fell seams and hemmed edges and casings for the drawstrings.

As the pictorial sources reveal, *şalvar* which had already become voluminous garments in the eighteenth century continued this development to even greater levels of extravagance in the nineteenth century. Charles White defines them:

> Salvars are loose trousers, nearly three yards wide at the waist, and diminishing to about eighteen inches at the extremity of the leg. They are drawn together and supported by an outchkoor, run through a broad hem, and richly embroidered at the ends. The extremities are fastened by loops over the ankles. Shalwar are made of various materials according to seasons, tastes and fortunes. First-class Odaliks of the Palace are celebrated for the splendour of their shalwars and indeed of their whole attire. The pieces of silk or brocade, called caftan, required for their shalwars and gown, and measuring eight yards, commonly cost from one thousand to one thousand five hundred piastres. Shalwars render the same service to Turkish and Armenian ladies as petticoats and slips to those of Europe . . .[60]

Both Allom's and Brindisi's engravings and the example in the museum's costume indeed confirm the comparison with a petticoat as their fullness makes them like a long bouffant skirt rather than trousers. The garment (Plate 48) is made in a brilliant lime green shot silk embroidered with floral sprays in *dıval işi* technique. The cut and construction are simple based on four rectangular pieces all alike (Diagram 7), joined at centre back and front from waist to crutch and from inner and outer leg with a crutch gusset inserted diagonally. The legs are threaded with drawstrings so that they can be gathered and tied just below the wearer's knee to billow in folds over the ankles. In these fashions the *şalvar* are put on over the *gömlek* and *dislik*.

Once underwear and *şalvar* had been arranged the main garment – the *anteri* in a long trailing graceful form with the skirt deeply slit at each side from hips to hem known as an *üçetek* – three skirts – could be worn. This style seems to have been a nineteenth-century development as it is well recorded in sources of this period though it may well have evolved from the long trailing *anteri* worn as an overgarment by the late

Opposite top left. Plate 46. Woman's *gömlek*. Turkey, c.1875–85.

Opposite top right. Plate 47. Woman's *dislik*. Turkey, c.1875–85.

Opposite bottom. Diagram 6. Woman's *dislik*. Turkey, Istanbul, c.1875–85. Scale – 1:13.

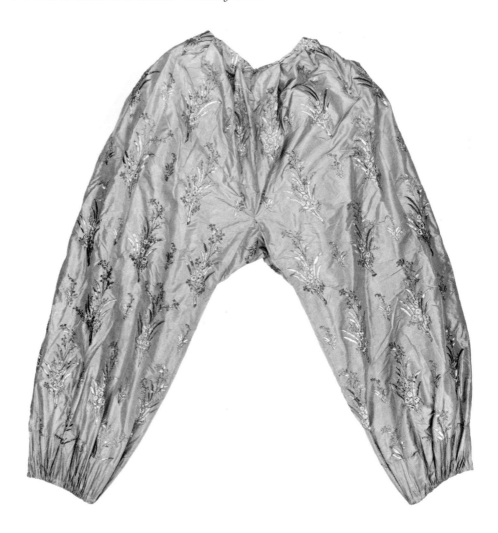

Plate 48. Woman's *şalvar*.
Turkey, *c*.1875–85.

eighteenth century *Servante d'une Sultane*. Charles White notes:

> Entary (gown) are most difficult to describe, the form, especially that of the skirt, being unlike anything within the range of European fancy. The back is closed, and adhere tightly to the figure. The front is open much cut away, and merely closed by three or four buttons at the waist; the sleeves are tight from the shoulder to below the elbow, and being much longer than the arm, hang down and exhibit the sleeve of the gömlek. The skirt is at least two feet longer than the person, and is divided below the waist into three breadths, the ends of which are tucked up when walking and secured beneath the waist shawl. Enteri are made of the same material as shalwars, and are lined with calico or silk, and trimmed with arf. They are worn at home and abroad, and in spite of their singular conformation, have a graceful and easy appearance.[61]

The museum's garment both confirms White's general description and supplements it by providing information on how the effect was achieved. Again the basic principles of cut are comparable with those found in seventeenth- and eighteenth-century examples, the garment depending on a central rectangle (Diagram 8) to which triangular side and front sections are added to produce a slim but flaring skirt and long pieces are set into the bodice at right angles to give sleeves. An additional construction device is also seen in the form of triangular sections inset at the underarm to give ease of movement. The fabric used is the same as that used for the *şalvar* with the addition of a deep border of coarse gold *arf* lace around all edges, thus neatly confirming White's account. The standard of the sewing is high with fine running stitch seams and careful matching of main fabric and lining so that no raw edges are visible.

Over the combined *şalvar* and *üçetek* was draped a *kuşak* here in the form of a folded cream silk fringed scarf. The style had developed from late eighteenth-century practice and had become the most usual form

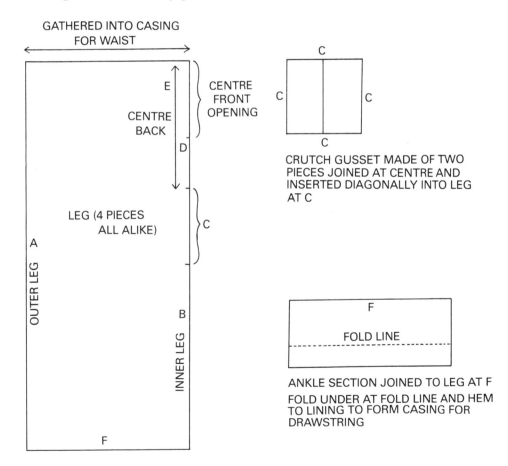

GATHERED INTO CASING
FOR WAIST

E

CENTRE BACK

CENTRE FRONT OPENING

D

LEG (4 PIECES ALL ALIKE)

A

OUTER LEG

INNER LEG

B

F

C

CRUTCH GUSSET MADE OF TWO PIECES JOINED AT CENTRE AND INSERTED DIAGONALLY INTO LEG AT C

F

FOLD LINE

ANKLE SECTION JOINED TO LEG AT F
FOLD UNDER AT FOLD LINE AND HEM TO LINING TO FORM CASING FOR DRAWSTRING

ALL PIECES CUT ON STRAIGHT OF FABRIC
LEG PIECES JOINED IN PAIRS AT A AND B THEN AT E FOR CENTRE BACK AND D FOR CENTRE FRONT
RUNNING STITCH USED FOR ALL SEAMS ALLOWING ¼ IN

Diagram 7. Woman's *şalvar*. Turkey, Istanbul, c.1875–85. Scale – 1:13.

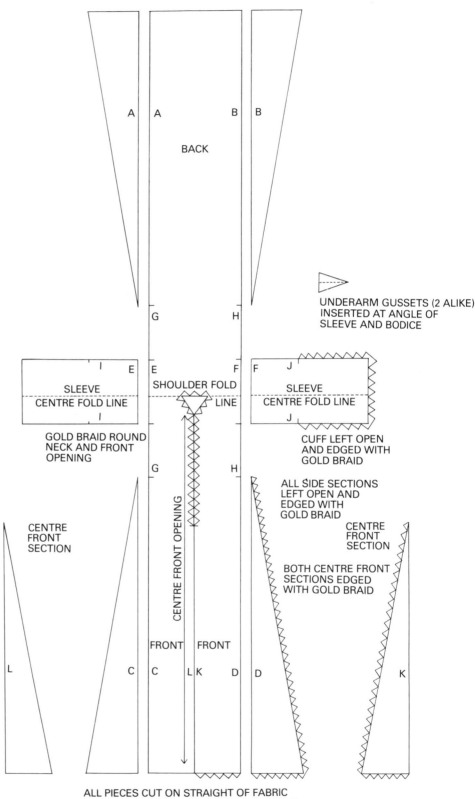

A A B B

BACK

G H

UNDERARM GUSSETS (2 ALIKE)
INSERTED AT ANGLE OF
SLEEVE AND BODICE

I E E F F J

SLEEVE SLEEVE

CENTRE FOLD LINE SHOULDER FOLD LINE CENTRE FOLD LINE

I J

GOLD BRAID ROUND
NECK AND FRONT
OPENING

CUFF LEFT OPEN
AND EDGED WITH
GOLD BRAID

G H

ALL SIDE SECTIONS
LEFT OPEN AND
EDGED WITH
GOLD BRAID

CENTRE
FRONT
SECTION

CENTRE
FRONT
SECTION

CENTRE FRONT OPENING

BOTH CENTRE FRONT
SECTIONS EDGED
WITH GOLD BRAID

FRONT FRONT

L C C L K D D K

Diagram 8. Woman's
anteri. Turkey, Istanbul,
*c.*1875–85. Scale – 1:19.

ALL PIECES CUT ON STRAIGHT OF FABRIC
SEAMS A-A TO L-L JOINED USING RUNNING
STITCH WITH ¼ IN SEAM ALLOWANCE

of waist decoration in the nineteenth century as recorded by Charles White.

The kuoshak is invariably of narrow shawl. It is fastened twice around the loins, and the ends are turned in, and rolled flat in front The kooshak is a receptacle for pocket handkerchiefs, and sometimes for the embroidered money bags. Few ladies wear watches, and none carry poignards.[62]

A further layer could be added to the costume a *yelek* – a short tight jacket though its use was optional and Charles White records that it is going out of fashion certainly in the capital.

These jackets are of light cloth, velvet or merino, of bright colours, richly embroidered in gold and coloured silks, without buttons, and with short half sleeves. They are worn over the entary in winter and form a picturesque addition to the rich and original costume of the fair sex. They are, however, more in vogue in the provinces than in

Plate 49. Woman's *çipşip*. Turkey, *c.*1875–85.

the capital. Ladies of fashion look upon them as gaudy and in bad taste . . .[63]

It is in this context perhaps significant to note that the *yelek* is a garment which could be and was replaced by a European style jacket among fashionable women such as Nazip Hanoum adopted daughter of Sultan Mahmut II's sister Asma Sultan. In 1835 she wore:

> . . . an antery of light green striped with white and edged with a fringe of pink floss silk; while her jacket, which was the product of a Parisian dressmaker, was of dove-coloured satin, thickly wadded and furnished with a deep cape and a pair of immense sleeves, fastened at the wrists with diamond studs.[64]

Remaining accessories were shoes and optionally fans. Turkish custom required different shoes for indoor and outdoor wear. At home ladies either went barefoot or wore various types of light slippers. The examples shown here (Plate 49) – flat purple velvet ballet shoes lavishly embroidered with gold thread and seed pearls are called *çipşip* described as:

> slippers without heels, extremely pointed, and somewhat curved at the extremity. They are of diverse materials and colours, richly embroidered in gold, silver or pearls with a border of coloured ribbon, and rosettes of silk, gold cord, or knots of pearls on the instep. The pearl-embroidered slippers are extremely rich and graceful, harmonising admirably with the general costume. From £10 to £20 is no uncommon price for Indjy (pearl) tchipship. They may, however, be purchased for 200 piastres; and then embroidered in gold and silver for 30 to 40 . . .[65]

Fans which added a graceful languid touch were always of the screen type known as *yelpaze* here made of a large circle of white ostrich feathers attached to a carved ivory handle.

Such a costume would not have been complete however without an appropriately elaborate hairstyle and a liberal application of cosmetics – topics on which the nineteenth-century sources are full of detailed information. Julia Pardoe describes the construction of a coiffure:

> We meanwhile amused ourselves with watching the slaves, who having left the bath and seated themselves in groups at the lower end of the apartment, combing, tressing and banding their dark, glossy hair; the younger ones forming it into one long thick plait hanging down the centre of the back, and twisting above it the painted handkerchief, so popular in the harem that it is worn equally by the Sultana and the slave; the others binding their tresses tightly about their heads and replacing the locks which they hide from view with a

profusion of false hair, braided in twenty or thirty little plaits, and reaching round the whole width of the shoulders.[66]

These hairstyles were adorned usually by an assortment of scarves wound round tasselled caps in many variations and proportions fastooned with jewellery according to the wearer's means, or by more modest lace trimmed handkerchiefs. Much time and energy was devoted to cosmetics and their application. Eye make-up was especially important as Julia Pardoe noted involving both the manufacture and application of kohl:

> In the course of the evening, the elder lady resumed her place at the tandour; and, in the intervals of the conversation, she amused herself by burning one of the nuts at a candle, and having reduced it to a black and oily substance with great care and patience, she took up a small round hand mirror, set into a framework of purple velvet, embroidered in silver that was buried among her cushions and began to stain her eyebrows, making them meet over the nose and shaping them with an art which nothing but long practice could have enabled her to acquire.[67]

Faces were also rouged

> Among other articles much in vogue with the Turks are – kissilyk yooz bouyoomaliky (rouge cottons for the cheeks). These cottons are steeped in a solution of cinnabar, and are then rolled in flat circles and dried. When used, the cheek is slightly moistened, the cotton applied, and the dye thus communicated to the skin upon which it leaves a soft carnation, that does not injure the epidermis by absorption.[68]

Charles White whose eyes missed nothing of the absorbing detail of Ottoman Turkish custom also noted that the traditional custom of staining the finger nails with henna was dying out among the wealthier classes who prefer instead to wear European gloves.

> It is amusing to observe the coquettish arts with which ladies of higher degree protrude their hands from beneath their ferijees, to show that they have renounced this filthy and unsightly custom. Still more diverting is the innocent variety with which some exhibit their adoption of silk or cotton web gloves purchased from the Frank traders of Pera.[69]

Despite the gradual introduction of European influences into Turkish urban costume social customs had not changed sufficiently to encourage the abandonment of discreet outdoor dress. Fashions here had modified, however, and the *ferace* was now a more frivolous

Plate 50. Women in outdoor dress. Amadeo Preziosi, Stamboul moeurs et costumes.

garment often in light coloured silks with a long frilled collar (Plate 50), while the *yaşmak* an arrangement of transparent veils was used to great effect as Julia Pardoe notes in her account of Turkish women on an excursion who

> sally forth, accompanied by two or three slaves, to pay visits to favourite friends; either on foot, in yellow boots reaching up to the swell of the leg, over which a slipper of the same colour is worn; or in an araba, or carriage of the Country, all paint, gilding and crimson cloth, nestled among cushions, and making more use of her eyes than any being on earth save a Turkish woman would, with the best inclination in the world be able to accomplish; such finished coquetry I never before witnessed as that of Turkish ladies in the street. As the araba moves slowly along the feridjhe is flung back to

display its white silk lining and bullion tassels; and should a group of handsome men be clustered on the pathway, that instant is accidentally chosen for arranging the yashmac.[70]

By the 1870s these attractive costumes were, at least in the main cities, giving way steadily to more European fashions. This is reflected at various levels in Turkish clothes, ranging from substituting European garments such as the Parisian jacket of Nazip Hanoum for Turkish garments, careful alteration of existing wardrobes in an effort to bring them up to date, curious amalgams of European shape with Turkish decoration, to sophisticated European clothes either commissioned from Paris by those of sufficient means such as the princesses of the Ottoman court or copied by enterprising Levantine dressmakers in the Pera quarter of Istanbul. The Royal Museum of Scotland's complete costume provides evidence of how an attempt was made to renovate a gown made *c.* 1875–85 to the fashion current in the 1890s for dresses with fitted bodices and nipped-in waists. Here the *anteri* was extensively altered by inserting darts at the back (Diagram 9), cutting close fitting curved armholes and sleeve tops and pleating the top of the *şalvar* in an effort to produce the right hourglass shape. Lucy Garnett writing in the late 1880s remarks:

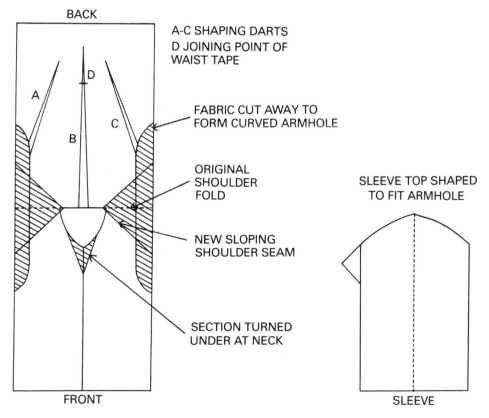

BACK

A-C SHAPING DARTS
D JOINING POINT OF
WAIST TAPE

FABRIC CUT AWAY TO
FORM CURVED ARMHOLE

ORIGINAL
SHOULDER
FOLD

NEW SLOPING
SHOULDER SEAM

SECTION TURNED
UNDER AT NECK

FRONT

SLEEVE TOP SHAPED
TO FIT ARMHOLE

SLEEVE

Diagram 9. Woman's *anteri*. Detail of alterations to bodice and sleeves. Scale – 1:13.

In September 1896, my parents' wedding took place at Emirgan. No pictures of my mother wearing her wedding dress were taken, but in photographs depicting her in the gown she wore on the day the marriage contract was signed, she looks charming. She wears a white dress of finest Brussels lace called Point d'Angleterre over cream satin and a short veil of matching lace, fixed with diamond flowers to her hair, which was dressed high on her head; white roses edge the low-necked bodice. Her actual wedding dress, which she later gave to me, might have been the gift of a fairy godmother. Of pale pink faille, ending in a very long train, it is entirely covered with embroidered floral designs in genuine gold thread, and so heavy that although supported by train bearers, my mother could hardly move and was afraid of falling backwards. Her veil, equally long, of palest rose chiffon, was held in place by a tiara and partly covered her face. Strands of flexible gold wire fell from the tiara on each side to the hem of her skirt, framing her face in a shining aura.[73]

Apart from this latter detail the dress would have been quite appropriate for a fashionable bride in contemporary Paris, London or Vienna. A surviving costume (Plate 52) in the Topkapi Palace attributed to Fehime Sultan daughter of Murat V (deposed 1876) dated to *c.* 1890 confirms this handling of European costume idiom.[74] It is an afternoon ensemble whose separate bodice and skirt are made of deep brown imported European velvet, decorated with appliqué motifs of silver

> With regard to indoor dress, it is difficult to say what is not worn at the present day by Osmanli women of the wealthier classes, as so many have, unfortunately, either wholly or in part, exchanged their own picturesque costume for what is only too often a caricature of Parisian fashions . . .[71]

A photograph of an Istanbul lady taken in 1873 (Plate 51) shows a reasonably graceful adaptation of her traditional costume.[72] Over voluminous *şalvar* she wears a trailing skirted *üçetek* but, instead of a bodice with long slashed sleeves wrapped with a bulky *kuşak*, she has a neat V-necked top with wide sleeves clasped at the waist by a belt in a style directly comparable with European fashions of the late 1860s. Her shoes, however, appear to be identifiable with a type of European style elastic-sided boot of which examples have survived. Here there is a confusion of tradition as the boots with their fashionable pointed toes and high heels have been made in purple velvet with uppers lavishly embroidered in gold thread; their European prototype would have been made in fine kid leather. The European costume worn by the upper classes showed a much more confident handling of the foreign styles – probably because their owners could afford to commission them direct from Paris. Emine Fogat Tugay charmingly describes her mother's wedding dress of 1896:

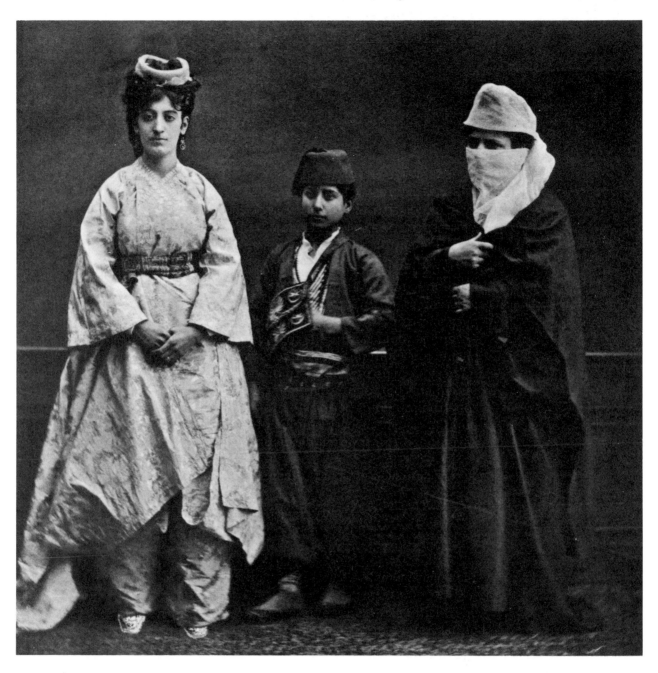

Plate 51. Woman in indoor dress. Istanbul, Turkey, 1873.

bugle beads. The bodice is tight fitting with back and fronts made up of several shaped pieces into which leg-of-mutton sleeves are fitted. All pieces are mounted on a white calico twill lining and vertical whalebone ribs stiffen the seams. To further ensure the tight fit a calico tape is attached to the centre back at waist level leaving the ends to be hooked in front. The bodice is lavishly decorated with frilled velvet epaulettes, beaded revers and brown corded silk ribbon bows. The bell-shaped skirt is made of five vertical sections pleated and tucked at the back and decorated with hem and side flounces at the front. This

Plate 52. Fehime Sultan's
afternoon dress with
brown velvet skirt and
jacket. Turkey, *c*.1890.

costume reveals the abandonment of traditional Turkish ways of cut and construction and, indeed, also of sewing methods since the neat narrow hand-sewn seams are replaced by wide machine stitches, ones whose edges are pinked and then simply opened and ironed flat.

Outdoor dress continued to develop along more modish lines.

The feridjes . . . of the wealthy are of fine cloth or silk, the younger and more fashionable ladies affecting light tints such as pink or lilac, often with trimmings of lace on the rectangular cape, and the elderly ladies more sober tints. The yashmak is composed of two squares of white tarlatan folded corner-wise. A small cap made of some bright coloured material and decorated with pearls, or diamonds, is placed on the top of the head and serves as a foundation for the upper part of the veil, the doubled edge of which is brought down to the eyes, the ends being pinned together at the back. The other and larger square is then placed with the folded edge upwards across the mouth and lower part of the nose the ends being pinned to those of the upper square . . .[75]

European fashions continued to set the style for well-to-do urban women in the early twentieth century. Emine Fogat Tugay provides an interesting description in 1913 of her Bayram festival dress in which modernity and tradition exist side by side.

Being too young for such functions, it was decided that I must stay at home. I was bitterly disappointed and begged and prayed until my Mother gave in, and had a long dress of flowered chiffon, over ivory satin, made for me by her dressmaker. With my hair dressed high for the occasion I felt completely grown-up. On the morning of the first day of Bayram, wearing yashmaks (still the correct thing when going to Court) and light silk cloaks over our dresses, and accompanied by women attendants and a eunuch, we proceeded on board our launch to the Dolma Bağçe Palace . . .[76]

Her dress resembled in style that made for Fehime Sultan (Plate 53) of printed cream voile and satin with loose bodice and bell-shaped skirt which was fitted over a pink silk lining and ornamented with bows and flounces.[77] Accompanying these lighter fashions was a change of outdoor dress known as the *çarşaf*.

The women of the poorer classes made it of black cotton, very voluminous with an impenetrable black veil. Not so the fashionable lady. Here was a silk dress of chic and elegance, with a short cape of the same silk, which she wore over her head and shoulders, together with a thin veil of lace and chiffon to hide her features. Long gloves completed the toilette.[78]

Above. Plate 53. Fehime Sultan's cream and pink silk dress. Turkey, *c*.1910.

Above right. Plate 54. Woman's *çarşaf*. Violet silk. Turkey, early 20th century.

A silk *çarşaf* (Plate 54) in the Royal Museum of Scotland's collection shows how it was constructed[79] and worn (Diagram 10). Made of brilliant violet silk, it is simply a rectangle with a drawstring at the waist gathered to produce a neat ankle-length garment draped over the head and falling in graceful folds around the body, its provocative and eye-catching colour effectively negating any concealing effect. As

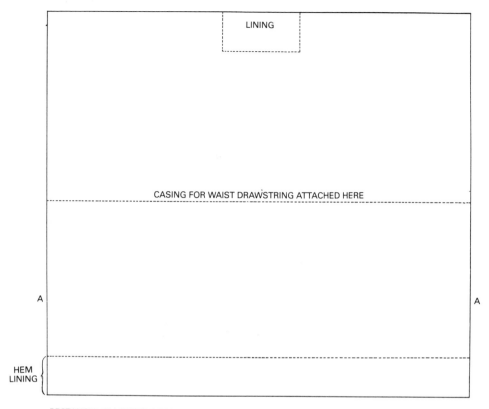

LINING

CASING FOR WAIST DRAWSTRING ATTACHED HERE

A

A

HEM
LINING

RECTANGULAR LENGTH OF FABRIC CUT ON STRAIGHT
ALL SEAMS HAND SEWN USING RUNNING STITCH – ½ IN SEAM
ALLOWANCE
FABRIC FOLDED OVER AND JOINED AT CENTRE FRONT A-A FROM
WAIST TO ANKLE
CASING FOR WAIST DRAWSTRING, FACINGS AT HEAD, HEM AND
OVER CENTRE FRONT SEAM SEWN DOWN WITH RUNNING STITCH

Diagram 10. Woman's
çarşaf. Turkey, early 20th
century. Scale – 1:20.

women's emancipation proceeded during the last years of the Ottoman Empire, and as the Turkish Republic became established, so their clothes changed. By 1921:

> The outdoor clothes of Turkish ladies were then undergoing a subtle change towards further emancipation. The tcharchaf had been discarded by the upper classes for a manteau, or coat, cut in accordance with the height of fashion, and worn with a turban covering the hair, with a dainty chiffon as a substitute for the veil. Some had even left off that graceful apology.[80]

As a final comment on the long evolution of Turkish women's clothes – from the layered garments preserving archaic Central Asian cut and construction methods to the ensembles of European style which inevitably quickened in pace and spread as women's emancipation advanced – are two garments, not from one of the main urban centres, but from a provincial town of Afyon traditionally famed for its felt

Above. Plate 55. Woman's *dislik*. Afyon, Turkey, *c*.1910.

Right. Plate 56. Woman's dress and jacket. Pink moire silk. Afyon, Turkey, *c*.1910–20.

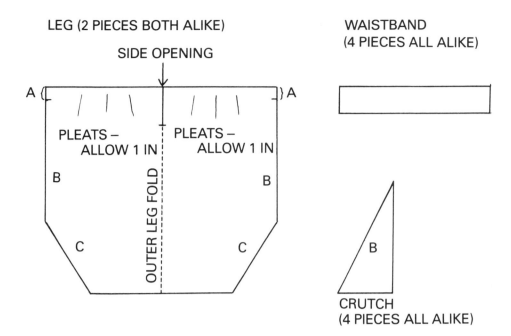

LEG (2 PIECES BOTH ALIKE)

SIDE OPENING

A PLEATS – ALLOW 1 IN   PLEATS – ALLOW 1 IN   A

B   OUTER LEG FOLD   B

C   C

WAISTBAND
(4 PIECES ALL ALIKE)

B

CRUTCH
(4 PIECES ALL ALIKE)

ALL PIECES CUT ON STRAIGHT OF FABRIC

ALL SEAMS MACHINE-STITCHED RUN AND FELL WITH ½ IN SEAM ALLOWANCE

CENTRE BACK AND FRONT JOINED AT A

CRUTCH SEAMED TO LEG PIECE AT B

INNER LEG JOINED AT C

EACH SECTION OF WAISTBAND MADE OF TWO PIECES MACHINED TOGETHER THEN ADDED RESPECTIVELY TO FRONT AND BACK OF GARMENT

PAIR OF TIES ADDED TO EACH SIDE OPENING

Diagram 11. Woman's *dislik*. Turkey, Afyon, early 20th century. Scale – 1:11.

making. These are both of European cut of First World War vintage, *dislik* (Diagram 11) in the form of knee-length drawers (Plate 55) trimmed with an airy version of Turkish needleworked lace – *oya işi* – and a costume in pink silk (Plate 56) with a fashionable hobble skirt and long fitted jacket.[81]

5

The Ottomans Abroad – South-East Europe

The costumes already discussed and which have shown the steady development of a sartorial tradition in the urban heartland of the Ottoman Empire, though in themselves of great richness and variety, are basically a carefully chosen selection of the infinite range of clothes worn in the Ottoman dominated world. For the sake of clarity the costumes of Muslim women of the main urban centres and, indeed, those only of the upper and middle classes were analysed because the documentation was reasonably complete and offered practical limits. Within mainland Turkey itself there were numerous gradations of fashion within the costume of this social class. Here as elsewhere in the world provincial fashions inevitably lagged behind metropolitan styles, as Julia Pardoe observed during her visit to Bursa in 1836:

> The city of Broussa is infinitely more oriental in its aspect than Stamboul; scarcely a Frank is to be seen in the streets; no French shops, glittering with gilded timepieces and porcelain tea-services, jar upon your associations; not a Greek woman stirs abroad without flinging a long white veil over her gaudy turban, and concealing her gay coloured dress beneath a feridjhe; while the Turks themselves almost look like men of another nation. I do not believe that, excepting in the palace of the Pasha, there are a hundred fez-wearing Osmanlis in the whole city. Such turbans! Mountains of muslin, and volumes of cachemire; Sultan Mahmoud would infallibly faint at the sight of them; worn, as many of them are, falling upon one shoulder, and confined by a string in consequence of their great weight . . . The women, meanwhile, except such as belonged to quite the lower orders, were almost invisible; I scarcely encountered one Turkish woman of condition in my walks, and those who passed in the arabas kept the latticed windows so closely shut, despite the heat, that it was impossible to get a glimpse of them.
>
> There is not a greater difference in the mode of wearing the turban by the one sex at Broussa, than in that of wearing the yashmac by the other. In Constantinople it is bound over the mouth and in most instances over the lower part of the nose, and concealed upon the shoulders by the feridjhe. In Asia, on the contrary, it is simply

fastened in most cases under the chin, and is flung over the mantle, hanging down the back like a curtain. In the capital, the yashmac is made of fine thin muslin through which the painted handkerchief and the diamond pins that confine it can be distinctly seen and arranged with a coquetry perfectly wonderful. At Broussa it is composed of thick cambric, and bound so tightly about the head that it looks like a shroud.[1]

Surviving costumes and illustrations confirm the wide differences between sophisticated Istanbul fashions and their provincial contemporaries. These provincial costumes, however, frequently display considerable panache and colour. The first example is an *üçetek* (Plate 57) in the Royal Museum of Scotland's collection probably from Bursa and of nineteenth century date.[2] It is made of a deep crimson rose silk woven with a design in damask weave of freely arranged roses and trailing stems, and decorated with large bouquets and sprays of flowers and a continuous scrolling border embroidered in the couched gold *dıval işi* technique. An examination of the construction (Diagram 12) shows that the garment was based on a central rectangular piece cut on the straight of the fabric and folded over at the shoulders. Following traditional methods of shaping, triangular sections were added to each front so that the garment could be wrapped over and belted while sleeves were set in at right angles to the body with triangular pieces added at underarm. An interesting touch of European influence is seen in the sleeves gathered into a narrow cuff. Apart from certain common

Below left. Plate 57. Woman's *üçetek*. Crimson silk. Bursa, Turkey, 19th century.

Below. Plate 58. Woman in striped silk costume. Sivas, Turkey, 1873.

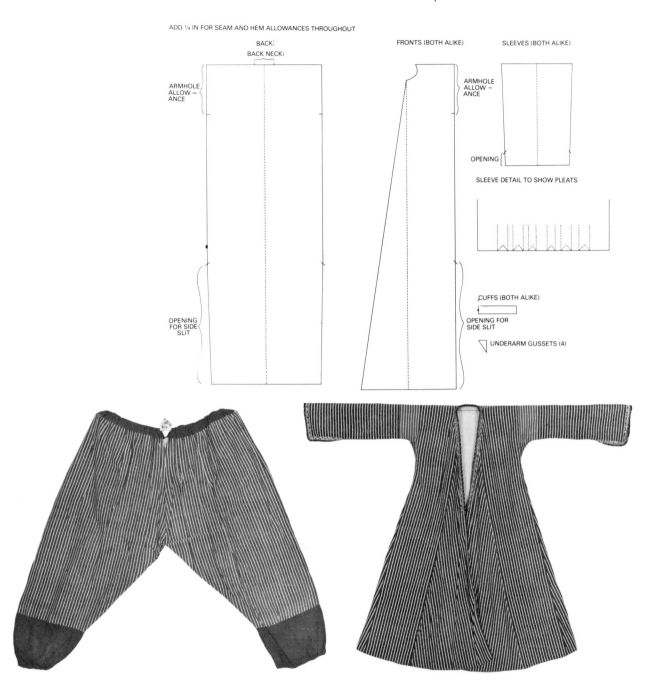

ADD ¼ IN FOR SEAM AND HEM ALLOWANCES THROUGHOUT

BACK
BACK NECK

FRONTS (BOTH ALIKE)

SLEEVES (BOTH ALIKE)

ARMHOLE
ALLOW –
ANCE

ARMHOLE
ALLOW –
ANCE

OPENING

SLEEVE DETAIL TO SHOW PLEATS

CUFFS (BOTH ALIKE)

OPENING
FOR SIDE
SLIT

OPENING FOR
SIDE SLIT

UNDERARM GUSSETS (4)

factors of construction the style of the *üçetek* differs from that of examples worn in the capital. The line of the garment is more square-cut, it is shorter and without the deep slits which would transform the skirt into a trailing series of trains.

Other examples of the variation in provincial costume are seen in a set of photographs taken for the Vienna exhibition of 1873 of the different costumes of the Ottoman Empire, a modern substitute for the books of miniatures on the same theme. Here the costume of a Muslim

Top. Diagram 12. Woman's *üçetek*. Turkey, Bursa, 19th century. Scale – 1:20. Sleeve detail scale – 1:10.

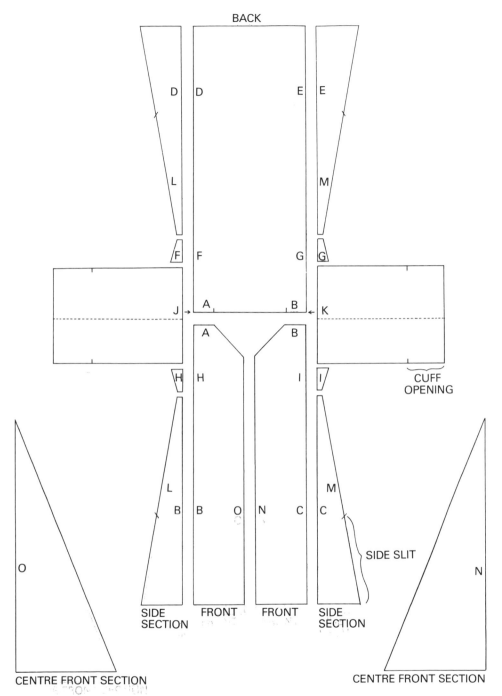

BACK

D D   E E

L   M

F F F   G G

J → A B ← K

A B

H H H   I I

CUFF OPENING

L   M

B B O N C C

O   SIDE SLIT   N

SIDE SECTION   FRONT   FRONT   SIDE SECTION

CENTRE FRONT SECTION   CENTRE FRONT SECTION

ALL PIECES CUT ON STRAIGHT OF FABRIC
SEAMS A-A TO O-O JOINED
ALL SEAMS AND HEMS MACHINE STITCHED
NARROW STRIP OF FABRIC ADDED TO NECK AND UPPER
FRONT EDGES AS FACING
BRAID TRIM ADDED TO NECK AND CUFFS

Opposite left. Plate 59. Woman's *şalvar*. Pink and white striped silk. Sivas, Turkey, early 20th century.

Opposite right. Plate 60. Woman's *anteri*. Pink and white striped silk. Sivas, Turkey, early 20th century.

Above. Plate 61. Femme d'Asie de condition and non mariée. Miniature from album of single figure studies, Turkey, c.1790.

Above left. Diagram 13. Woman's *şalvar*. Turkey, Sivas, early 20th century. Scale – 1:18.

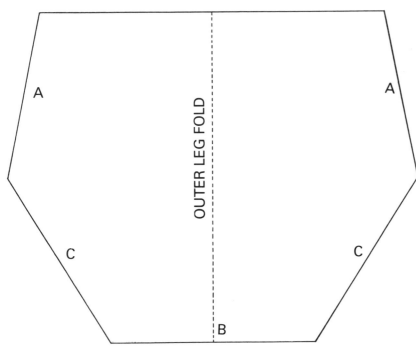

LEG (2 PIECES BOTH ALIKE)

A   A

OUTER LEG FOLD

C   C

B

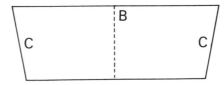

LOWER LEG (2 PIECES BOTH ALIKE)

B

C   C

ALL PIECES CUT ON STRAIGHT OF FABRIC
ALL SEAMS AND HEMS MACHINE STITCHED
EACH LEG JOINED AT CENTRE BACK AND FRONT AT A
LOWER LEG ATTACHED AT B
INNER LEG JOINED AT C
STRIP OF RED FABRIC (17 IN × 3 IN) FOLDED IN HALF AND
ATTACHED AT WAIST TO FORM CASING FOR DRAWSTRING
DRAWSTRING THREADED THROUGH CASING AT ANKLES

Above. Plate 62. Perotte, Dame de Pera. Miniature from album of single-figure studies, Turkey, *c*.1790.

Above right. Diagram 14. Woman's *anteri.* Turkey, Sivas, early 20th century. Scale – 1:12.

woman from Sivas in Eastern Turkey (Plate 58) is especially striking, with its short *anteri* and matching *yelek* of striped silk and the large headdress consisting of numerous *yemenis* – block printed cotton scarves – wound over a foundation cap to produce a stylish turban.[3] A set of garments – *şalvar* and *anteri* – in the Royal Museum of Scotland's collection[4] are interesting not only in their own right but as pieces which may be identified with the costume worn by the girl from Sivas

(Plates 59 & 60), thus completing the picture of material, construction and final appearance. They are both made of a finely striped silk in white and deep rose pink. The *şalvar* are voluminous (Diagram 13) but of different proportion from those worn in the capital, and less exaggerated in length so that they fall in manageable folds around the ankles. The *anteri* is again short with neat proportions and simple sleeves, constructed (Diagram 14) from triangular sections added to the sides and centre front of a straight central piece and of a width to produce a bell-shaped skirt. All are neatly machine stitched, a guide to the lateness of their date, but in proportion and shape preserve archaic features more common to eighteenth-century dress. A painting in the Diez album of *c.* 1790 may be compared here (Plate 61) depicting 'Femme de Asie de Condition et Non Mariée'.[5] The style of the *anteri* in its close fit and comparatively short skirt may be readily identified in the nineteenth-century photograph and garments, while her cumbersome bulbous headdress is clearly a rather inadequately drawn version of the Sivas-style turban of several patterned and twisted scarves.

Plate 63. Woman in outdoor dress. Trebizond, Turkey, 1873.

Plate 64. Perotte, Dame de Pera sur la rue. Miniature from album of single-figure studies, Turkey, c.1790.

Outdoor costume in the provinces, more opaque and concealing in the nineteenth-century, than in the capital, continued these conservative trends. A photograph of a girl from Trebizond of 1873 (Plate 63) shows her wearing a voluminous *çarşaf* and a black veil — *petçe* — of a stiff black mesh — a contrast to the graceful *yaşmak* and also to the dashing indoor costume.[6]

Julia Pardoe in her acutely observed account of the more conservative provincial fashions of Bursa comments that even the Greek women were obliged to modestly cover themselves when out of doors.[7] Greeks were among the many ethnic and religious minorities who inhabited the Ottoman Empire who in turn contributed their own version to the procession of fashion. In Istanbul the Greek community along with the European trading, diplomatic and commercial missions lived in the section across the Golden Horn known as Pera. They played an active role with Armenians and Jews in the trade of the empire and rendered themselves indispensable in transactions between visiting European delegations and the Ottoman court. Evidence of the style of dress among the Greek women of Pera is provided by more paintings in the Diez album. Both their indoor and outdoor costumes show an interesting combination of Turkish styles of garment with innovation resulting from outside influence and difference of custom. The 'Perotte, Dame de Pera'[8] follows the same basic principles of dress as her Turkish neighbour (Plate 62) in that she has assembled her costume by layering the garments. She wears a pleated V-necked *gömlek* with an ankle-length *anteri* of white silk which is figure hugging, and tight-sleeved with a low cut neckline and encircled by a pink *kuşak* caught up into a looped knot. Over this she wears a light blue silk coat cut along the same lines as the *anteri* but with short tight sleeves and narrow front which is clearly meant to be worn open to reveal the garments beneath. This garment is comparable in shape to the fur-trimmed coat — *kırk* — worn by wealthy Turkish women in winter. The light colour scheme, the lack of *şalvar* and touches such as the ribbon bow at the neckline of the white *anteri*, and the choker all combine to give a European flavour to garments which are basically foreign in cut. Contemporary European influence is also seen in the accessories from the neat high heeled shoes, to the stick fan, and the extraordinary headdress of a dark turban strewn with feathers and ropes of pearls which surely should be compared with the exaggerated hairstyles current among fashionable aristocratic women in Europe during the 1780s and 1790s. When going out, the Pera Greek (Plate 64) simply put on a *ferace* with long sleeves and collar comparable to that worn by a Muslim Turk but instead of concealing her face with the *yaşmak* she draped a long scarf[9] — here obviously in the form of a Kashmir shawl with decorated borders — over her head and threw one end under her chin and the other over her shoulder since neither orthodox Christianity nor social custom required her to conceal herself.

Other minority groups also adapted Turkish costume by adding their own fashions. Julia Pardoe visiting the daughter of Mustafa Paşa – the Paşa of Skodra in Albania – at her Istanbul home, notes

> Heymine Hanoum dispatched a slave for a handkerchief with which she was in the habit of binding up her hair, in order to show us one of the Albanian fashions. It was of black muslin, painted with groups of coloured flowers, and bordered all round with a deep fringe of fine pearls; I never in my life saw any mixture which produced a more striking effect; and when she wound it about her head – the dark glossy tints of the flowers, and the whiteness of her clear brow rivalling the pearls that rested on it – I thought that earth could hold nothing more lovely than Heymine Hanoum.[10]

It is clearly established that a vital and dominant costume tradition flourished in the mainland of Turkey comprising many parallel strands such as metropolitan, provincial, urban and rural styles, all enriched by specific details of the costumes of minority races. It was unlikely, then, that such a tradition would not have influenced or interacted with the costume styles of the many territories which were under Ottoman domination both in Europe and Asia. Here one of the most interesting areas of interface as yet comparatively unexplored is that of the Balkans – Turkey in Europe. From the time of their first military excursions into Thrace in the mid-fourteenth century, the Ottomans gradually and relentlessly pursued a policy of conquest until in the early sixteenth century all of South-Eastern Europe from Hungary through to Southern Greece was under their control – a situation which was to basically endure until the late nineteenth and early twentieth centuries. The area ruled by the Ottomans now the modern states of Hungary, Albania, Bulgaria, Greece, Jugoslavia and Romania corresponded approximately to the old Ottoman provinces of Rumeli (Albania, Thrace, Serbia, Macedonia, Montenegro, North and South Greece), and Bosna (Bosnia-Hercegovina), Eğri and Timişvar (Hungary) and the autonomous Christian states of Bogdan (Moldavia), Eflak (Wallachia) and Erdel (Transylvania).

This large area in South-Eastern Europe was of vital importance to the Ottomans and valued probably more highly than many of their Asian provinces. It was not only a source of tribute and manpower but also provided indispensable reserves of food such as wheat from Thrace and the Dobruja, and sheep and cattle from Bulgaria, Macedonia and Eastern Thrace, and essential links in Ottoman trade with Europe and the Black Sea area. Consequently Ottoman Turkish and established traditions intermingled. Here conditions were flexible – Rumeli, Bosna and Eğri and Timişvar were ruled as Ottoman provinces under direct rule which naturally meant a civil and military administration staffed by Turkish officials and officers, while the Romanian principalities of Bogdan, Eflak and Erdel were treated as autonomous or Christian vassal states with the privilege of electing their own rulers in return for supplying tribute and levies of troops. These differences of status are visible today in the distribution patterns of architecture. Rumeli and Bosna's towns still preserve the distinctive buildings of Ottoman architecture – the mosques with their great domes and rocket-like minarets, the *medresses* – Moslem theological colleges, and the *hamams* – public baths, and the *bedestens* – covered markets. These also survive in Hungary in Budapest, Eger and Peç even though here the Ottoman occupation was relatively short, extending from 1526 to 1699 when Hungary together with Erdel was handed over to the Austrian Hapsburgs. In Erdel itself, however, and in the two principalities of Bogdan and Eflak there are no buildings of Ottoman Turkish architecture except in the Black Sea coastal area of the Dobruja which was under direct rule.

Costume together with architecture was one of the more obvious and striking visual symbols of Ottoman influence. Broadly speaking before the advance of the Ottoman, South-Eastern Europe had fallen under two spheres of cultural influence which can be traced in costume: that of the Byzantine and Orthodox world in the lands extending from the province of Serbia eastwards, and that of Western Europe and the Roman Catholic tradition from North Albania, Croatia and through Hungary. Since, however, the entire area was of great importance in West-East trade, oriental textiles and influences in costume were apparent before the Ottoman invasion – certainly in the clothes of the landed aristocracy and wealthy urban classes. Country people, however, wore clothes which although not of luxurious silks and furs were remarkable for their regional variation and lively embroidered and woven decoration, whose descendants may still be seen today in the costumes of Balkan villagers brought out for festivals and holidays.[11]

It is essential to determine how Turkish influences contributed to this rich indigenous tradition. While there is considerable evidence it is not always even in concentration and range; there is not, for example, the equivalent of the series of Turkish miniature paintings recording the activities of the rulers, and European illustrations and travellers' accounts are less abundant because many regarded South-Eastern Europe mainly as a necessary transit area on the road to Istanbul. Despite these reservations, certain developments may be traced closely linked to the pattern of Turkish occupation. In the areas under direct control two factors were important: the presence of a Turkish population mainly consisting of the administrative personnel and their families who were concentrated in key towns – Beograd, Sarajevo, Skopje, Salonika, Shoumen, Budapest – whose costumes followed Turkish styles and provided models to be copied, and the presence of a large Muslim population of local origin such as occurred in Bosna where many Slavs had converted to Islam and formed a class distinct by their dress and social customs from their Christian neighbours. Consequently, certain common patterns may be traced in the costumes of Rumeli and Bosna the areas longest under direct rule.

Plate 65. Vue de Belgrade – la ruine de Prince. . . . Watercolour, *c.*1860. Carl Goebel (1824–99).

To a traveller arriving anew in one of the main towns the streets would present a lively and remarkably varied picture where different nationalities and classes of society mingled wearing their distinctive costumes. Goebel's view of Beograd in the 1860s, for example (Plate 65), successfully captures the atmosphere of a busy attractively dilapidated town and its inhabitants.[12] Among the shoppers and strollers on the left are peasant women from the Danube area of Posavina in the neighbourhood of Beograd wearing distinctive high circular caps known as *konda* whose colourful costumes contrast with the sober *feraces* and *yaşmaks* of the two Turkish women shopping on the right. Yet it would be a naive simplification to assume that sartorial difference could be neatly divided between Christian and Muslim women, and, indeed, there is evidence of the influence of Turkish tradition on Christian women. Milovan Djilas remembering his Orthodox Christian aunt, a native of Montenegro, as late as the early twentieth century states: 'She dressed like the Moslem women in baggy trousers and cloak. From 1912 onwards, however, she did not wear the veil. Like other Orthodox women from Turkish towns, such as Prizren and Peć, she had Muslim ways, but she was more liberal in outlook.'[13]

The Posavina peasant women in Goebel's picture also wear tight short sleeveless waistcoats called *jelek* which are clearly taken from the Turkish garment – *yelek* – which occurs in both sleeved and sleeveless versions.

Direct Turkish influence is seen in the costume of a Serbian city girl[14] as painted by the Transylvanian artist Charol Popp de Szathmary (Plate 66) who visited Beograd several times between 1849 and 1885 and has left an animated and attractive record of the people he encountered there. The girl's articles of costume and the terms used to describe them are heavily indebted to Turkish contemporary fashions, from her voluminous red *şalvar* to her short sleeveless underjacket – *mintan* and the fur-lined and fur-edged upper garment the *curce* or Turkish *kırk*. Her costume, however, shows local adaptations of Turkish styles notably in the simplified headdress consisting of a blue tasselled red fez worn over long bobbed and fringed hair simply and without elaborate scarves. This costume serves to introduce the pattern of women's dress in the provinces under direct rule, where Ottoman Turkish styles were worn not only by the Turkish population but also adapted in varying degrees by the native urban élite. In Greece, for example, Turkish Muslim women of Salonika (Plate 67) took to the streets in the fashion of *ferace* and *yaşmak* as worn in contemporary

Above. Plate 66. A town girl, Belgrade. Watercolour, *c*.1849–85. Charol Popp de Szathmary (1812–87).

Right. Plate 67. Woman in outdoor dress. Salonika, Greece, 1873.

Istanbul. Salonika as a thriving city close to the capital could be expected to follow its styles. Earlier in the nineteenth century Baron Broughton gave an account of Greek women's city dress which closely parallels in every detail that of a Turkish woman.

> The dress of the females does not vary materially from the Turkish, of which there is so exact an account in Lady M. W. Montagu's Letters. The vest fits quite close to the bosom, but becomes larger and wider a little below the waist. The gown, which is sometimes made of fine flowered silk, flows off loosely behind, and the sleeves of it which widen and are slit towards the waist, are made much longer than the arm, and are turned back. There is sometimes a ribbon, or other girdle, under the bosom; but the zone, a rich shawl, embroidered with gold and flowers, is nevertheless worn, loosely resting on the hips, and either tied in a spreading knot, or fastened before with a large plate, ornamented with false or real jewels.
>
> The female zones are not, like those of the men, wrapped many times round the body, but only once, and are put for ornament, not use, as they do not bind or support any part of the dress . . .
>
> The whole dress of the richer females is swollen out and ornamented with gold and silver trimmings to a very unbecoming excess. They wear bracelets of precious stones, and strings of gold coins, round their arms and necks. The headdress of the younger girls is tasty; their hair falls down their backs in profusion, generally straight, but sometimes plaited for the sake of adding false tresses, and is combed straight over their foreheads and the sides of the cheeks: a little red cap with a gold tassel, studded with zequins, is fixed on one side of the crown, and adorned, by the girls with flowers, by the matrons with heron's feathers or a bouquet of jewels.
>
> It is at Athens, and I believe elsewhere, a very prevailing fashion for the young women to dye the hair of an auburn colour with the plant called henna. The matrons, by another process, give a dark black tinge to their tresses. When abroad the Greek ladies are muffled up in a wrapping-cloak, much like the Turkish, except that they have not a square merlin hanging behind, and, instead of a hood over the face, generally wear a long veil, which, however, they frequently throw aside when not in the presence of any Turks.[15]

Plate 68. Femme de l'ile de Tino. Miniature from album of single-figure studies, Turkey, *c*.1790.

Greek women's costumes in the islands also mirrored Turkish fashions especially in those situated close to the Turkish mainland. Here a woman of Tinos (Plate 68) portrayed in the Diez album of the 1790s[16] resembles her Turkish neighbour in the main garments of her dress differing, however, in detail such as the European heeled shoes and the sugar loaf hat.

A comparable phenomenon is seen in the Jugoslav province of Bosna, centre of a large native Muslim population, where the town costume of Sarajevo followed Turkish fashions closely. At the end of the

Plate 69. Woman's *anteri*.
Sarajevo, Bosnia, late 19th
century.

nineteenth century (Plate 69), women who could afford it were wearing
the *üçetek* type of *anteri* usually of light coloured silk embroidered with
floral sprays in couched gold *dıval işi* technique[17] with deeply slit skirts
and long trailing sleeves with slashed cuffs which could be thrown
back to reveal either the lace trimmed or gold embroidered borders of
the *gömlek*. The *anteri*, however, did not have the exaggeratedly long
skirt associated with the Istanbul style, and was cinched at the waist
with a narrow filigree gold or silver belt with a decorative buckle
instead of being enwrapped in the folds of a shawl-like *kuşak*.

Headdresses also were never as elaborately swathed, neat jewelled fez-like caps being preferred which could be decorated with jewellery or borders of gold coins to suit the wearer's taste and means. Voluminous *şalvar* were also worn either beneath an *anteri* or as a complete costume in their own right over an elaborately decorated *gömlek* worn together with a short sleeveless jacket or *yelek*.[18]

The elaborate materials for such costumes were probably commissioned in Istanbul or could be bought directly in the market of Sarajevo which was a thriving international trade centre. As European influence infiltrated in varying degrees into the costume of Turkish women so did it also into the Balkan variation, though at a slower rate than in Istanbul. In Sarajevo, for example (Plate 70), by the early twentieth century Muslim women were wearing garments which attractively blended Turkish and European elements – a voluminous *şalvar* usually of a light flowered material so shaped that it seemed more like a long

Below left. Plate 70. Women's costumes. Sarajevo, Bosnia, late 19th–early 20th century.

Below right. Plate 71. Croat and Serb women's costumes. Jajce and Mostar, Bosnia – Hercegovina, late 19th century.

full skirt, topped by a blouse of matching fabric with full sleeves and flounced neck and shoulders inspired by contemporary Western styles.[19] Further fashions to be considered were those worn by the Christian Serb and Croat population of Bosna (Plate 71) which also showed evidence of Turkish influence, a taste for voluminous skirt-like *şalvar* worn with varying types of *yelek* according to region. Croats of Jajce, for example, wore a tight *décolleté* jacket with long slashed sleeves in a colour and design contrasting with the *şalvar*; a Serbian woman of Mostar might choose a jacket of the same colour as her *şalvar* but looser in shape and open at the centre front.[20]

Paradoxically, the two Romanian principalities of Eflak (Wallachia) and Bogdan (Moldavia) which were never under direct rule and, therefore, did not have the living Ottoman presence to inspire new fashions provide the most continuous chronological documentation of the influence of Turkish costume traditions in South-East Europe.[21] Hungary, in contrast, while a province under direct occupation only experienced this status for a comparatively short period from 1526 to 1699; Turkish influence is found more in men's garments, in furnishings such as carpets and in domestic embroideries which were greatly influenced by Turkish designs rather than in women's dress. The two principalities, however, by virtue of their greater proximity to the Caucasus and Black Sea regions and the strategic importance of their Danube ports, had long been familiar with the products of Seljuk Persia and Turkey and later the Ottoman world in the centuries before they were conquered. As their dependence on the Ottoman political system lasted effectively until the mid-nineteenth century so did its visible expression in the form of costume. The presence, however, of the princely courts of the Romanian voivodes and their boyars meant that there was a native aristocracy to set a standard for luxury fashion which was based on that of the Ottoman world, the dominating cultural and artistic influence of the Balkan area. Consequently, the furnishings and appurtenances of the courtly life of the principalities whose capitals were established at Tirgovişte and then Bucharest in Wallachia, and Suceava followed by Iaşi in Moldavia often consisted of imported Ottoman Turkish objects. The shards of sixteenth-century polychrome Iznik pottery excavated from the Curtea Vecche at Bucharest provide evidence of this.[22] In the absence of a direct Ottoman presence, the princes were able to build up feudal estates for themselves which in a fertile and abundant land yielded revenues from agriculture and fishing. Monastic foundations were also endowed, which in turn flourished as centres of culture and scholarship, amassing their own collections of manuscripts and treasures which again included Turkish Iznik pottery such as the pieces preserved in the monasteries of Neamţ and Putna in Moldavia.[23] Also stored in the monasteries are lengths of Turkish fabrics from which it is possible to reconstruct the costumes of the princes and their womenfolk, and embroideries showing the influence of Ottoman designs.[24] Additionally fresco paintings of rulers and their families have survived, as it was the custom in Romanian Orthodox churches always to have a complete portrait of the founder and his dependants at the west end just inside the entrance.[25]

Probably the earliest evidence of the presence of Turkish textiles in Romanian court costume is that provided by the embroidered grave cover of Maria of Mangop (Plate 14), the second wife of the prince of Moldavia Stefan the Great who died in 1477 and was buried at the monastery of Putna.[26] While Romanian ecclesiastical embroideries reached a high standard in the vestments required for the divine liturgy employing traditional themes of iconography common to the Eastern Orthodox world, their repertoire was extended also by the apparently unique theme of portraying on a grave cover the dead person richly dressed in court robes. Apart from the stylised posture, great care was taken to use stitches which would accurately recreate the texture of the fabrics used and the shape of the garment. The material of Maria's robe has already been discussed in the section on Turkish costume and identified with the luxurious brocade known as *zerbaft*. Apart from her crown and jewellery, her costume is dominated by this robe which is cut and shaped to take maximum advantage of the bold patterns of the fabric. Its cut and construction is identical with that of the Turkish masculine garment known as a *caftan* – a generic term used to denote a heavy outer garment – fastened from neck to hem which as is seen here was made distinctive by the fashion of long false sleeves extending to the hem of the robe; the wearer's arms appeared through deep slits at front armhole level. The cut of such a garment followed traditional Turkish methods of adding shaping to a straight length folded in half at shoulder level to form centre back and front. Maria's robe shows the care taken to match up patterns, and how all edges are neatly bound with a broad facing in a plain fabric. It is especially interesting because as yet no evidence has survived to document the wearing of such a garment by contemporary Ottoman Turkish women.

A further example of a garment made in both Turkish fabric and style depicted in embroidery is seen in the grave cover (Plate 72) of Prince Ieremia Movila who became ruler of Moldavia in 1595.[27] An ambitious and cultivated man, he endowed the monastery of Suçevita, which he and his two equally ambitious brothers Gheorge and Simion had founded in 1581, with many treasures – silver objects, manuscripts, and embroideries. On his death in 1606, he was buried in the monastery church and his grave was covered with an embroidered portrait which also has an inscription naming him and the date of his death. Ieremia is portrayed as a striking dignified personage elaborately costumed as befitted his rank in Ottoman-inspired court dress. The dominating garment is a long-sleeved outer robe of the *caftan* type as worn by Maria of Mangop in her funeral costume and here fashioned of brocade patterned with bold repeating motifs of peony sprays interwoven with curving serrated leaves and stems of open roses. His brother Simion

who died in 1609 is also commemorated in a grave cover in which he wears a robe of the same material.[28] Did the two brothers commission a long length of brocade from one of the Bursa looms and have them made up there into costumes, or was the brocade transported as an uncut length to distant Moldavia? Certainly the design is to be identified with Turkish brocades of late sixteenth-/early seventeenth-century date indicating that the Moldavian nobility kept abreast of current fashion.

Evidence of the Turkish-inspired costumes of the Romanian nobility does not depend on representations in other media alone, as examples of actual garments worn by both men and women have survived. They have been reconstructed from textiles collected together from Romanian monasteries – such as Cozia, Bistriţa, Voroneţ and Dragomirna – by the Romanian scholar Alexandru Odobescu in 1864 and deposited in the National Museum of Antiquities, which is now part of the Museum of Art of the Socialist Republic of Romania at Bucharest. Many of these textiles had survived as altar vestments which on examination were found to have been garment sections and capable of restoration into their original form. They are made either from imported Italian or Turkish brocades ranging in date from the sixteenth to the seventeenth century, in designs of large bold spot and crescent motifs, repeated ogival motifs enfolding stylised carnations and tulips and rippling designs of graceful stems of carnations.[29]

Among the garments worn by women is the robe known as a *conteş* whose shape, cut and construction are indebted to Turkish styles. One handsome example made of *zerbaft* (Plate 73) shows this clearly.[30] Like the children's garments of the early seventeenth century (Diagram 15), the main pattern parts are three – a rectangular central back, and two front pieces all extended at waist level, joined at the shoulder with straight seams. Extra shaping was achieved by adding triangular sections to the sides of the skirts, while wide and straight sleeves were set in at right angles to the body and curved at the inner wrist. Unlike the Turkish prototypes, however, which have pockets set into side seams, pocket slits were prominent vertical openings on each front at waist level. Sometimes the *conteş* was fastened with frogged loops and buttons. Plenty of pictorial evidence is available to show how the Romanian noblewoman wore such a garment and also the long-sleeved *caftan*. A fresco painting of Princess Roxanda dated to *c.* 1530 from the episcopal church at Curtea de Argeş,[31] a manuscript portrait of Princess Elina, wife of the voivod of Wallachia Matei Basarab (1632–1654) dated to *c.* 1644[32] and another fresco painting of Princess Roxanda from the chapel of Cozia monastery dated 1543[33] show these royal ladies wearing the long-sleeved *caftan* draped over the shoulders as a resplendent cloak, or the *conteş* neatly fastened over knife pleated voluminous robes with full sleeves decorated with embroidery. Their heads are adorned with heavy radiating faceted crowns balanced by long pendant gold earrings reaching to their shoulders. The entire

Opposite. Plate 72. Embroidered tomb cover. Portrait of Ieremia Movilă Suceviţa Monastery, Moldavia, Romania, 1606.

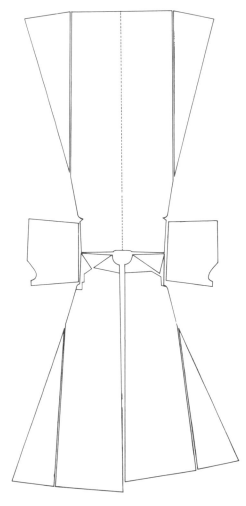

Above left. Plate 73. Woman's *conteş*. *Seraser* woven in silver with large spots enfolded in ogival palmette medallions. Romania, late 16th–early 17th century.

Above right. Diagram 15. Pattern for woman's *conteş*. Romania, late 16th–early 17th century. Scale – 1:22.

costume is a blend of provincial Byzantine survivals with garments which still survive today in Romanian peasant costume such as the pleated dress with full sleeves, given a sophisticated finish by the Turkish-inspired over robe.

Such robes continued to be worn throughout the seventeenth century, but accessories became neater and on a smaller scale as is shown by the family group of voivod Constantine Brincoveanu with his wife Maria and their children (Plate 74) painted in the church of the monastery of Hurez (constructed 1691–1703).[34] Maria and her seven daughters are portrayed in *conteş* robes of either gold brocade – possibly *zerbaft* – or what seems to be deep crimson brocade patterned with large ogival flower medallions. All their robes are edged with contrast facing and fasten at the neck. Their hair is caught up and concealed under gold crowns while the long pendant earrings have given way to neat hoops.

During the eighteenth century the costume of the upper classes was subject to another wave of Turkish influence which furnishes an excellent example of the effect of political change as visibly mirrored in fashion. From 1711 to 1821 the two Romanian principalities were no longer ruled by native princes but by rulers – *hospodars* – appointed directly by the Ottoman administration at Istanbul. These hospodars were invariably recruited from the more prominent and wealthy members of the families of Istanbul's Greek minority known as Phanariots; consequently their period of rule in the principalities is known as the Phanariot period. Whatever its political problems it was a brilliant period culturally and intellectually in which literature, architecture and painting flourished. These Phanariot Greek princes and their families dressed in the style of costume worn by the Greek communities of Istanbul which, although essentially Turkish in basic principles, showed the variations in proportion and headdress which

Plate 74. Voivod Constantin Brîncoveanu and his family. Wall painting, Hurez Monastery, Romania, 1691–1703.

Above right. Plate 75. Erotokritos and his parents. Illustration to the Romanian translation of the Cretan Vincenzo Cornaro's romantic poem *The Erotokritos* commissioned in 1787 for the voivod Nicolae Mavrogheni.

Above. Plate 76. Femme Valáque ou Moldave mariée, riche et en Galla. Miniature from album of single-figure studies. Turkey, *c.*1790.

were distinguishing features; some have already been noted in the costume of the Greek girl from the district of Pera. The costumes are well documented in various pictorial sources. As an example of the new stimuli and influences in Romanian life and literature during the Phanariot period the *Erotokritos*, a romantic poem written by the Cretan Vincenzo Cornaro in the seventeenth century, should be mentioned. This poem was translated into Romanian between 1770 and 1780 and proved to be very popular. A manuscript version of this Romanian translation copied for the voivod Nicolas Mavrogheni in 1787 is illustrated with characters dressed in contemporary costumes.[35] The illustrations are charming and naively direct (Plate 75) indicating the layers of costume clearly. Here the women are clad in the familiar *gömlek* with a low V-neck, a long-sleeved *décolleté anteri* reaching to the ankles cinched at the waist with a buckled belt or swathed with a shawl-like *kuşak* draped modishly to one side of the hip. Over the *anteri* is worn a sleeveless pelisse – a *kırk* – lined with fur and with a deep fur collar. The headdress resembles the swathed turban of the girl from Pera. As the Romanian principalities during this eighteenth century period of direct rule were regarded properly as part of the Ottoman Empire, portraits of Romanians featured in the albums painted from the sixteenth century onwards. The Diez album of *c.* 1790 features two supposedly typical Romanian women among its cast of characters[36] – a married lady and an unmarried girl (Plates 76 & 77) – clearly intending to show them as more provincial than the sophisticated ladies of the Phanariot courts, as their costumes are a combination of traditional Romanian and Turkish garments. Instead of the Turkish style *gömlek*, their undershirts drawn tightly at the neck and with long full sleeves gathered at the wrist and decorated with embroidered bands are related to the garments worn by the princesses of the sixteenth and seventeenth centuries, and survive today in the many elaborate versions of contemporary village dress. Instead of an *anteri* they wear waisted sleeveless pinafore dresses whose *décolleté* bodices, however, show Turkish influence. The married woman's fur-trimmed coat with its tight cap sleeves and skirt slit at the side, however, is directly related to the pelisse of the Phanariot style, while the unmarried girl wears a hip-length sleeveless jacket. The accessories are much less flamboyant either than those of a contemporary Turkish or Pera Greek woman, being either a fur hat or neat skull cap. A perceptive touch is the high heeled court shoes of the married woman, a foretaste of the European influence which eventually dominated in the nineteenth century.

Plate 77. Fille de Moldavie ou Valachie, non mariée. Miniature from album of single-figure studies. Turkey, *c.*1790.

Turkish styles of dress continued into the early nineteenth century and were attractively recorded in the detailed studies in oils painted by the Austrian artist Mihail Töpler (1780–1820) whose skill and deftness in rendering the materials and ornaments of his sitters' costumes made him popular with the aristocracy at the court of Prince Constantine Ipsilanti and his wife Safta.[37] Töpler was active in Iaşi and Bucharest after 1800 and has left a series of portraits of the wives of contemporary officials. His portrait (Plate 78) of Safta Ipsilanti[38] dressed in a décolleté robe of green velvet worked in *dıval işi,* swathed in a *kuşak* of Kashmir shawl and finally covered with a closely cut pink silk robe with a deep fur collar and cuffs, her hair flowing around her shoulders and back barely covered with a small red cap decorated with jewelled pendants is an accurate well-interpreted portrait showing the persistence of Turkish fashion. In certain details, however, such as the white undershirt with a deep rounded neck edged with a lace frill the costume shows the beginnings of European influence. In urban and upper class costume the principalities were to follow the same process as Turkey in adopting European dress though they assimilated its idioms more rapidly, for several reasons. The Phanariot period witnessed an influx of European, particularly French, cultural ideas and influences into the

Above left. Plate 78. Portrait of Safta Ipsilanti. Oil painting, Mihail Töpler, 1780–1820.

Above right. Plate 79. Woman in blue. Oil painting, *c*.1860. Anton Chladek (1794–1882).

principalities, as the princes maintained connections with the diaspora Greek communities of Russia and Vienna and after the French revolution employed French *émigrés* as tutors to their children. After the re-establishment of native Romanian rulers in 1821 this process of Europeanisation quickened – wealthy Romanians travelled to Europe and certain enlightened aristocrats such as Dinu Golescu[39] were generous patrons of writers and painters and encouraged the foundation of schools organised on Western lines teaching subjects such as French and mathematics. This process was again reflected visually in costume so that by 1860 the lush Turkish-style beauty of Safta Ipsilanti was replaced by the intricate detail of fashionable European dress as observed by the Czech painter Anton Chladek (Plate 79) in his portrait of a wealthy Bucharest lady dressed in blue.[40]

6

The Ottomans Abroad – The Arab World

As they expanded their empire into the Middle East the Ottoman Turks came into contact with yet more costume traditions. After the completion of their conquests of the Balkans and Anatolia by the early sixteenth century, they turned their attention to the lands of the Eastern and Southern Mediterranean and their hinterlands. Sultan Selim I (1512–1520) after marching first on Aleppo and defeating the Mamluk ruler Al-Ghawri, then advanced relentlessly taking Damascus and Jerusalem until he reached Egypt which he subdued in 1517. This conquest gave him control of the holy cities of Mecca and Medina and adjacent areas of the coastal regions of Arabia. Eventually the Ottomans extended westwards along the North African coast until by the reign of Süleyman the Magnificent (1520–1566) they held Libya, Tunisia and Algeria. Süleyman penetrated further into the Arab world and conquered Baghdad which meant that he effectively annexed Iraq to the Ottoman realm. In social and cultural terms these accessions meant that the Ottoman Turks now controlled areas which were predominantly Arabic and Muslim in religion, but included substantial minority communities such as the Jews of Iraq and Yemen, and the Christians of Egypt and Syria.

Similarly to the Balkan provinces, an Ottoman administrative military élite was established which added a Turkish presence to such main towns as Aleppo, Damascus, Cairo, Baghdad, Jerusalem, Tunis and Algiers; it is in these urban centres that the influence of Turkish dress on local costume is seen. The sources, however, for an evaluation of the costumes of the Arab provinces both before and after the Turkish conquest are very variable. Surviving garments are comparatively few and erratic in provenance. The tradition of manuscript illustration did not provide the realistic detail which makes Turkish painting so valuable as secondary source material, while the majority of European illustrations date from the late eighteenth and nineteenth centuries when these areas became more accessible to travellers who had the time to record the local scene and its inhabitants. Written sources again vary in both quantity and quality, from references in Arabic texts to the more objectively recorded and annotated accounts of European visitors, principally of the nineteenth century.

Plate 80. Woman's dress.
Cream linen. Egypt,
c.3100–2810 BC.

For various reasons the most complete picture of women's costume
may be reconstructed from Egyptian sources. Egypt, because of its
particularly favourable hot and dry climatic conditions, is unique in the
textiles which have been preserved and excavated from burial sites to
reveal an impressively long historical sequence for the materials and
construction of dress, with the result that it is possible to trace the
features which appeared in women's costume before the arrival of the
Ottoman Turks and which were, at certain levels of society, to change
as a result of their conquest. Egypt's reputation as a centre of textile
weaving was to endure from Pharaonic times through its history as a
province of the Roman and Byzantine Empires, and after its conquest
by the Arabs in AD 641 when the products of its workshops were in
demand throughout the Islamic world. Early evidence of both the type
of textiles and style favoured in women's dress may be attributed to the
first dynasty of the Old Kingdom of Pharaonic times in the form of a
woman's dress (Plate 80) found in one of the graves excavated at the site
of Tarkhan thirty-seven miles south of Cairo, and dated to *c*. 3100–2810
BC.[1] The fabric has been identified as plain weave linen of cream
slubbed thread in a loom width of seventy-six centimetres with plain

selvages. The dress is long and straight with a tight high-waisted skirt and a pleated V-necked bodice with long sleeves, achieved by using simple methods of cut and construction. The skirt, for example, is basically a single loom width folded at the right side and joined at both selvages, while the bodice is made of two straight pieces pleated horizontally, doubled over at the shoulders and attached to the waist at back and front leaving a deep V-neck. The long tight sleeve is shaped by cutting the fabric in a curve at the underarm. The garment is interesting both because of its state of preservation and for the information it reveals about dressmaking techniques. Clearly the aim was to use the material as much as possible with minimal seams. Sewing details show the use of edges rolled and whipped with small neat stitches to avoid fraying of the linen before seams were joined, techniques which continued into Christian and Islamic costume.

These dressmaking traditions continued as is shown by the remains of two dresses attributed to the fifth dynasty *c.* 2494–2345 BC excavated from a burial at Deshasheh a provincial necropolis in the Fayum.[2] Again they are both of cream coloured linen in which the entire loom width is used. The skirt is a single loom width folded over at the right side and seamed at the left, while the high waist is joined to two identical pieces each forming bodice and sleeve with a deep V-neck at centre front and back. There is evidence of other fashions contemporary with these linen dresses. A shift-like garment made of a mesh of blue and black faience beads with a deep fringe at the hem of mitra shell equipped with a brassière made of two circular sections of blue faience was found in a tomb at Qau in Middle Egypt.[3] This dress might have been worn over a linen petticoat-like garment or simply over the naked body. It clearly was a garment worn by a professional dancer, and should be regarded as an exotic exception, rather than as an example of everyday dress. A much later dress excavated from a cemetery of the seventh century BC also at Tarkhan indicates the continued use of cream coloured linen in wide loom widths but with extremely simple cut and construction. A single loom width is used consisting of a wide rectangle folded over at the shoulders with a keyhole opening at the neck, and joined at the sides leaving openings for the arms to which optionally sleeves could be sewn. This dress is especially interesting as it is mentioned in contemporary inscriptions from the site of Deir el Medina – a town of workmen employed in tomb building at the nearly royal necropolis and was a working-class garment worn equally by both sexes, adults and children.[4] The garment preserved its simple shape and was certainly worn in the nineteenth century as recorded by William Lane in his encyclopaedic study of nineteenth-century Egyptian society.[5]

Most surviving garments, however, date from late antiquity – a period broadly extending from the late third to the seventh century AD, when Egypt was a province of both Roman and Byzantine Empires. An enormous quantity of textiles has been excavated from both pagan and

Christian burial grounds. Two sites in Upper Egypt were especially productive: the burial grounds of Akhmim, the site of the Greek city of Panopolis which was one of the most important centres of linen manufacture, and the city of Antinoe built by the Emperor Hadrian in AD 140. Both sites were in continuous use until after the Muslim conquest and have yielded rich finds of textiles woven in linen, wool and silk.[6] Unfortunately, the majority were excavated hastily and unsystematically to satisfy the demand of the antiquities market, with pieces even being cut up and divided for easy sale; it was not until 1881 that controlled excavation of the sites was begun under the direction of the French Egyptologist Gaston Maspero. In the absence, therefore, of accurate provenance, dating and attribution are by no means definite as the textiles have been classified mainly by comparative stylistic analysis which has yielded a chronological scheme broadly spanning the fourth to the twelfth century.[7] Traditionally these textiles have been conveniently classified as Coptic, because most of them were allegedly produced when Egypt's population was predominantly Coptic Christian. The definition is not strictly accurate since on examination many of them are ornamented with designs which are more closely related to the repertoire of the pagan Graeco-Roman world, while others were made long after the Arab conquest and the gradual conversion of the population to Islam. Bearing the reservations of the problems of chronology and attribution in mind, they still, however, provide invaluable evidence of both the techniques of manufacture and decoration of textiles and of their use in costume. They are especially important in the absence of comparable material from other areas of the late Roman and Byzantine world. This very absence, however, means that they should be interpreted with caution and not used as evidence of dress traditions for an area beyond Egypt because, in the absence of comparative material, it is not possible to determine whether they document fashion in general or only a specific provincial version.

In broadest terms the costume of both men and women in the Late Roman and Byzantine world was based on garments of comparatively simple cut and shape developed from those of classical antiquity and were basically variations on a tunic-like draped robe and a wrap or cloak. The tunic was ornamented with decorative bands and medallions and became the most important part of the costume. The mosaic of San Vitale at Ravenna of 548 (Plate 1) shows the Empress Theodora wearing this type of garment with decorative hem and medallions and a full purple cloak draped over it fastening on the right shoulder.[8] The textiles enable the appearance and texture of this costume to be reconstructed as most of them are either complete tunics or fragments in the form of bands of decoration. The tunic was woven as a single loom width in a cross shape which when folded in half at the shoulders and seamed at underarm and sides produced a T-shaped garment with a wide opening at the neck.[9] The direction of the weaving was from sleeve to sleeve so that the normally vertical warp threads were aligned horizontally. This part of the tunic was usually woven in natural or bleached linen in plain weave. If woven in wool a wider range of colours was used including a deep olive green and purple.

Individual styling in such garments depended on the decoration of which the main element was a pair of long narrow bands – *clavi* – which extended at both back and front from shoulder to hem. Bands also extended along each sleeve to form a decorative cuff. Later a band around the neck opening and a range of circular or square medallions at shoulders and front chest were added. Eventually, the decoration dwindled to shorter *clavi* and a pair of medallions at knee level. This decoration was woven in brightly coloured wools or in silk in close tapestry weave, thereby contrasting in both colour and texture with the linen background. The bands and medallions are characterised by a versatile repertoire of design motif which could draw on a heritage of ancient Egyptian themes, blended with subjects of Graeco-Roman origin and later incorporating Christian iconography. Ornament was trained into borders, medallions and continuous repeats of interlaced geometrical motifs and fluent yet disciplined leaf and floral scrolls. Figure designs include creatures from Graeco-Roman classicism – cupids, hunters, dancers and musicians clad in fluttering draperies, lively animal motifs such as birds, lions and hares.[10] A popular motif

Plate 81. Tunic medallion depicting a goddess riding on a dolphin. Slit tapestry weave in coloured wools. Egypt, 8th century.

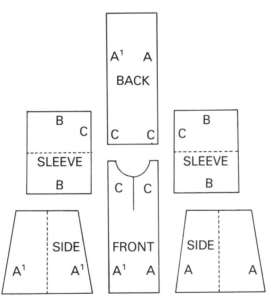

ALL PIECES CUT ON STRAIGHT OF FABRIC

ALL SEAMS HAND SEWN IN CREAM LINEN
THREAD

RUN AND FELL WITH ½ IN ALLOWANCE
JOINED A-A, A¹-A¹, C-C

CUFF AND HEM EDGES WITH ¾ IN ALLOWANCE

TURNED UNDER TWICE AND OVERCAST

NARROW BINDING STRIPS HEMMED OVER RAW
EDGES OF NECK AND FRONT OPENING

Above right. Plate 82.
Child's tunic. Cream
linen. Shoulder bands
woven in brown silk. El-
Drounka, Egypt, 9th–10th
century.

Right. Diagram 16. Pattern
from same child's tunic.
Scale – 1:12.

(Plate 81) was a synthesis of the classical theme of a goddess riding a dolphin among the fish and aquatic creatures[11] of the Nilotic river-scapes derived from Ancient Egyptian wall paintings. Several complete garments indicate the progressive evolution of this linen garment in shape and decoration and in methods of cut and construction. A child's garment in the Royal Scottish Museum's collections (Plate 82) excavated from El-Drounka and dated to about the ninth or tenth century illustrates these points well.[12] It is made of natural cream coloured linen in a plain weave cut into a straight rectangular piece (Diagram 16) folded over at the shoulders to form the centre front and back, with loose straight sleeves inserted at right angles and triangular sections added to each side at skirt level for shaping. The woven decoration by this period has become more modest and is confined to a narrow band on each shoulder of alternating hexagon and S-motifs worked in brown silk. The garment is neatly seamed and hemmed with linen thread using run-and-fell seams.

As the date of this garment indicates, textiles made for the Coptic Christian community continued to be made long after the Arab conquest because, although conversion to Islam was encouraged and did indeed flourish, both Muslim and Christian communities lived side by side. On a practical level, this co-existence is to be seen in the influence of Coptic weaving on the textiles and costumes commissioned by Muslim patrons who were quick to appreciate the highly-developed skills of the indigenous population. Another child's garment in the Royal Scottish Museum (Plate 83) excavated from the Muslim cemetery at El-Drounka[13] and dated to the eleventh or twelfth century demonstrates this point, as it is very similar to the earlier Coptic example. It is also woven in natural cream coloured linen in plain weave cut into a rectangular (Diagram 17) piece folded over at the shoulders to form the centre back and front. Straight loose sleeves and additional shaping pieces are added at the armhole and skirt of the central section. The decoration is again restrained consisting of narrow spaced vertical stripes and small lozenges in brown wool worked in satin stitch. Other than such isolated examples, recognisable surviving garment fragments are rare for the early centuries of Muslim Arab rule in both Egypt and the neighbouring territories of North Africa and Syria. It is clear, however, that the Arab conquerers and their successors were satisfied to continue the textile industries already in existence. In Egypt this naturally involved capitalising on the skills of the Coptic weavers which meant that their designs and techniques influenced the commissions undertaken for their Muslim customers. In turn their requirements modified the basic Coptic repertoire. Although complete garments are lacking and there is as yet little evidence of the survival of a highly developed school of narrative painting, documentation may be gained from surviving examples of lustre-painted ceramics dating from the Fatimid period (909–1171). These depict figures wearing plain wide-sleeved robes ornamented with narrow

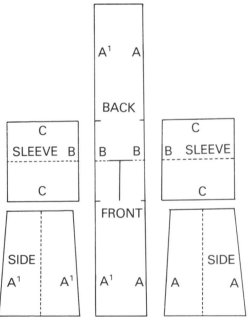

Above right. Plate 83. Child's tunic. Cream linen. Narrow bands embroidered in brown wool. El-Drounka, Egypt, 11th–12th century.

Right. Diagram 17. Pattern for same child's tunic. Scale – 1:12.

ALL PIECES CUT ON STRAIGHT OF FABRIC

ALL SEAMS HAND SEWN IN CREAM LINEN THREAD

RUN AND FELL WITH ½ IN ALLOWANCE

SEAMS JOINED AT A-A TO C-C

decorative bands arranged in a pair vertically down the front and along the seam joining sleeve to body, or long wide-sleeved dresses patterned with flamboyant repeating designs of fan-shaped palmettes encircled and linked by twining stems.[14] The plain robes are indebted to the T-shaped Coptic garments but the decoration has been modified to narrow bands along front, shoulders and neck of Arabic inscription which replaces the exuberant plant and animal motifs.

Large numbers of textile pieces have survived consisting of background fabric and inscription which provide a great deal of information about the textile industry in Egypt during the centuries of its history as a client colony of the Abbasid rulers based at Baghdad (749–1258), and later under the independent Fatimid dynasty (909–1171) who also controlled Syria. This distinctive group of textiles is known collectively as *tiraz*, a term originally referring to the decorative bands but later adapted to mean the workshop or factory where they were woven. They are classified into two types the *tiraz al-khassa*, the private factories in the ruler's palace reserved exclusively for garments for the royal household and robes of honour awarded as gifts, and the *tiraz al-amma*, public factories owned by merchants who sold their goods in a wider market.[15] Among the fabrics used were linen in Lower Egypt and wool in the Fayoum and Upper Egypt woven in a close plain weave. The decorative bands could be worked in a range of techniques – woven in tapestry weave, embroidered in flat outline stitches – split chain and stem stitches and couched in gold thread, painted or block printed in outline. The colours always contrasted distinctly with the background fabric in shades of brown, ranging from golden to deep red. The Arabic inscriptions of these decorative bands in angular Kufic calligraphy recorded information which not only enables a chronological sequence of textile styles to be established, but also provides information about conditions of manufacture. A complete *tiraz* inscription includes the following elements – the Bismillah formula 'In the name of God the Merciful the Compassionate', the ruler's name and titles, some complimentary and benedictory phrases, the name of the *tiraz* factory and the date of manufacture. Using the evidence of these dated inscriptions, it has been possible to trace a sequence beginning with a piece of linen woven in 854 in the reign of the Abbasid ruler Al-Mutawakkil[16] and finishing three centuries later with textiles from the reign of the Fatimid ruler al-Hafiz (1131–49).[17] During this time-span an evolution in the style of Kufic calligraphy from bold angular letters through graceful curved forms interlaced with vines and palmettes to more debased cursive forms is seen.

After al-Mustansir's reign apparently the detailed and informative inscription is replaced by a string of pious formulas. From the inscriptions it can be deduced that the *tiraz* factories of Egypt were situated at Alexandria, Bahnasa, Damietta, Fayoum, Qais and Tinnis,[18] while the use of the term *misr* somewhat confusingly can be used for the capital Cairo or for the entire country. Inscriptions also provide the

Plate 84. Border woven in yellow and crimson silk. Design of bands of Arabic calligraphy alternating with guilloche scroll enclosing motifs of running animals. Egypt, mid-12th century.

names of factory owners or supervisors in some instances.[19] Running parallel with the comparatively austere or at least restrained elegance of the *tiraz* productions was a second group of textiles with more flamboyant decoration more closely resembling Coptic types which may be compared with the patterned robes depicted on contemporary ceramics. A group dating from around the eleventh to twelfth century in the Royal Museum of Scotland's collections demonstrates the main features.[20] They are woven in plain weave either in linen or silk (Plate 84), with decoration in plain weave stripes of tapestry weave bands in linen wool or silk in bright colours of blue, red, green and yellow. Motifs include mixed themes of scrolling foliage, twisted ribbon borders and medallions enclosing running animals and birds mingled with bands of stylised Kufic calligraphy creating a final effect of both richness and delicacy.

The main problem of women's dress in Egypt during the Abbasid and Fatimid periods derives from the lack of surviving garments and comprehensive pictorial evidence. To a certain extent the situation is clearer from the thirteenth to early sixteenth centuries when Egypt together with Syria was under the rule of the Mamluk Sultans (1250–1517), as the source materials are more extensive although there are too few surviving garments – tunics, caps, shoes and a veil.[21] To supplement these modest examples, there are the costumes depicted in the paintings illustrating Arabic manuscripts produced in both Egypt and Syria which, once their conventions are understood, yield information at least about shapes and types of garment and how they were assembled into complete costumes.

A different viewpoint on these costumes is provided by representations in European paintings of the fourteenth and fifteenth centuries. Written sources include descriptions in contemporary Arabic chronicles and official manuals, though here the information is selective rather than systematic, lists in marriage contracts[22] and European travel accounts. Extant manuscripts are comparatively few in number mainly illustrating collections of fables and anecdotes. The paintings impose by their stylistic conventions certain limitations on their value as costume documents; they do not show the varied and meticulous detail of Ottoman Turkish and Persian miniature paintings. Little attention, for example, is paid to background scene. The figures tend to be in stooped or crouching poses usually in three-quarter view and drawn in fluent outline using a single red line. These outlines served as a foundation for details of feature and costume built up by the application of opaque colours. Here certain conventions are repeated from manuscript to manuscript. Flat washes of colour are used for certain items such as white for trousers and black for shoes. Monochrome garments with folds are painted in a schematised manner using up to three shades of the same colour. The folds are depicted as parallel double vertical bands opening into horizontally aligned curves and ripples, which are painted in the lightest shade occasionally highlighted by fine strokes of white and then outlined in the darkest tone. A comparable technique is used for patterned textiles especially those with repeated motifs such as hexagons and interlocked Y-shapes. Here the background is painted in one shade and the design details are outlined in a darker one. Where, however, textiles are patterned in more fluent spiralling foliate designs these are painted in colours contrasting with that of the background. Accessories and decorative details are painted in opaque ochre yellow – hats, cuffs, armbands – probably intended as a foundation for gold leaf which would have been worked into a series of patterns.

It is useful to look at selected examples of these paintings to see how much of women's dress can be reconstructed. Two manuscripts illustrating the *Maqamat* or *Seances* of al-Hariri dated to *c.* 1275–1300 copied in Syria show women in various styles of Mamluk costume.[23] One of the miniatures (Plate 85) depicting a reclining girl gives a general picture of indoor dress and accessories.[24] The girl is dressed in plain white pyjamas-like trousers (*sarawil*) over which is worn a knee-length long-sleeved pink robe (*thaub*) which from the disposition of the folds is belted at the waist. Decoration is confined to gold bands across the upper sleeves and at the hem. In its unstructured shape and from the position of the decoration this garment is closely related to the Coptic tunic prototype which continued to be worn with modifications. The girl's eyes are outlined in black kohl and her hair is dressed to fall smoothly around her face and over her shoulders. Alternatively the hair could be dressed in long braids and swathed with a turban.[25] This presentation of female dress should be compared with that seen in a single miniature dated 1315 from a manuscript copied in Egypt of

Plate 85. Girl in indoor dress. Miniature painting from a manuscript of the *Maqamat* of al-Hariri. Syria, *c.*1275–1300.

al-Jazari's *Kitab fi ma'rifat al-hiyal al-handasiya*.[26] This depicts an automation of a girl offering wine to a ruler and is distinguished by the clear and schematic way in which the costume is shown (Plate 86). She also wears a combination of trousers and robe. The trousers, however, are more voluminous and in a bright orange-red fabric. The robe of deep olive-green colour is also knee length falling from a belt at the waist, and is decorated with gold borders at cuffs and skirt hems and patterned gold bands along the upper sleeves. The sleeves, however, have stylised rippling lines extending from the cuff which may indicate underarm seams, and the skirt hem has a short slit which would normally be at the side of the garment and balanced by a corresponding one on the other side. It is possible to hypothesise that the painting represents a T-shaped garment with a rectangular centre piece folded over at the shoulders into which straight sleeves are set. The pieces would then have been seamed at the armholes and at underarm and sides leaving a slit at the hem. The decorative sleeve bands could have been inset tapestry weave or embroidered, but there is no way of identifying the technique from the painting. It is possible too that the gold bands at hems and cuffs functioned also as facings made by seaming the border to the garment, and then pulling it to the right side and neatly hemming it to avoid raw edges. Comparable sewing and tailoring techniques are observable in surviving Turkish and Persian clothes. The headdress here consists of a tightly wound shawl framing the face kept in place by a knotted scarf with trailling ends tied like a bandeau.

Miniatures in the second manuscript of the *Maqamat*[27] while providing more information about outdoor dress as the women are depicted in public situations rather than in private domestic scenes, also show patterned dress fabrics as revealed beneath the wrap. A miniature of al-Harith (Plate 87) discovering the principal character of the *Maqamat*, Abu Zaid, disguised as an old woman in a ruined mosque shows this. Beneath a blue wrap, Abu Zaid wears[28] a long dress with tight sleeves in an elaborately patterned material in which interlocking repeated Y-motifs in green and red outline are reversed against an ochre yellow background. Although the weave and texture of the material cannot be identified, it is possible that the technique of painting the motifs in fine outline is a convention used for depicting floating welf-brocaded fabrics in which the design wefts are taken straight across the main weave. Over the dress, a long blue wrap (*izar*) is swathed covering the body from head to ankle showing well the conventions used for indicating ample folds.

Other miniatures in the same manuscript are, however, more informative about details of outdoor dress. Here a scene of mourners at a graveside[29] includes two women crouched over the tomb (Plate 88). Following accepted social custom as they are in a public situation, they are enveloped in concealing garments and closely veiled. They are both shrouded in voluminous wraps one in blue, the other in white. As to the construction of these wraps, were they simply long rectangular lengths of cloth or were they made in a semi-circular shape like the outdoor veil or *chadar* which is much easier to drape and fold and still worn by Persian women today? A closer examination reveals that the woman in white had pulled her wrap tightly around her face and knotted it under her chin while the woman in blue lets it fall more casually over her face veil. Both women are wearing variants of a face veil (*burqu*). Their hair seems to be confined beneath tightly wound black headscarfs which are pulled well down over their foreheads; it also serves as a means of preventing the outer wrap from slipping off the wearer's head. The woman in blue wears a *burqu* which, consisting of a narrow red band from which a long rectangular white cloth is suspended leaving a space above for the eyes, effectively conceals her face from the forehead to below the chin. The woman in white seemingly wears a simpler version – a plain white veil extending from below the eyes to cover the lower part of her face.

Certain questions of how such veils were constructed and fastened may be resolved by comparison with finds from Mamluk levels of the excavations of Quseir al-Qadim – a port site on the Red Sea from which two veils were found, and at Qasr Ibrim situated on the Nile in South Egypt.[30] From associated material the veils have been dated to *c*. the fourteenth to fifteenth century. The most complete example from Quseir al-Qadim is made of two pieces of undyed linen which in its construction most closely resembles the *burqu* worn by the woman in blue. A narrow rectangular piece hemmed along all four edges may be identified in function with the red forehead band. A longer piece is attached to it at the sides and centre leaving two narrow eye slits. A vertical tuck stitched to the centre of both pieces produces a ridge over the nose to keep this veil taut. A plaited cord attached to each upper corner of the veil enables it to be fastened at the back of the head. Once in position the wrap was draped over it. Further variations and accessories of outdoor dress are seen in a painting depicting Abu Zaid and his wife (Plate 89) in dispute before the Qadi of Tabriz.[31] Abu Zaid's wife is enveloped in an *izar* of white cloth patterned in repeating checks of black and purple edged with a deep black border. She wears this wrap in loose folds around her head over a plain white face veil; it is then wrapped over her arms and finally reaches to her ankles. From the treatment of the folds in a somewhat heavy manner instead of the ripples seen in the wraps of the women mourners, it is possible that the material is probably of a denser and thicker texture. Also the way in which the folds fall indicates that the garment may be of a semi-circular shape. The outdoor dress is completed by a pair of black boots (*khuff*).

This necessarily incomplete and perhaps generalised impression of Mamluk women's dress at least shows the main components of their costume in which garments of ancient origin such as the knee-length dress (*thaub*) are mingled with those of later introduction such as voluminous trousers and all enveloping cloaks and veils. After the

Opposite top. Plate 86. Girl offering wine. Miniature painting from a manuscript of the *Kitab fi ma'rifat al-hiyal al-handasiya* of al-Jazari. Egypt, 1315.

Opposite bottom. Plate 87. Abu Zaid disguised as a woman. Miniature painting from a manuscript of the *Maqamat* of al-Hariri. Syria, *c*.1275–1300.

Top. Plate 88. Mourners at a graveside. Miniature painting from a manuscript of the *Maqamat* of al-Hariri, Syria, *c*.1275–1300.

Above. Plate 89. Abu Zaid in dispute. Miniature painting from a manuscript of the *Maqamat* of al-Hariri. Syria, *c*.1275–1300.

Above left. Plate 90. Indoor gossip, Cairo. Oil painting, 1873. John Frederick Lewis (1805–72).

Above right. Plate 91. Lilium Auratum. Oil painting, 1871. John Federick Lewis (1805–72).

conquest of Egypt by the Ottoman Turks in 1517 women's costume underwent further development as the ruling élite and urban classes absorbed and adapted Turkish fashions. Here the documentation, especially for the nineteenth century, is more plentiful as not only have examples of the costumes themselves survived but there are also detailed paintings and descriptions by the increasing numbers of Europeans who chose to live in Egypt or take employment there as teachers or technical experts during the reign of Mohammad Ali (1805–1848) and the Khedive Ismail (1863–1879). Among the paintings those of the English artist John Frederick Lewis (1805–1872) who lived in Cairo from 1841 to 1852 are remarkable both for the precision of the costume detail and the romantic manner in which they evoke local colour epitomising contemporary European visions of Egypt.[32] Lewis dressed and lived in local style tirelessly observing and sketching his neighbours and collecting an invaluable archive of source material which he worked up into paintings after his return to England. The visual impact of his paintings act as a useful supplement to the detailed descriptions of costume found in such written accounts as Edward Lane's classic study of contemporary Egyptian life, based on his stay there from 1825 to 1849.[33] Later accounts, notably those of two governesses Emmeline Lott[34] and Ellen Chennells, document the changes of fashion between 1860 and 1871.[35]

As shown in Lewis's paintings and Lane's account, the costume of upper-class Egyptian women closely resembled that of their contemporaries in Istanbul of the first half of the nineteenth century with some differences of accessory and vocabulary. Two of Lewis's paintings 'Indoor Gossip Cairo' and 'Lilium Auratum' (Plates 90 & 91) demonstrate how the complete costume would have been worn.[36] Like the Turkish woman the Egyptian arranged her elaborate costume over a set of underwear whose details are supplied by Lane's descriptions.

'Their shirt is very full, like that of the men, but shorter, not reaching to the knees; it is also, generally of the same kind of material as the men's shirt, or of coloured crape, sometimes black.'[37] It would have been made of linen, cotton, muslin, silk, or cotton and silk mixed – but usually in white. In this it resembles the Turkish woman's undershirt (or *gömlek*) but information, however, about its cut and construction are lacking. The women in 'Lilium Auratum' are wearing such undershirts as the loose sleeves can be seen edged with gold lace. As yet no evidence has come to light of the use of underpants comparable to the Turkish *dislik* and the next garment to be worn are full voluminous trousers – *shintiyan* – comparable in fabric and cut to the Turkish *şalvar*. According to Lane they were worn tied under the undershirt, whereas the Turkish fashion, as seen from the late eighteenth century onwards, was to tie them over. The *shintiyan* were extreme in length with drawstrings at their ends so that they could be tied up under the knee, thus creating a graceful bouffant effect as they trailed in folds over the wearer's ankles. A wide range of materials was used for them ranging from light printed cottons or muslins to heavier silks in rich colours of violet, blue and deep pink. Patterned in gold and worn over the *shintiyan* was a robe corresponding to the *üçetek* form of the Turkish woman's *anteri* though here confusingly called a *yelek*. It was a long robe of slender and elegant proportions whose trailing skirts were deeply slit at the sides up to hip level. Equally long sleeves had deeply slashed cuffs which fell back over the wrists to reveal the sleeves of the undershirt. Similarly to the *shintiyan* a wide choice of fabrics was available. A matching fabric could be selected, or silks ranging from lightly coloured ones with striped designs picked out in gold to deep rich colours with patterns embroidered in gold couching – *dıval işi*. In Egyptian fashion a short jacket here called an *anteri* could be worn instead of the long trailing robe. The waist was encircled by a shawl-like girdle swathed as in the Turkish costume.

Over the combination of voluminous trousers and robe or jacket, further layers could be worn either another long robe of comparable cut to the *yelek* but with tighter and shorter sleeves usually in a plain fabric, or a short coat – *salteh* – often of velvet or broadcloth in deep colours such as green or blue lavishly embroidered with stylised foliate motifs in fine couched gold thread; this garment corresponds to what the Turks identified as a *yelek*. Headdresses, while consisting of the same elements as the Turkish headdress namely a foundation cap wrapped with scarves, were much smaller and neater never reaching the extravagant proportion of those worn by the Istanbul women depicted by Thomas Allom.[38] Hairstyles were based on variations of numerous long braided plaits hanging down the back threaded with cords to which little gold ornaments were attached, while liberal use of kohl and henna embellished the face and hands. Often a rectangular white scarf of cotton embroidered at each end was thrown over the headdress – a practice which was not found in contemporary Turkey. Flat embroidered yellow or red slippers (*mezz*) completed the indoor costume. An evocative impression of its total effect is found in the account told to Emmeline Lott by an old Frenchwoman who had attended Princess Nazli Hanim the daughter of Mohammad Ali in the 1830s.

> As to her costume, I remember it as well as if she now stood before me. She wore, over a pair of wide bright amaranthus coloured silk trousers, a large white Cashmere dress, the loose sleeves of which displayed her well-formed arms, and which being open in front, made her train a yard, and a half in length. A waistband of splendid large pearls, fastened with two large diamond clasps, encircled her waist. Her tiny feet were encossed in a pair of satin slippers, almost as small as those of a child, embroidered with costly pearls. Her headdress consisted of a large fillet of golden-coloured crape Cashmere, which was twisted very prettily around her head. Her long black hair, neatly plaited, was rolled up behind and fastened with large diamond pins. Her bracelets consisted of strings of enormous pearls; her necklace was composed of some of the finest pearls imaginable, which fell negligently on her clear alabaster skin, and half-disclosed her bust . . .[39]

In outdoor dress, however, Egyptian fashions showed more continuity with the Mamluk past, as Lane shows:

> Whenever a lady leaves the house, she wears, . . . first a large, loose gown (called 'tob', or 'sebleh'), the sleeves of which are nearly equal in width to the whole length of the gown; it is of silk; generally of a pink, or rose, or violet colour. Next is put on the 'burko', or face-veil, which is a long strip of white muslin, concealing the whole of the face except the eyes, and reaching nearly to the feet. It is suspended at the top by a narrow band, which passes up the forehead, and which is

sewed, as are also the two upper corners of the veil, to a band that is
tied round the head. The lady then covers herself with a 'habarah',
which for a married lady, is composed of two breadths of glossy,
black silk, each all-wide, and three yards long; these are sewed
together, at or near the selvages (according to a height of the person);
the seam running horizontally, with resepct to the manner in which
it is worn; a piece of narrow black riband is sewed inside the upper
part, about six inches from the edge, to tie round the head . . . The
unmarried ladies wear a habarah of white silk, or a shawl. Some
females of the middle classes, who cannot afford to purchase a
habarah, wear instead of it an 'eezar' or 'izar'; which is a piece of
white calico, of the same form and size as the former, and is worn in
the same manner. On the feet are worn short boots or socks (called
'khuff'), of yellow morocco, and over these the 'baboog' (yellow
leather mules with pointed toes).[40]

Emmeline Lott, who was employed as governess to Ibrahim Pasha,
the son of the Khedive Ismail, in the 1860s, had the time and opportunity to observe upper class Egyptian women's dress as it evolved and
incorporated European influences. She notes of one princess's costume:

Her Highness, the widow of Said Pacha, one of the handsomest
women I had yet seen in any of the Harems, sat reclining on a
divan . . . Her dress was composed of a very long maroon-coloured
silk dress which trained upon the ground, very full bright crimson
silk trousers, over which costume she wore a chocolate-coloured
velvet jacket.

Her head was covered with a dark silk handkerchief, a plume of
ostrich feathers hung down over the right ear, and a beautiful
artificial damask-rose, highly perfumed, drooped down as it were on
the left.

A black spot was painted in the centre of her forehead. In her small
ears hung magnificent diamond drops; and her alabaster-looking
neck was encircled with a necklace of brilliants. Her small hands
were as white as snow; her finger nails were tinged with *henna*, and
several large diamond rings of the finest water sparkled on the little
fingers of each hand.[41]

At the festivities accompanying the ritual of Kurban Bayram costumes were even more lavish:

Her Highness, the Princess Epouse, the mother of my Prince, was
attired in a rich blue figured silk robe, trimmed with white lace and
silver thread, with a long train; full trousers of the same material,
high-heeled embroidered satin shoes to match the dress. On her
head she had a small white crape handkerchief, elegantly embroi-

dered with blue silk and silver, and round it was placed a tiara of May blossoms in diamonds. She wore a necklace to correspond, having large sapphire drops hanging down on her neck. Her arms were ornamented with three bracelets composed of diamonds and sapphires, and an armlet entirely of sapphires of almost priceless value . . .[42]

However, once again European influences gradually intruded on these costumes. They are already observable in the high-heeled shoes worn at the Kurban Bayram festivities instead of the traditional

Plate 92. Princess Zeyneb. Egypt, 1871.

flat-soled leather slippers. On a visit to another household Emmeline Lott notes of a lady otherwise attired in a patterned muslin robe and trousers that 'Her feet were encased in white cotton stockings and black patent leather Parisian shoes'.[43] She also recalls the avid interest which her own clothes evoked:

> Some took up the black straw hat which I had taken off and laid upon the divan at my side. This, they passed from hand to hand, gazing with pleasure and delight at that specimen of English manufacture. After this they examined the whole of my costume from head to foot. What seemed to attract their notice the most was the crinoline I wore, which was by no means a large-sized one; and yet many of the Turkish and Egyptian ladies of the present day may be seen in the streets of Alexandria and Constantinople walking about in that appendage.[44]

Presumably she means here women of Armenian and Greek origin as Muslim women however European their indoor dress would still have been cloaked and veiled in the streets, but the point is made that such fashions were by no means strange and were avidly adopted. Within a few years completely Europeanised costumes were worn by the Khedive's family. Ellen Chennells in 1871 describes her pupil Zeyneb, daughter of the Khedive Ismail as:

> The Princess was magnificently dressed in black velvet, made in the last Parisian fashion. The trimming was of white ostrich feathers; a diamond brooch, which with the pendants attached to it, was as large in circumference as an orange, sparkled on her chest. She wore diamond earrings, a clasp of the same precious stones at the waist, black velvet boots with diamond buckles, and a velvet hat with the same feather trimming as on the dress. She had a weary look, as if all this adornment did not add to her happiness, and taking my hand, she asked me to go upstairs with her and read a story to her![45]

Apart from the excess of jewellery she is clearly dressed in the manner of any contemporary affluent Western European child while her photograph (Plate 92) showing her in another of her many outfits confirms the impression she made on her governess.[46]

7

Close and Distant Neighbours— Persia and Afghanistan

As an intimate neighbour rather than a permanent accession of empire Persia exerted a great influence on Ottoman Turkish culture. Many Ottoman sultans included fluency in the Persian language among their intellectual accomplishments, and the illustrated Persian manuscripts in the collections of the Topkapi Palace library bear witness to their appreciation of the exquisite art of miniature painting. Classics of Persian literature, such as the great romantic poems of Nizami of Ganjeh (1115–1202) which blend fantasy and the exploits of Persian kings, were much enjoyed by the educated élite who commissioned sumptuously illustrated copies from Turkish artists. Persian grammatical forms and vocabulary penetrated the Turkish language contributing to the development of Ottoman Turkish whose richness and sophistication when used by the administrative and literary classes separated it from the dialects of the majority of the empire's population. Apart from these cultural advantages of neighbourhood, at times the Ottoman Turks intermittently controlled areas of North and West Persia. As an extension of his campaigns to subdue Eastern Anatolia, for example, Sultan Selim I defeated the Safavid ruler Shah Ismail at the battle of Çaldiran in 1514 between Erzincan and Tabriz. The victory, however, did not result in permanent absorption of North Persia into the Ottoman domains as Shah Ismail managed to rally successful resistance, but Selim I had occupied Tabriz and had deported many of its inhabitants including merchants, artists and scholars to Istanbul. Throughout the sixteenth century there was an uneasy tension between the Ottoman Turks who could attack Persia from both Eastern Anatolia and further south from Iraq, and threaten the silk trade, and the Safavids who often resorted to a scorched earth policy. Active war with Persia was resumed under Sultan Murat IV (1623–60) who occupied Erivan and Tabriz in 1634, and a century later under Sultan Ahmet III (1703–25) when Ottoman forces occupied Georgia, Shirvan and Azerbaijan in 1723–25 until driven back by Nadir Shah.

Apart from fluctuations in cultural and political relationships, Persian sartorial traditions closely paralleled those of the Ottoman Turks in that costumes were built up of carefully chosen and assembled layers of tailored and fitted garments. This is hardly surprising since both cultures shared a common ancestry in dress which can be traced from Central Asia through to Sassanian, Abbasid and Seljuk Persia and Anatolia. A careful examination of the surviving source materials, however, reveals that Persian costume evolved in an individual manner. It is, however, more difficult to trace its history as the evidence is less complete than that for Ottoman Turkey.

There are sound historical reasons for this. After the Ottoman Empire established its capital in Istanbul its history was remarkable for its basic stability. Despite boundary changes related to the ebb and flow of Ottoman political fortunes Istanbul always retained its position as the administrative, legislative and cultural heart of the empire; it was never submitted to attack or destruction by occupying forces. The Topkapi Palace, for example, has a history of more or less uninterrupted residence from its foundation in the late fifteenth century until the Sultanate was formally abolished with the creation of the Turkish Republic in 1925, which has meant that its furnishings, library and costumes have been preserved in relatively secure conditions. Persian history during the same timespan has in contrast been chaotic and disturbed – at least five dynasties were in control compared with Turkey's one. Persia also suffered from the Mongol invasions of Genghis Khan in the thirteenth century whilst Turkey was left untouched. Also during the late fifteenth century and most of the eighteenth century, political control was bitterly contested between rival warring leaders and their factions. To match this instability the capital was moved many times from Tabriz, briefly to Qazvin, then to Isfahan, Shiraz and finally Tehran. Such mobility does not encourage the preservation of a well-documented wardrobe, so that there is nothing among surviving garments comparable to the sequence of costumes stored in the Topkapi Palace. The only Persian building which may be compared in status and scale with the Topkapi Palace is the Gulestan Palace at Tehran, which is in any case of recent foundation dating from the late eighteenth century at the earliest, and has been subjected to drastic alteration and rebuilding.[1] If any costumes were located in its storerooms their existence has not been recorded. Despite this initially discouraging impression it is, however, possible to trace the sequence of development of Persian women's costume from the early fourteenth century onwards through the interpretation of a range of sources.

Surviving garments today are divided between museums and private collections, and date from the late seventeenth to the nineteenth century. Persia, like Turkey, was a famous centre of textile manufacture whose products in addition to their use in the domestic market had long been exported to admiring customers in the medieval world of the Byzantines and their Muslim neighbours of Iraq and Egypt. Silks woven in a range of complex and sophisticated weaves have survived from the tenth century onwards, many in the type of repeating pattern suitable for making up into clothes. Velvets were also woven of which a particularly striking and handsome group of seventeenth century date featured designs of large scale human figures which may also be linked to actual garments. Embroidered textiles were also used for clothes in techniques ranging from covering a firmly woven linen foundation with floral designs worked in tiny stitches in coloured wools and silks, to delicately worked cut and drawn threadwork.

The garments and textiles are conveniently supplemented by pictorial and literary secondary sources of both Persian and European origin. One of the most important pictorial sources is the series of Persian miniature paintings illustrating manuscripts whose beginnings at present have been traced to the late thirteenth century. Various schools flourished depending for patronage on the ruler's court, until by the early fifteenth century meticulously detailed and refined work was produced. In contrast to many of the Ottoman Turkish paintings, however, the aim of these Persian miniatures was not to illustrate historical chronicles, but rather to embellish manuscripts of the famous poetic classics of Persian literature especially the national epic, the *Shahnamah* or Book of Kings of Firdausi of Tus (936–1020) completed by 1010, the *Khamseh* of Nizami of Ganjeh (1115–1202) and later the *Yusuf and Zuleikha* of Jami (1414–1492).

It is instructive to compare these classics which were copied again and again both for the choice of scene and episode and the treatment of costume throughout the centuries. Although they did not aim to illustrate reality, the artists depicted the characters in the contemporary fashions of their time and, as many of them were female, it is possible to trace through these Persian miniatures the sequence of women's fashions from an earlier period than for Ottoman Turkey. From the late sixteenth century a taste developed for albums depicting aristocratic beauties as single figures dressed in the height of fashion. This continued through the seventeenth century being transformed eventually into the large scale studies in oils which were produced from the late eighteenth through to the early twentieth century.

To a superficial observer this art of the Persian miniature would seem precious and self-contained which once fully developed would admit little outside influence. However, by the second half of the seventeenth century, when European visitors – diplomats, merchants and craftsmen – were actively encouraged to visit Isfahan, the capital of the Safavid rulers, evidence of this contact is seen in Persian paintings which begin to show the results of experimentation with technical devices such as shading to create volume and the use of oil pigments as a medium. These trends reached fruition in the series of oil paintings dating from the late eighteenth and nineteenth century which are excellent sources of realistic detail of the costume accessories and cosmetics of the court beauties which they portray. Another series of Persian paintings comparable with the Turkish albums of typical characters and nationalities of the Ottoman Empire and aimed at satisfying the curiosity of European visitors, were volumes of single-figure studies in clear bright watercolours on fine paper of women in different costumes and craftsmen at work, painted in the nineteenth century to cater to a similar market. While of limited artistic importance, they usefully document costume styles.

Again European illustrations complement local paintings. They are, however, less abundant in both number and quality of interpretation because although Persia was known to European travellers since the expedition of the Venetian merchant Marco Polo from 1252 to 1298, the flow of visitors was not as consistent or steady as it was to Turkey. Persia was more remote and more difficult of access bearing in mind the slow and cumbrous means of transport available, and political conditions were less stable than in the Ottoman Empire. Apart from a few Spanish and Italian travellers in the fifteenth century, it was not until the late sixteenth to early seventeenth century that efforts were made to establish permanent diplomatic and commercial relations, which in turn dwindled owing to the unsettled conditions of the eighteenth century before being re-established in the early nineteenth century. Consequently, there are not the series of costume engravings so valuable as a source of Turkish costume from the sixteenth century onwards. At best, European views of Persian life and costume are the illustrations accompanying the account of Sir John Chardin a Huguenot jeweller at the Safavid court of Shah Abbas II[2] who lived in Persia from 1666 to 1669 and again from 1672 to 1676 and, of later visitors, the superb drawings of Sir Robert Ker Porter whose travels took place from 1817 to 1820.[3] Otherwise, the somewhat mundane drawings and engravings accompanying the written accounts of travellers have to suffice.

In the late nineteenth century photography arrived in Persia as an aid to recording its environment, life and customs. The as yet earliest record of the use of photography in Persia is seen in the album of the Italian diplomatic mission of 1862 which includes evocative views of buildings and gorgeously costumed court officials.[4] Most of the travel accounts from this time onwards were illustrated with photographs which included costume studies, and there are also the delightful photographs taken by Ernst Hoeltzer, superintendent of the Isfahan Telegraph Office who took advantage of his work there to affectionately record his environment.[5] Finally, the skill of photography was studied eagerly by Persians themselves. Nasiruddin Shah Qajar ruler of Persia from 1848 to 1896 was a keen amateur, who arranged for one of his courtiers Agha Reza to be instructed in photography at the newly established technical college in Tehran, the Dar ul-Funun, and appointed him court photographer in 1863.[6] Nasiruddin Shah's own photographic albums have been preserved in the Gulestan Palace at Tehran,[7] and include among their subjects studies of the ladies of his household whose somewhat homely appearance provides a salutary corrective to the idealised fashions of the glamorous court beauties of the oil paintings.

The most abundant written sources are the accounts of successive European travellers which range from the brief notes in the diaries of the Italian envoys of the late fifteenth century to the intelligently observed and detailed description of Chardin in the seventeenth century. These accounts are, naturally, more numerous for the nineteenth century and are generally variable in quality and accuracy. Among the most useful for an assessment of costume are those of Lady Sheil, wife to the British envoy to the court of the Qajar rulers in the 1850s, Dr C. H. Wills, physician to the staff of the Persian Telegraph Department from 1866 to 1881 stationed in Tehran, Hamadan, Shiraz and Isfahan and Ella Sykes who spent eight years as housekeeper to her brother Percy Sykes, British consul in Kerman.[8] Persian sources have as yet been less exploited. Occasionally, there are references in Persian poetry to certain garments such as women's veils as often a significant twist in the story depended on identity confused through concealment but, unfortunately, there are no memoirs comparable with those of the Ottoman court ladies of the late nineteenth century. It is clear from this general survey of the source materials that it is easier to document Persian women's costume from the seventeenth century onwards, especially when European women began to accompany their menfolk to Persia and were able, as in Turkey, to gain access to the private quarters of households. The area of public life was a masculine domain which continued into the home as the *biruni* – the men's quarters – also functioned as a reception area where business was conducted and guests entertained. The women, however, were restricted to the *anderun* – the inner quarters reserved for close family members and female visitors. In urban areas they maintained this seclusion by veiling themselves when they went out on shopping expeditions or to visit women friends. While village and nomad women were segregated from men in certain situations, they did not shroud themselves in veils as their way of life would have made this impractical. The distinction between the external and internal worlds is consistently maintained in the depiction of women in the miniature paintings: in situations taking place in house or garden they are unveiled, whereas in the street and market place they are veiled.

Evidence of the development of women's costume during the late thirteenth and fourteenth century is sporadic and in the main dependent on representations in miniature paintings. The illustrated frontispiece (Plate 93) to a manuscript of the *Kitab al-diriyak* of mid-thirteenth century date depicting entertainments and processions of court life portrays women in both indoor and outdoor dress.[9] The flat schematised style of painting at least enables the basic shapes of the garments to be understood. The main item of indoor clothing is a belted crossover robe reaching to mid-calf with long tight sleeves, decorated with contrast facing along all borders and cuffs. The fabrics used are either plain – olive green, blue or orange in which folds are indicated by stylised ripples, or covered in small repeating patterns such as

Opposite. Plate 93. Court entertainment. Frontispiece painting of the *Kitab al-diriyak*, Mosul, Iraq, mid-13th century.

interlocking octagons and Y-shapes in outline against purple and blue grounds. Hair is dressed in long thick braids which fall over shoulders and back and is swathed in striped or plain turbans. The make-up appears to be correspondingly bold stressing arched and sweeping black brows plucked into a fine line, slanting eyes outlined in black and brightly rouged mouths. It is not, however, clear from the painting whether they are wearing knee-length boots or trousers gathered into flat slippers. If comparison with later examples is considered as a valid argument for continuity certainly the latter choice is found in the *chak-chir* – combined slippers and trousers worn as outdoor dress by Persian women in the nineteenth century. Women in their outdoor dress are shown in procession riding in pannier-type litters on camels. They are wrapped in all-enveloping cloaks while their heads are covered in tightly swathed shawls in contrasting colours – red, orange, blue – which also function as veils as one end is pulled across to conceal the lower half of the face and then tucked up into the narrow fillet bound over the forehead. Another thirteenth century painting an illustration to al-Tabari's *Annals* depicts three women wearing a different style of cloak – *chadar* – of white which covers their heads and is wrapped tightly around their faces over a white veil extending from nose to chin, before falling over their shoulders and arms.

Fourteenth-century fashions may be traced in a series of dated Persian miniatures. The birth of the Prophet Mohammad (Plate 94) from the *Jami al-Tawarikh* or *World History* of Rashid al-Din dated 1306[10] naturally portrays women in an interior environment and consequently unveiled. A group of three women standing on the left present the clearest details of costume. They appear to be dressed in two visible layers of modest clothing – an ankle-length dress covered by a coat which appears to be of straight narrow cut with long wide sleeves. One of these coats is of special interest because it reveals information about the use of contrasting textile patterns and thus of construction. The main fabric is a regular lattice of checks, but the lining is patterned in a fluent design of what appears to be tendrils trained into palmette loops. The lining has been cut larger than the coat so that it can be folded back over the front and neck edges to form a deep facing band. All the women wear similar headdresses in the form of long rectangular scarves whose decorated and sometimes fringed edges enable the line of the draping to be traced. First one end is pulled across the breast wound tightly round the head, crossed again under the chin and then folded over the head so that the other end hangs over the shoulder, giving the effect of a close fitting wimple.[11] A miniature from the *Al-Athar al-Bagiya* of Al-Biruni dated 1307[12] of a couple feasting confirms the style of a long narrow unbelted robe and a tightly wound headshawl for women, though the representation is more impressionistic and careless of detail. Both manuscripts are also informative about outdoor dress which follows the main lines of development outlined for the thirteenth century. Women cover themselves from

head to foot in long chadars which could be pulled tightly together and swathed across the face at will. Women's costume continued to develop along these lines throughout the fourteenth century stressing clear flowing lines of dress. As an alternative to the headshawl, women are sometimes shown with their hair arranged to frame the face coiled from a central parting and then extending in long plaits down their backs. This hairstyle might be ornamented with strings of jewellery or covered with a fluttering long scarf pinned lightly to the top of the head.

The continued evolution of women's fashions through the fifteenth century may be traced through a series of dated miniatures painted at Tabriz, Herat and Shiraz. All these centres are widely separated geographically which would normally argue for representation of certain regional differences in costume or at least conventions for symbolising them. In general, however, the styles are notable for their similarity mainly because the miniatures were the work of court artists trained in a common tradition who inherited certain ways of depicting costume detail which had the effect of overriding local variations. A miniature (Plate 95) portraying the introduction of the sculptor Farhad to Shirin from a manuscript of Nizami's poem *Khusrau and Shirin* painted at Tabriz *c.* 1405–1410 illustrates the basic principles of costume composition. Garments continue the narrow elegant line already established throughout the fourteenth century and depend for effect on accumulated layers, a fashion idiom already seen in Ottoman Turkey. The seated figure of Shirin reveals, for example, at least three visible layers of clothing. First she wears a light round-necked undergarment – *pirahan* – which is covered by a V-necked long robe in light mauve lined in green; this is turned back at the neck to reveal the undershirt and to create contrast revers. The final garment is a plain

Plate 94. Birth of the Prophet Mohammad. Miniature painting from a manuscript of the *Jami al-Tawarikh* of Rashid al-Din, 1306.

Plate 95. Farhad brought before Shirin. Miniature painting from a manuscript of the Khusrau and Shirin of Nizami. Tabriz, 1405–10.

orange coat lined with ermine which is indicated by a discreet edging at the centre front and long narrow sleeves extending well over the wrists to conceal the hands. Such coats could be worn in various ways – draped nonchalantly over the shoulders with the sleeves trailing behind, or worn so that the hands were covered. Similar garments are known in Ottoman Turkish costume where a slit for the arms is positioned at the underarm so that the exaggeratedly long sleeves have become decorative rather than functional. A possible explanation for this curious survival is that originally such garments were used as riding coats which required close fitting long sleeves to protect the wearer's wrists and hands in harsh weather conditions. This was certainly the function of such long sleeves in the coats worn by Manchu nomads which later survived in the court costume of the Qing dynasty of China as it was worn from the seventeenth to nineteenth century. Shirin's costume is completed by a headdress consisting of a filmy purple scarf secured to the top of her head by a curved pin, from which a narrow jewelled string passes down the sides of her face and under the chin. The hair is still coiled and looped in front of the ears.

Evidence of continuity in this basic style of court dress is seen in later miniatures from Shiraz and Herat (Plate 96). A painting *c.* 1440[13] from Shiraz portraying Iskander and the Indian princess (from Nizami's poem the *Iskandarnameh*) shows that two female attendants are wearing costumes very similar to that of Shirin. As the figures are on a larger scale, however, it is possible to gain more information about the shape and volume of the garments. One of the girls wears the complete assemblage of high-necked undergarment, V-necked robe and fur-lined coat with the long sleeves which conceal the hands. Her companion, however, does not wear this coat which reveals that the robe could have short sleeves and was loose enough to be gathered into

Below left. Plate 96. Iskandar and the Indian princess. Miniature painting from a manuscript of the Iskandarnameh of Nizami. Shiraz, *c.*1440.

Below right. Plate 97. Mahan in the enchanted garden. Miniature painting from manuscript of the Khamseh of Nizami. Shiraz, 1491.

folds at the waist when belted. As a contrast, the undergarment is in a darker fabric and has long tight sleeves. Their hairstyles are conservative continuing the fashion for front hair smoothly groomed from a centre parting and coiled in loops framing the cheeks. Their headdresses are of interest as they seem to consist of scarves knotted over a face-framing transparent shawl indicated by a convention of reticulate white dots which possibly may be identified as a *charghat* – worn by Persian townswomen in the nineteenth century and still surviving today among Qashqa'i tribal women of South-West Persia.

A series of miniatures also painted at Shiraz in 1491 of scenes from Nizami's poems of *Khusrau and Shirin*, and *Layla and Majnun* (Plate 97) clarifies the problem of this headdress as it is more clearly depicted. In this later group all the women have long black hair dressed so that plaits trail down their backs while the front locks are trained into the now familiar coils framing the face.[14] Over the hair a white transparent shawl is pulled tightly round the face and fastened under the chin. The area and outline of this shawl are indicated by painting a white open lattice over the hair and neck and using a definite white line to indicate its border. In one of the series of miniatures this *charghat* is seen continuing to trail behind the wearer ending in a point which, by analogy with later examples, gives the impression that the shawl was triangular in shape. Wrapped around the *charghat* forming a type of bandeau swathing the forehead and tied in a knot at the back so that the ends hung down and fluttered behind the wearer was a twisted scarf in a bright contrasting colour – red, blue, purple.

The same series of miniatures also clarifies further detail of the main costume garments. Colours are bright and intense – scarlet, royal blue, orange, light purple, golden yellow, turquoise green – combined to give striking contrasts of, for example, red and yellow, turquoise green and royal blue, and green, orange and red. Either at least two or all of the three co-ordinating garments are worn. The undergarment follows the already established pattern of an ankle-length garment with neat round neck and long tight sleeves. The robe worn over it may have long or short cap sleeves, and may extend to the ankles or to mid-calf, and be worn belted or unbelted. This robe may also be decorated with what appears to be designs worked in gold embroidery, perhaps using couching methods similar to those which have been seen on surviving Ottoman Turkish textiles, or woven in weft-floated brocade technique. The motifs seem to be cloud bands trained into a shawl-like collar shape over the front and back of the robe's neck and shoulders and into a deep band at the hem. The long fur-lined coat may have either the long trailing sleeves, long sleeves fitting in to the wrist or short sleeves reaching to the middle of the upper arm.

Although the series of miniatures is extremely informative, once its costume conventions can be understood and interpreted, it provides little information about methods of pattern construction. By analogy with Ottoman Turkish garments and surviving Persian garments of

Plate 98. Shirin receives the portrait of Khusrau. Miniature painting from a manuscript of the Khusrau and Shirin of Nizami. Herat, 1494.

later date, and from the shape as depicted in these miniatures, it would be reasonable to hypothesise that their main pattern unit was a long rectangular centre piece folded over the shoulders to which sleeves and shaping sections were added. A miniature painted at Herat in 1494 (Plate 98) of Shirin looking at the portrait of Khosrau shows a comparable style of dressing[15] although differing in certain conventions of rendering fabric; for example, the headdress is the *charghat* but depicted as being made of an opaque white fabric demurely knotted under the chin, whilst the confining scarf is much neater with short rather than fluttering ends tied at the back of the head. A further variation of the long-sleeved outer coat is seen in which there are openings at underarm so that the wearer's arms can pass through them leaving the surplus length of the sleeve to fall behind her.

In all these fifteenth-century miniatures depicting the progression of women's dress certain conventions were used to indicate make-up. Eyebrows were painted and shaped into arched black lines sometimes joined over the bridge of the nose to give a continuous undulating curve. The upward slant of the eyes was accentuated with a black outline, while black beauty spots and moles were dotted about cheek and neck. In some examples an elongated deep blue pendant was painted on the forehead in line with the bridge of the nose possibly indicating a tattoo or hennaed pattern. Small heartshaped red mouths continued to be admired. These cosmetic fashions closely mirror the standards of feminine beauty repeatedly praised in Persian poetry in which broad moon faces, bold black eyebrows and slanting eyes, red mouths and long black hair were paramount.

The outdoor costume which concealed these strikingly painted and dressed beauties naturally continued more sober traditions. The all-enveloping cloak – *chadar* – continued to be worn. When pulled tightly round the head a fold could also be pulled across the mouth to conceal the lower part of the face. The *chadar* was also worn over a separate face veil. There is, however, literary and pictorial evidence for the use of another form of concealment – the black horsehair face mask or *picheh*. It was noted in Tabriz by Ruy Gonzales de Clavijo, Castillian ambassador to Timur 1403–1406: 'These women go about, covered all over with a white sheet, with a net made of black horse hair before their eyes . . .'[16] Its use is again remarked on in 1471 by Caterino Zeno, Venetian ambassador to Uzun Hassan Khan '. . . they cover their faces with nets woven of horsehair, so thick that they can easily see others, but cannot be seen by them'.[17]

This face mask is clearly to be identified with a black band folded back over the forehead in miniatures (Plate 99) depicting women otherwise enfolded in a white *chadar*. The conventions of Persian painting which can make folded scarves appear as curious cockscombs also coped with a black face mask by representing it as turned back from the wearer's face and foreshortened.

Although Persia had long been famous for its textile manufacture, consecutive documentation in the form of actual fabrics is sporadic. Pieces of silk highly sophisticated both in weaving technique and design survive from the Sassanian and Seljuk periods, but as yet few examples have been attributed to the centuries following. It seems, therefore, that only with the period of Safavid rule – concentrated on the brilliant court at Isfahan – a period which gave Persia two centuries

Plate 99. Rustam rescuing Bizhan from the well. Miniature painting from a manuscript of the Shahnameh of Firdausi.

of stability and prosperity can the history of Persian textiles be resumed by studying existing examples. These have survived both as lengths and pieces of fabric and more rarely as garments, and have mainly been attributed to the late sixteenth and seventeenth century. Certain features are outstanding such as great technical accomplishment in weaving technique, use of luxurious materials such as silk, gold and silver threads, and designs which exhibit a wide range of elegant and graceful motifs. Techniques included reversing motifs in coloured silks against backgrounds of fine silk or continuous gold and silver thread, weaving in fine velvet pile which could be mingled in cut and voided designs with brocade backgrounds. Colour schemes tended to be softer and perhaps subtler than those of contemporary Ottoman Turkish textiles and, depending on taste, perhaps lacked their strength and vigour. Design motifs, however, included a greater range of subject and theme from repeating sprays of flowers, birds and trees to complex schemes of human figures sometimes depicting popular scenes from the great Persian romantic poems. Here both subject and treatment closely paralleled that of contemporary miniature painting making it tempting to speculate that, at least in ateliers working for the court, weavers had design cartoons prepared for them by the painters.

Certain textiles are inscribed with dates which enable some sequ-

Plate 100. Apricot silk brocade woven with repeated panels containing seated girls. Persia, 1646.

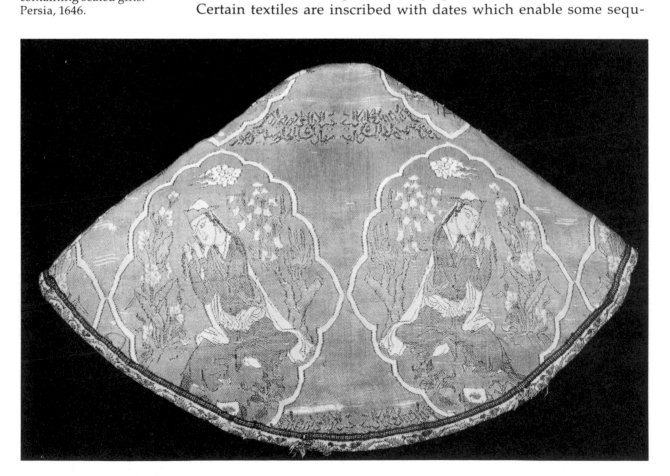

ence of both stylistic and technical evolution to be established. An example (Plate 100) now in the Royal Museum of Scotland's collections furnishes a convenient example of technique, design and date.[18] It is a piece of silk woven in fine twill weave with a design of repeating lobed panels against an apricot background. Within each panel is a graceful young woman dressed in a deep pink robe with white veil and sash, plaiting her hair in a garden of flowering trees and clouds. Details characteristic of this type of silk brocade are the use of separate wefts in black silk to outline the design in a manner recalling the miniature painters' technique and the smooth balance of areas of colour. A repeated inscription in Persian woven in black letters gives an exact date 'This was made by order and was finished on the eleventh day of Sha'ban in the year 1056 (AD 1646).' The nature of the design would make this fabric equally suitable for use in a garment such as a sumptuous outer robe or as a furnishing fabric. Figure designs woven in silk brocades all tend to be supple and delicate in scale. In velvets, however, they are boldly depicted groups or pairs of elegantly dressed young men and women. The effect and proportion of these figured velvets in costume may be seen in a coat presented by the Czar of Russia to Queen Christina of Sweden in 1644.[19] Apart from the existence of textiles, the source materials of Safavid costume are more abundant because the paintings provide a more careful rendering of pattern and design, and from the late sixteenth century there developed the fashion of single-figure studies which naturally present costume detail in a notably enlarged format, while the written sources include reports by European visitors who stayed in Persia long enough to make accurate observations.

A series of sixteenth-century miniatures reveals certain changes in the fashions of women's costume, especially in the choice of fabric and the treatment of headdresses. These changes are well illustrated in a miniature of *c.* 1540 (Plate 101) painted by Aqa Mirak of Shirin and Khusrau seated with their court being entertained by storytelling.[20] Shirin and her attendants all wear variants of the same dress, beginning with the round-necked undergarment already noted in fourteenth- and fifteenth-century costume. Here the garment is simply fastened at the neck with a single clasp from which the front opening falls as a narrow vertical décolleté to waist level. The long tight sleeves of this garment are visibly creased and folded at the wrists. The robe which is worn over this continues in the shape of the fifteenth-century garment but has been cut so that the fronts slant inwards from the shoulders to the waist giving a deep V-neckline and effectively revealing the undergarment. Some of the robes are of plain fabric while others are patterned in designs of graceful floral stems and repeated lobed panels which can be matched with surviving silk brocades. Over the robe the short sleeved version of the coat is worn which can again be of plain or patterned material with deep cape-like collar and looped braid fastenings. Headdresses have undergone a transformation to

what appear to be small embroidered skull-caps over which the *charghat* – now a neat triangular scarf – is draped and secured in place by a single string of jewels passing from the temples and under the chin. The hairstyle is correspondingly lighter as the heavy coiled bobs give way to wavy strands falling casually on each side of the face. Other cosmetic details worth noting are the elaborate patterns of henna covering some of the girls' hands, a fashion which though it may well have occurred before the sixteenth century has not previously been depicted in such detail. A single-figure painting of a seated princess (Plate 102) by Mirza Ali contemporary with the miniature of Khosrau and Shirin provides the detail which completes the picture of early sixteenth-century dress.[21] It is, for example, possible to see through the front opening of the undergarment that a white filmy shirt is worn which is not necessarily a sixteenth-century innovation but had not been discernible in earlier miniatures.

The three main garments – undergarment, robe and coat have all been made of fabrics carefully chosen to both harmonise and contrast in their colour and pattern. Undergarment and robe are each in shades of blue patterned in gold with delicate floral tendrils and ducks among grass respectively. The coat is a brilliant orange also patterned in gold with peony sprays and ducks. Probably all three fabrics are to be identified with plain silk brocaded with motifs in lustrous contrasting silks woven in weft float. The robe's lining, a soft fine dark fur, peers through at the front hem, border and sleeve edges. This robe also clearly shows how the shawl-like collar functioned. Here it is of black material and has probably been embroidered with the design of spiralling arabesque tendrils. It has been neatly sewn into place over the orange robe and in this technique and shape resembles the so-called cloud collar found on Chinese robes. Finally, details of the headdress including the pearl strand passing under the chin, and the jewellery – pendant earrings, a double-stranded bead choker and a finger ring are seen. The style of beauty continues in the well-established tradition of full face with accentuated arched black brows and eyes.

Miniatures painted *c.* 1565–70 indicate that the general lines of the fashion as outlined here continued with the addition of accessories such as tie belts over the long-sleeved robe, sometimes a jewelled spray pinned to the headdress, an extra scarf tied to the *charghat* and the variation of a short knee-length version of the fur-lined coat which could have either long or short sleeves. They also show that ankle-length white trousers were worn thus completing the set of underwear. Colourful and pretty variations on the main costume style are seen in a miniature painted *c.* 1575 (Plate 103) at Qazvin of ladies preparing a picnic,[22] whose garments and headscarves are patterned with crowded floral and star motifs. As they are busying themselves with cooking, lighting fires and other tasks, they have tucked their robes up into their belts so the miniature also gives an idea of how these clothes worked in

Opposite. Plate 101. Khusrau and Shirin listening to stories. Miniature painting from a manuscript of the Khusrau and Shirin of Nizami, *c.*1540.

Above. Plate 102. Seated princess. Persia, *c.*1540.

Plate 103. Ladies' picnic.
Miniature painting,
Qazvin, *c.*1575.

action. They also make a feature of the long pointed end of their *charghats* by twisting it over their shoulders and diagonally into their belts like a bandolier. A later sixteenth-century miniature painted *c.* 1590 to 1600 (Plate 104), illustrating one of the heroes of the Shahnameh Faridun attacking the tyrant Zahhak, again is informative about additional detail rather than the general assemblage of costume.[23] The two ladies anxiously watching Faridun are fashionably dressed in the layered look, but indicate that by the late sixteenth century skirts were shorter at least in the undergarment and robe as here they reach to just below the knee revealing tight trousers patterned with oblique flowered stripes. These are of interest not only because they add still more information to the picture of sixteenth-century costume, but because they survive until the early nineteenth century where they are made either from brocaded silk or closely embroidered linen.

Women's outdoor dress, while in the main continuing the fashions

Above left. Plate 104. Faridun striking Zahhak. Miniature painting from a manuscript of the Shahnameh of Firdausi. Persia, *c.*1590–1600.

Above right. Plate 105. Rustam rescuing Bizhan from the well. Miniature painting from a manuscript of the Shahnameh of Firdausi. Persia, late 16th century.

Plate 106. Arrival of Zulaikha. Miniature painting from a manuscript of the Yusuf and Zulaikha of Jami. Persia, *c.*1556–65.

that were already well established, did present some innovation to accompany the new styles of headdress. The plain white *chadar* worn over the face veil was the most usual fashion as attested by a series of miniatures from the 1540s onwards. The example (Plate 105) here of the mid-sixteenth century in which the hero of the Shahnameh, Rustam, rescues Bizhan from the pit also shows Manizeh watching his progress.[24] She is clearly shown closely wrapped in her *chadar* which she has folded over her arms to give an appearance of a sleeved coat

while her face veil conceals her from nose to chin. *Chadars* in colours other than plain white were also worn; the girl in a miniature of the old man declaring his love from the fifteenth-century poet Jami's work *Tuhfat al-Ahrar* is about to conceal her face with a *chadar* patterned with small sprigs of flowers. An alternative to the all-enveloping *chadar* and face veil is seen in a miniature dated *c.* 1556–65 (Plate 106) illustrating the arrival of Zuleikha the heroine of Jami's most popular and frequently illustrated poem *Yusuf and Zuleikha*.[25] While ladies peering out from the castle wall are muffled in *chadar* and veil, Zuleikha's attendants have merely tied a brief face veil over the scarves of their headdresses. This fashion was probably short lived as there seems to be no evidence of it in later pictorial and written sources. The black horse hair mask – *picheh* – continued to be worn as noted by the Venetian ambassador to Shah Tahmasp in 1571 Vincentio d'Alessandri, 'And I saw the mother of the Sultan Mustaffa Mirisce, who was slightly indisposed, come out with her face covered with a black veil, riding like a man, accompanied by four slaves and six men on foot'.[26] It also seems that the requirements of modesty in outdoor dress could be satisfied by wrapping a white shawl around the head and so arranging it that the

Plate 107. Princess Duvulrani riding. Miniature painting from a manuscript of the romance Mihr u Mishtari. Persia, 1596.

lower part of the face was concealed. This is shown in a painting dated 1596 (Plate 107) from the Persian romance *Mihr u Mishtari* showing Princess Duvulrani out riding.[27] Apart from the white headshawl, her outdoor dress consists of a long-sleeved discreetly closed ankle-length coat.

After the establishment of Persia's capital at Isfahan in 1597 by Shah Abbas I (1587–1629), the documentation of fashions in dress may be drawn from a greater choice of source materials. Shah Abbas found outlets for his energy in both planning and constructing magnificent buildings in his new capital and in pursuing diplomatic and commercial relations with Europe, which he further accelerated by allowing legations and trading factories to be established. Together with diplomats and merchants, missionaries and craftsmen came to Isfahan often staying there several years like the Huguenot jeweller John Chardin. They were encouraged by the positive reception they received from Shah Abbas and his court to explore and observe Persia and to record its institutions and customs. Their reactions varied from wonder at seemingly strange and bizarre ways to admiration and perceptive interest depending on their intelligence and ability to record their observations accurately. Naturally, costume of both men and women was a readily accessible subject so that descriptions of it both enliven these European accounts and provide an individual source to supplement the evidence of miniature paintings and pieces of contemporary textile. Persian costume was indeed much admired in Europe, though not everyone went to the extent that King Charles II of England did as recorded by the diarist John Evelyn on 18 October 1666 'To Court, it being the first time his Majesty put himself solemnly into the Eastern fashion of vest, changeing doublet, stiff collar, bands and cloaks, into a comely vest after the Persian fashion, with girdle or straps and shoe strings and buckles of which some were set with precious stones'.[28] Sir Anthony van Dyck's glamorous paintings of 1622 of Sir Robert Sherley, adventurer and self-styled British envoy to the Safavid court, and his wife Teresa both resplendent in Persian costume make it easy to sympathise with Charles II.[29] Additional to these more extensive written sources, textiles have survived made up into complete garments.

Miniature paintings continue to provide the meticulously detailed information about the composition of female costume as observed in the sixteenth century. Book illustrations continued the tradition of the single-figure study where, portrayed as finely rendered drawings or finished paintings, they enjoyed great popularity. Here favourite subjects were charming girls immaculately dressed and accessorised in elegant fashions. By the second half of the seventeenth century a new influence is seen in Persian miniature paintings which expresses itself in exquisitely graduated colours, use of shading and stippling and subtly individual treatment of features. This style is very much the result of the assimilation of contemporary European methods which had been introduced to Persia through both imported paintings and the presence of foreign artists at the Safavid court. Three painters especially, who are known from signed and dated works, eagerly adopted the new technique – Mohammad Zaman, Ali Quli Jabbadar and Shaykh Abbasi. Related to this period of European innovation is the introduction of painting in oils which could only have been learnt from Europe. As yet relatively few Safavid oil paintings have been identified, and in some cases it is open to question whether they were painted by European or Persian artists. At their best they resemble provincial versions of the works of Lely and Kneller, two of the most fashionable and accomplished Restoration portrait painters, in their attention to the detail of the sitter's appearance. For this reason they supplement the miniature paintings as sources of costume study.

Plate 108. Girl in violet robe. Miniature painting from an album of single-figure studies. Isfahan, *c.*1630.

Plenty of single-figure studies depict attractive girls in languid poses alternatively coy and pensive or holding wine flasks and glasses, writing or reading letters, stretched out in invitingly flowery gardens or simply showing off their clothes. A study of a girl painted *c.* 1630 (Plate 108) indicates clearly how these clothes were worn.[30] She wears first a round-necked undershirt fastened by a single clasp and then an ankle-length robe with long tight sleeves of plain violet fabric with an embroidered border at the hem. A light contrasting colour is chosen for the lining which is turned back at the deep V-neck to form the revers of the collar. Other decorative and functional items are combined in the form of the frogged braid fastening from neck to waist. The robe is swathed with a long scarf in ample folds low on the hips. While none of these elements are new the emphasis is different. Instead of the slim straight lines of sixteenth-century fashions curves are stressed and accentuated by use of accessory and finishing detail. Comparison with the shapes of surviving garments and also representations in the more realistic oil paintings indicates that shaped pattern pieces were used to give the desired effect. The headdress shows an interesting variation on the neatly wrapped scarves of sixteenth-century costume. Here the *charghat* is a patterned square folded in two diagonally and tied round the head over a full-length pale green *chadar* so that the points cover the head and the ends flutter behind. The use of an indoor *chadar* does not seem to have occurred before the Safavid period and certainly survived into the nineteenth century. It was usually made of a light material in attractive subtle shades of grey, light orange, blue, white and green. Other accessories include pearl necklaces and earrings and also cuban heeled shoes worn over brocaded ankle socks or indoor boots which can be documented in detail again from the oil paintings and surviving examples.

Late seventeenth-century costume reconstructed from Persian painting, European illustrations and descriptions and surviving garments presents a more flamboyant fashion in which richly patterned fabrics and a bell-shaped line dominated. One of the series of life-size oil paintings displaying European influence (Plate 109) serves as the

Plate 109. Woman in
Persian dress. Oil
painting, Isfahan, *c.*1650–
80.

equivalent of a fashion plate to give the total ideal look. It depicts a young woman holding a bowl of flowers standing on a balconied terrace overlooking a pastoral landscape.[31] She is posing in a rather self-conscious manner well aware of the magnificence of her costume. At first glance, it follows the long established principles of layers of different garments in carefully chosen fabrics, but their proportions and shape have altered. The most obvious difference is in the skirt which now flares out over the hips in a stiff bell shape to a hem reaching just below the knee. This shorter length has been noted in a late sixteenth-century miniature but does not on evidence available seem to have become fashionable until a century later. The undergarment is made of a light blue silk woven with repeated rosette flower motifs. It still has a round neck but now is fastened at the side and has an edging of black piping, a finishing technique suitable for brocade. Her robe is of white silk woven in what is probably a complex twill weave with a graceful repeating pattern of floral arabesque in which tendrils spring from peony and lotus motifs. The bodice is provocatively tight with a deep V-neck and long sleeves. The deep border of floral scroll on a gold ground is woven in a bias twill weave and can be matched up to surviving pieces. The sash draped and looped around her hips is also of silk with a deep border of rose sprays. Instead of a long outer coat she wears a hip-length jacket of gold brocade patterned with floral sprays and lined with fur draped over her shoulders to function as a cape. Her legs are covered in tight red trousers over which are fitted brocaded silk sock-boots which are then thrust into high-heeled leather shoes for outdoor wear. Here the headdress is simply a white *charghat* held in place by a ribbon fillet over long wavy strands of hair. Variations on the headdress may be chosen from small patterned triangular headscarves secured under the chin or a loose swathed turban. The costume is completed by discreet jewellery – a gold choker, a long string of red beads – possibly carnelian – terminating in a gold plaque, and a small single-bezelled ring on the little finger of each hand.

The significance of this splendid fashion plate is that its fabrics and some of its garments can be matched up with surviving pieces. The gold and silver brocades of robe, jacket and boots all display the variations on combinations of flower tendril and spray characteristic of late Safavid textiles, in which neat disciplined arrangements of motif on an even background were favoured. A robe (Plate 110) of late seventeenth- or early eighteenth-century date in the collections of the Victoria and Albert Museum[32] demonstrates the methods by which the tight bodice and bell-shaped skirt were made. The robe is of comparable shape with a short tight low-necked bodice into which a long skirt is gathered. It is open at the centre front. Long tapering sleeves are set into straight armholes with a detail not visible in the painting of a horizontal slash above the cuff, presumably so that the arm could be pushed through here if a shorter look was required. Two fabrics are used. The bodice, sleeve and skirt are made in a warp-faced beige silk with wefts of silver metallic thread wrapped around a yellow silk core, the combined effect of which is a rich silver beige. The pattern is woven by using additional silk wefts in blue, salmon pink, apricot and silver, and consists of repeated motifs of serrated leaves enfolding a spray of roses. All borders are edged with a continuous band of deep yellow silk woven on the bias with a zigzag scroll of pink lotus and blue carnation alternating, very similar to that of the robe in the oil painting. Probably the garment had a lining but all traces of the original have disappeared.

Plate 110. A woman's coat. Beige silk woven with repeated motifs of rose sprays. Persia, late 17th- early 18th century.

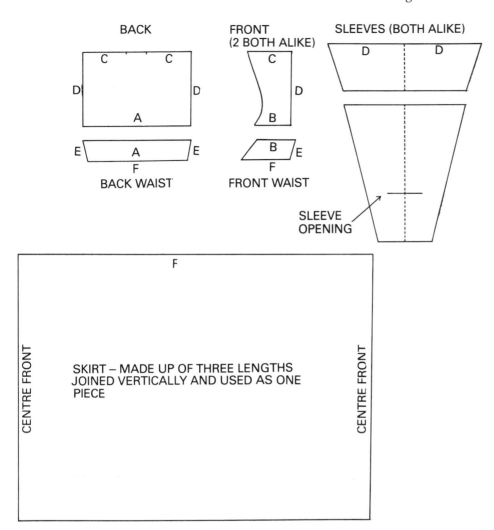

ALL PIECES CUT ON STRAIGHT OF FABRIC
½ IN SEAM ALLOWANCE
ALL SEAMS HAND SEWN IN DOUBLE RUNNING STITCH
SKIRT GATHERED ON TO WAIST WITH OVERCAST
SMOCKING STITCH
ALL EDGES FACED WITH DIAGONAL SILK BINDING

Diagram 18. Woman's coat. Persia, late 17th–early 18th century. Scale – 1:15.

A close examination (Diagram 18) of the cut and construction of the robe naturally supplements the information supplied by the paintings. One feature which continues to be found in surviving garments of later date is the use of a patchwork of skilfully joined scraps of material to make up the required shape of a pattern piece; the material was too expensive and valuable to waste. In this robe the back only shows this economy measure. The construction is basically simple. The bodice is made of three pieces joined at the shoulders – an almost rectangular piece for the back and two fronts shaped to give the deep *décolleté* neck. They are all seamed to a broad waistband which in turn is fitted to a gathered skirt made up of three vertically joined pieces. All seams are naturally hand sewn using yellow or beige silk thread in a double running stitch, while the facings are held in place with a single row of running stitch at each edge. An examination of the seams indicates the order in which the robe was built up. First, the shoulders were joined and the waistband attached, then the sleeves were inserted and the skirt sections gathered to the waist. Finally, the underarms, sides of bodice and skirt were joined in one long continuous seam and the facings added. This order of construction continued to be used in eighteenth- and nineteenth-century garments, and is still found today in rural and tribal areas where traditional costumes are worn even though they are made of modern machine-made synthetic fabrics.

A further example of the correlation between painting and surviving garment is seen in accessories, where again the object enables the pictorial representation to be correctly interpreted. The pieces here are a pair of sock-boots (Plate 111), made of a brocaded cloth of pink silk warps and silver wefts wrapped around a white silk core, decorated with repeating ogee-shaped lozenges each containing a rose spray all worked in supplementary wefts in pink, green and blue silks.[33] The boots are bordered at the ankle with a rose scroll against a gold ground. They are of simple shape and construction, with flat pointed soles and straight sides reaching to mid-calf. Each boot has a leather sole saddlestitched to a pointed and curved upper which fits over the instep and is in turn joined to a single leg piece which is seamed together at the back. The back of the heel is made into a decorative feature as it is covered with a piece of white leather and embroidered in gold. The boots are lined with red cotton block printed with floral sprigs, a material frequently used for lining all types of garment. The leather soles enable the silk boots to be worn as durable indoor footwear, and as they were also soft and flexible they could be easily fitted into the high-heeled leather shoes worn out of doors. Here the survival of the

Plate 111. Pair of boots. Pink silk and silver brocade woven with rose motifs. Persia, late 17th century.

actual garment enables the painting to be accurately interpreted, as it would otherwise be possible to mistake the boots either for contrast trouser cuffs or as decorative uppers to the high heeled shoes without realising that two pairs of footwear are in fact worn.

Sir John Chardin in late seventeenth century gives his impression of women's dress.

The Habit of the Women resembles, in a great many things that of the Men; the *Drawers* fall in the same manner down to their Ancles, but the Legs of them are straiter, longer and thicker, because the Women wear no Stockings. They cover their Feet with a Buskin, which reaches four Fingers above the Ancle, and which is either Embroider'd or of the richest Stuff. The Shift which they call *Comis*, from whence, perhaps the Word Chemise or Shift comes, is open before down to the Navel: their Vests are longer, and hang almost down upon their Heels: Their Girdle is small, and not above an Inch wide: Their Head is very well cloath'd, and over it they have a Vail that falls down to their Shoulders, and covers their Neck and Bosom before. . . . The Women wear four Vails in all; two of which they wear at Home, and two more when they go Abroad. The first of these Vails is made like a Kerchief, falling down behind the Body, by way of Ornament; The second passes under the Chin, and covers the Bosom: . . .

The Head-dress of the Women is plain; their Hair is all drawn behind the Head, and put in a great many Wefts; and the Beauty of that Head-dress consists in having those Wefts thick, and falling down to their Heels; and if the Hair be not long enough, they tie Wefts of Silk to lengthen them: They trim the Ends of these Wefts with Pearls, and a Knot of Jewels, or Ornaments of Gold and Silver. he Head is no otherwise dress'd under the Vail or Kerchief, but from the End of a Fillet, cut or hollow'd Triangularwise; and this is the Point that covers the Head, being kept upon the top of the Fore-head by a little Fillet, or String about an Inch broad. This Head-band or Fillet, which is made of several Colours is small and light; The little Fillet is Embroider'd, in Imitation of Needlework, or cover'd with Jewels, according to the Quality of the People. This is, in my Opinion, the ancient *Tiara* or Diadem of the Queens of *Persia*; none but the Married Women wear them: and this is a Mark whereby they are known to be under Authority. The Girls have little Caps instead of the Kerchief, or the *Tiara*.

They wear no Vail in the House, but they cause Two tresses of their Hair to hang down upon their Cheeks. The Cap of young Women of Condition, is fasten'd with a Stay of Pearls. They don't shut up the young Women in *Persia*, till they are six or seven Years of Age; and before they come to that Age, they go out of the *Seraglio* sometimes with their Father, insomuch that one may see them. I have seen some of them prodigiously Handsom; one may see their Neck and Breast, than which nothing in Nature can be finer. The *Persian* Dress gives one the Liberty of seeing much more of the Waste than ours does.[34]

Chardin is also informative about details of cosmetics and jewellery:

Black hair is most in Esteem with the *Persians*, as well the Hair of the Head, as the Eye-brows and Beard: The thickest and largest Eye-brows are accounted the finest, especially when they are so large that they touch each other. The *Arabian* Women have the finest Eye-brows of this kind. Those of the *Persian* Women, who have not Hair of that Colour, dye and rub it over with Black to improve it. They make themselves likewise a black Patch or Lozenge, not so big as the Nail of one's little Finger, a little under the Eye-brows; and in the dimple of the Chin another little Purple one; but this never stirs, being made with the point of a Lancet. They likewise generally annoint their Hands and Feet with that Orange-colour'd Pomatom, which they call *Hanna*, which is made with the Seed or Leaves of *Woad* or *Pastel* ground . . . which they make use of to preserve the Skin against the heat of the Weather. Observe likewise, that among the Women, the smallest Wastes are the most esteem'd.

The Ornaments of the *Persian* Women are very different; they dress their Head with Plumes of Jewels pass'd into the Fillet of the Fore-head; or with knots of Flowers instead of them: They fasten a Crotchet of Precious-Stones to the Fillet, which hangs down between their Eye-brows; a row of Pearl, which is fasten'd to the Top of the Ears, and goes under the chin . . . Besides the Jewels which the *Persian* Ladies wear at their Head, they were Bracelets of Jewels, of the bigness of two, and almost three Fingers, and very loose around the Arm. The People of Quality wear Rows of Pearl: the young Girls have nothing commonly but little Manacles of Gold, about the thickness of a tagg'd Point, with a Precious Stone, at the Place where it shuts. Some of 'em likewise wear Fetters made like these Manacles, but that is not usual. Their Necklaces are either chains of Gold or Pearl, which they hang to their Neck, and which fall below the Bosom . . .[35]

As in previous centuries there was a marked contrast between the splendour of this indoor costume and the discreet seclusion of the outdoor clothes. As Chardin again observes: 'When they go out, they put over all, a great white Vail, which covers them from Head to Foot, not suffering any thing to appear, in several Countries, but the Balls of Their Eyes.'[36] This custom is equally quaintly and graphically confirmed by John Fryer a surgeon who was in Persia from 1672 to 1681. 'The Plebean Women walk without Doors, either on Foot, or else ride on Horse-back covered with White sheets, with Holes for their Eyes and Nose; content to enjoy Day at a little Hole rather than prostitute their Face to the publick View.'[37]

In these basically conservative garments where function was more important than style a change of fashion is noticeable in the seventeenth century which is documented by a series of miniatures painted in Isfahan dating from 1612 to 1693. The *chadar* continued to be worn as an all-enveloping cloak covering the wearer from the top of her head to her ankles. The change is in the form of the face veil (Plate 112) which takes the form known as the *ru-band*, consisting of a rectangular piece of white fabric fastened over the *chadar* leaving a slit for the eyes, which could be flipped back over the head when the lady wished to reveal herself. Chardin again succinctly describes this type of outdoor dress in his listing of the four layers of veils worn: '. . . The third, is the White Veil, which covers all the Body; And the fourth is a sort of Handkerchief, which goes over the Face, and is fasten'd to the Temples. This Handkerchief or Vail, has a sort of Net-work, like old Point, or Lace, for them to see through . . .'[38]

Following the abundant documentation of the seventeenth century, material for the study of women's costume dwindles to a disappointing trickle during the eighteenth century only to emerge again in comparable detail in the nineteenth century. The basic reasons for this sparseness are to be found in the chaotic and confused political situation of Persia of the eighteenth century during which conditions were obviously unfavourable for the pursuit of fashion whether through the medium of court painters, weavers and dressmakers or the observations of travellers. During this period commercial relations with the outside world declined so much that apart from a few determined merchants such as Jonas Hanway[39] few people visited Persia. Scattered pieces of evidence, however, seem to indicate that women's costumes experienced no startling innovation but continued steadily along familiar lines. A miniature, for example, of an old man among young men and women, an illustration to the *Divan* of Hafez dated 1717[40] shows the girls dressed in long patterned robes with hip-length long-sleeved jackets worn over them and white veils draped over their heads. After a long interval, life-size oil and fresco paintings attributed mainly to Shiraz which enjoyed a period of relative stability and prosperity in the late eighteenth century under the rule of Karim Khan Zand (1750–1779) provide fresh information about costume development. Most of these paintings depict pretty girls playing musical instruments (Plate 113), eating fruit or simply reclining in carpeted and curtained interiors. Their costumes all consist of hip-length diaphanous undershirts with long flowing sleeves and jewelled openings at neck and centre front worn over wide but straight trousers of the type seen first in the late sixteenth century, patterned with obliquely arranged stripes of contrasting floral garlands and scrolls. Such trousers could be made of finely woven silk brocade or of linen covered in small stitches embroidered to stimulate a woven texture. The long robe, however, is no longer worn and has been replaced by a tight short jacket flaring over the hips made of a flowered silk brocade. Headdresses consist of a small cap adorned with strings of jewels over

Plate 112. Veiled girl. Miniature painting, Isfahan, *c.*1640.

which a long indoor *chadar* is draped to trail behind the wearer. Alternatively a large patterned turban is worn. Hair is artfully dressed with casually dishevelled fringes and side curls combined with numerous plaits displayed over the shoulders.

With the establishment of internal security again in Persia at the end of the eighteenth century by Agha Mohammad the first ruler of the Qajar dynasty (1794–1797) and its maintenance by his successors, which was also accompanied by a renewal of diplomatic and commercial relations with Europe, a suitable environment was created for the development of fashion, which can be followed consistently through the sources of Persian painting, surviving garments and European accounts and illustrations supplemented by photographs. Life-size oil and fresco paintings especially provide a spirited and engaging guide to the eccentricities of ninteenth-century Persian female clothing, which underwent some extraordinary changes in shape and propor-

Plate 113. Lovers sharing a bottle of wine. Oil painting, Persia, late 18th century.

tion. Many such paintings have survived of bold handsome girls gorgeously dressed and involved in such activities as playing a range of musical instruments, dancing, precariously balancing upside down on their hands and doing other acrobatic tricks, pouring wine or reclining in the company of personable young men. They functioned as superior items of interior decoration in the houses of wealthy Persians where they were seen by European guests such as Sir Frederick Goldsmith when he was given hospitality at Enzeli.

> He places at my disposal the traveller's room in his house, an apartment about 14 feet by 6, with pictures of flowers and females. A décolleteé beauty on the ceiling is rouged up to the eyes, and surrounded with miniatures of attendants in all kinds of impossible positions and attitudes, to say nothing of the flying charmers supporting her.[41]

Plate 114. Girl serving wine. Oil painting, Persia, early 19th century.

Such paintings were also seen in the winter and summer palaces of Fath Ali Shah (1797–1834) and, while they vary in both quality and technical skill, they are excellent sources of costume garment, jewelled accessory, cosmetics and hairstyles because the artists were required to include every detail. They reveal that by the early nineteenth century Persian women's fashions had undergone a definite change which has already been seen in the late eighteenth-century oil paintings of Shiraz. The mid-calf length coats of stiff brocade of Safavid times were out of date soon to be followed by the straight trousers with their oblique stripes of floral pattern. Instead the favoured silhouette is of a continuous bell shape flowing from a tightly confined waist to the ankles. This was basically to stay in fashion throughout the first half of the nineteenth century. The costume, however, relied on conservative tradition in that it was still assembled from layers of garments. These began with the undershirt – *pirahan* (Plate 114) – which is represented as hip length and with long loose sleeves made of a transparent gauzy fabric.[42] The round neck is no longer followed by a single centre front opening. Instead the *pirahan* is slashed with several jewel-edged and revealing openings which caused much comment among Europeans '. . . the gauze perhan, quite transparent, leaves nothing to the imagination. The breasts and chest are very visible, and the abdomen is quite bare.'[43] Over the *pirahan* was worn a pair of flaring voluminous trousers which could be of plain fabric edged with a decorative border or of splendidly patterned brocade, and a short tight fitting jacket with long sleeves, in material which either contrasted with or matched that of the trousers. This costume was festooned with lavish jewellery – ropes of pearls, armbands, bracelets and necklaces of rubies and emeralds and pearl studded caps – if worn by court favourites. Hairstyles were extravagant based on cascades of thick waves falling around face and shoulders and in long plaits at the back. The jewelled cap could be worn alone or with a *charghat* draped becomingly over it.

Contemporary with these flamboyant paintings of Fath Ali Shah's reign are surviving garments, which enable details of fabric, cut and construction to be acurately surveyed. A pair of trousers and a jacket in the Royal Museum of Scotland's collections well illustrate both the appearance and the practical details of the glamorous clothes of the portraits.[44] The main fabric of the trousers (Plate 115) is a stiff patterned brocade. The weaving technique is sophisticated using wefts of yellow silk wrapped with metallic gold strip worked closely over silk warps to give a subdued shimmering background. The design woven in smooth weft-floated silks in blue, green, pink and white consists of a stylised floral cone motif repeated in rows. Small cones and crescent-shaped floral sprays function as undergrowth and foliage to the principal motifs. The fabric in both technique and design is in the direct line of development from the Safavid textiles but the patterns have become smaller and more self-contained. The trousers extend from waist to ankle and are of loose fit with wide legs. They are attached to a broad waistband of crimson silk of double thickness to form a casing for the drawstring. The pattern and construction details are basically simple (Diagram 19). Two leg pieces which are both alike are cut as rectangles but shaped at the top by tapering them obliquely inwards. Each piece is folded in half vertically at the outer leg and joined together with an inner seam. The oblique edges of each piece are joined one to the other at centre front and back giving a neat V-shaped waist. All the seams are hand sewn using neat small running stitches. As the trousers are mounted on a block printed cotton lining all raw edges are concealed. Finally, the trouser hems are finished with black silk facing.

Plate 115. Woman's trousers. Gold brocaded silk patterned with repeated floral cones. Persia, early 19th century.

ADD ¼ IN FOR SEAM AND TURNING ALLOWANCE THROUGHOUT

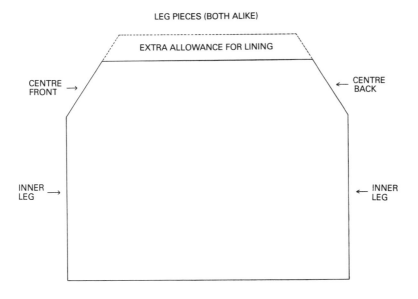

LEG PIECES (BOTH ALIKE)

EXTRA ALLOWANCE FOR LINING

CENTRE FRONT →

← CENTRE BACK

INNER LEG →

← INNER LEG

WAISTBAND (BOTH PIECES ALIKE)

CENTRE FRONT →

← CENTRE BACK

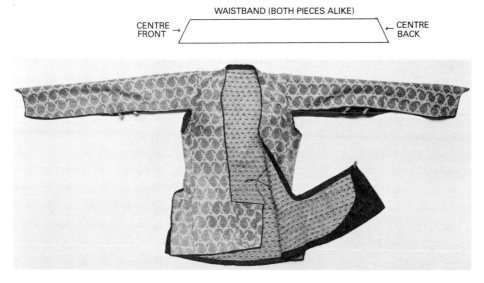

Above left. Diagram 19. Woman's trousers. Persia, early 19th century. Scale – 1:8.

Left. Plate 116. Woman's jacket. Gold brocaded silk patterned with repeated floral cones. Persia, early 19th century.

The jacket has been made to match the trousers in a silk brocade identical in colour and weave (Plate 116). The design motifs, however, are subtly worked on a smaller scale more suitable for a jacket than the bold sweep of large floral cones running the length of the trousers. The feature already observed in Safavid garments of economically piecing together scraps of material to make up a pattern shape is continued here. The jacket is short with a tight bodice tapering into the waist and then flaring out in a short curved peplum. The centre front opening takes the form of a deep V-shaped exposed neckline. Long narrow

Above. Plate 117. Woman's skirt and blouse. Blue and pink silks. Persia, *c.*1840.

Plate 118. *Above right.* Ladies around a samovar. Oil painting, Persia, Isma'il Jala'ir, *c.*1865.

sleeves taper to a point covering the wrists; they are completely open at the underarm being held in place only by a short horizontal band above the elbow. The jacket is fastened at the waist by crossing the left over the right front to be joined by a pink silk cord frogged loop. Construction details (Diagram 20) show how traditional methods were adapted to create the new shape. The centre bodice consists of three pieces joined at the shoulders, a rectangular piece for the back and two shaped fronts, to which extensions are added at waist level to make the wrapover. Further shaping is achieved by adding indented pieces and curved triangles at the sides of body and waist respectively. Finally, the long sleeves are attached to the bodice at right angles. The use of a block printed cotton lining, black silk facings and neat running stitch seams match those of the trousers. Another set of garments now in the Victorian and Albert Museum dated to *c.* 1840 (Plate 117) shows certain variations in this type of costume. It consists of a hip-length long sleeved *pirahan* with slashed and ornamented openings but made in a more modest blue silk worn over an ankle length pink silk gathered skirt instead of the wide trousers. The total effect of this striking costume, however, often created mixed feelings in the Europeans who saw them. Lady Sheil, wife of the British Minister of Tehran, after a visit to Nasiruddin Shah's mother on 12 January 1850 records her impressions in an account where an honest desire to carefully note all that she has seen struggles with disapproval.

> I do not admire the costume of the Persian women. The Shah's mother was dressed with great magnificence. She wore a pair of trousers made of gold brocade. These Persian trousers are always, as I have before remarked, very wide, each leg being, when the means of

the wearer allow it, wider than the skirt of a gown, so that they have the effect of an exceedingly ample petticoat; and as crinolines are unknown, the elegantes wear ten and eleven pairs of trousers, one over the other in order to make up for the want of the above important invention. But to return to the Shah's mother: her trousers were edged with a border of pearls embroidered on braid; she had a thin blue crepe chemisette, also trimmed with pearls; this chemisette hung down a little below the waist, nearly meeting the top of the trousers, which are fastened by a running string. As there was nothing under the thin gauze, the result of course was more display than is usual in Europe. A small jacket of velvet was over the chemisette, reaching to the waist, but not made to close in front, and on the head a small shawl, pinned under the chin. On the shawl were fastened strings of large pearls and diamond sprigs; her arms were covered with handsome bracelets, and her neck with a variety of costly necklaces. Her hair was in bands, and hung down under the shawl in a multitude of small plaits. She wore no shoes, her feet being covered with fine Cashmere stockings. The palms of her hands and tips of her fingers were dyed red, with a herb called henna, and the edges of the inner part of the eyelids were coloured with antimony. All the Kajars have naturally large arched eyebrows, but, not satisfied

Diagram 20. Pattern and layout for woman's jacket. Persia, early 19th century. Scale – 1:14.

GATHERED INTO KNIFE PLEATS ¼ IN DEEP AND ATTACHED TO CAP WITH ½ IN SEAM AT

ATTACHED TO CAP AT F

GATHERED, ETC, AS FOR BACK

GATHERED, ETC, AS FOR BACK

GUSSET – DOUBLE THICKNESS CUT AND QUILTED INSERTED INTO FRONT MATCHING B¹-C¹ TO B-C ON EACH SIDE

SELVAGE

BACK
(5 PIECES ALL ALIKE)

SELVAGE

SELVAGE

B

C

FRONT
(1 PIECE)

SELVAGE

A

B¹

FRONT
GUSSET
(BIAS CUT)

C¹   C¹

CROWN OF PILLBOX
CAP – DOUBLE THICKNESS
QUILTED

D¹

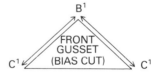

SIDE OF CAP – BOTH ENDS
JOINED – D ATTACHED TO D¹
ON CROWN

D

E   F

CONSTRUCTION – 5 BACK PIECES AND FRONT PIECE ALL JOINED VERTICALLY TO FORM 'TENT' WITH BACK STITCHED ⅛ IN SEAMS

1¾ IN TURNED UP ALL ROUND FOR HAND SEWN HEM

A-B SLASHED FOR FRONT OPENING, GUSSET INSERTED B-C ON EACH SIDE WITH ¼ IN RUN AND FELL SEAM A-C FINISHED WITH ¼ IN HEM

WHEN CAP AND BODY PIECES JOINED CAP LINED WITH STRIP OF CLOTH TO COVER ALL SEAM EDGES with this, the women enlarge them by doubling their real size with great streaks of antimony: her cheeks were well rouged, as in the invariable custom among Persian women of all classes.[45]

From the mid-nineteenth century onwards changes of fashion may be seen in Persian women's costume mainly in the shape and length of the skirts which have replaced the wide trousers. At first these seemed modest enough as depicted in an oil painting of *c.* 1865 (Plate 118) by Isma'il Jala'ir who had studied European techniques at the Dar ul-Funun technical college.[46] The ladies enjoying an informal tea party are wearing full skirts which vary in length between knee and mid-calf and are gathered on to a tight waistband. Ankle-length trousers are tight and of light colour functioning now as undergarments. Jackets continue in the neat tight shape of the early part of the nineteenth century but may either be short, stopping at the waist, or long with a full skirt. Heads are covered with the *charghat* – now a triangular shawl draped over the head and fastened under the chin so that the three points are distributed evenly around back and chest. Dr C. J. Wills a medical officer with the Persian Telegraph Department from 1866 to 1881 had ample opportunity through his profession to observe Persian women. '. . . two young ladies entered, aged from sixteen to eighteen, though they seemed some three or four-and-twenty to me. I must acknowledge that I was unprepared for such a free display of loveliness, and it was the first time I ever saw Persian ladies in their very becoming, if slightly indelicate, home-dress.'[47] So he wrote of his visit to the household of the official Eyn ul-Molk at Tehran in 1867. He soon accustomed himself to this style of dress, however, and progressed to write lively and observant accounts of Persian costume including some of its more daring variations.

> The garment doing duty as a chemise is called a perhan; it is, with the lower orders, of calico, white or blue, and comes down to the middle of the thigh, leaving the leg nude. Among the upper classes it is frequently of silk. At Shiraz it is often of fine cotton, and elaborately ornamented with black embroidery: among the rich it is frequently of gauze, and much embroidered with gold thread, pearls, etc. With them it often reaches only to the navel.
>
> The head is usually covered with a charghat, or large square of silk or cotton, embroidered. These chargats are folded, as were shawls amongst us some years ago, thus displaying the corners, two in front and two behind; it is fastened under the chin by a brooch. It is often a considerable value, being of Cashmere shawl, embroidered gauze, etc.
>
> A jika, a jewelled, feather-like ornament, is often worn at the side of the head, while the front hair, cut to a level with the mouth, is brought up in love-locks on either cheek.
>
> Beneath the chargat is generally a small kerchief of dark material,

worn to set off the complexion, and preserve the chargat: only the edge of this is visible. The ends of the chargat cover the shoulders, but the gauze perhan, quite transparent, leaves nothing to the imagination. The breasts and chest are very visible, and the abdomen is quite bare.

A very short jacket of gay colour, quite open in front, and not covering the bosom, with tight sleeves with many metal buttons, is usually worn in summer: a lined outer coat in cold weather.

In winter a pair of very short white cotton socks are used, and tiny slippers with a high heel; in summer in the house ladies go often barefoot.

Plate 119. Persian lady in indoor costume.

The rest of the costumed is composed of the 'tumbun', or 'shulwar'; these are simply short skirts of great width, held by a running string; the outer one usually of silk, velvet, or Cashmere shawl, often trimmed with gold lace, according to the purse of the wearer; or among the poor, of loud-patterned chintz or print. Beneath these are innumerable other garments of the same shape, and varying in texture from silk and satin to print.

The whole is very short indeed; among the women of fashion merely extending to the thigh, and as the number of these garments is amazing, and they are much *bouffée*, the effect of a lady sitting down astonishes the beholder, and would scandalise the Lord Chamberlain. As the ladies are *supposed*, however, to be only seen by their lords in these indoor dresses, there is perhaps no harm done.[48]

The short full skirts which so caught his eye had shrunk even more by the end of the century as demonstrated by Ella Sykes' photograph (Plate 119) and description of 1894.

All the Persian ladies wore loose-sleeved jackets of the richest brocades and velvets, and had short, much-stiffened-out trousers, which did not reach to the knees, the costume being completed with coarse white stockings or socks. Before the Shah went to Europe the Persian ladies all kept to the old national costume of long, loose, embroidered trousers, but on the return of the monarch, this present ungraceful costume became the fashion in the royal *anderoon*, and has spread throughout the whole country; it being, I believe, a fact that the dress of the Parisian ballet-girls so greatly fascinated the Oriental potentate that he commanded it to be adopted by his wives.[49]

Two skirts in the Royal Museum of Scotland's collection (Plate 120) demonstrate both shape and construction.[50] One is of fine white calico made of numerous widths joined and gathered in close pleats to a broad waistband, and probably functioned as a foundation for skirts made in more luxurious materials. The other skirt is of similar construction but made of red wool with a border of trefoil foliage embroidered in white cotton thread.

Plate 120. Pair of women's skirts. White cotton calico and red wool. Isfahan, late 19th century.

An accessory first noticed in Persian women's costume only in the nineteenth century was the jewelled brassière, a scanty decorative item rather than a practical foundation. It is first seen in an oil painting of a dancing girl of Fath Ali Shah's reign (Plate 121) who is dressed in an exotic costume based on Indian prototypes of tight brocade trousers worn with a tight short red blouse and a transparent skirt.[51] Over the blouse she wears a brassière consisting of two circular pearl-encrusted cups linked together to give a deep cleavage and secured by a string of pearls attached at each side which passes round her back. Such a brassiere was, however not simply a rare eccentric titillation but was worn in more sober circumstances as a photograph of Shukuh es-Sultaneh, Nasiruddin Shah's cousin and principal wife, taken in *c.* 1880 shows her as a stolid middle-aged woman wearing a glittering brassière beneath the transparent pirahan of her costume.[52] The actual appearance of such a brassière is seen in an example in the Royal Museum of Scotland's collection (Plate 122) acquired in 1889. It is of surprisingly petite proportions with neat triangular cups of blue silk mounted on a lime green silk lining lavishly embroidered with bands and circles couched on silver and gold metallic threads.[53]

All these costumes would have been incomplete without a correspondingly lavish facial make-up and hairstyle, projects to which Persian women devoted much time and effort as Ker Porter noted during his travels.

> The Persian ladies regard the bath, as the place of their greatest amusement. They make appointments to meet there; and often pass seven or eight hours together in the carpeted saloon, telling stories, relating anecdotes, eating sweetmeats, sharing their *kaliouns*, and completing their beautiful forms into all the fancied preparations of the East; dyeing their hair and eye-brows, and curiously staining their fair bodies with a variety of fantastic devices, not infrequently with the figures of trees, birds and beasts, sun, moon and stars. This sort of pencil-work spreads over the bosom, and continues down as low as the navel, round which some radiated figure is generally painted. All this is displayed by the style of their dress, every garment of which, even to the light gauze chemise, being open from the neck to that point . . .[54]

A comparison of this description with contemporary oil paintings shows the results of all this attention (Plate 123). Eyebrows have been groomed and pencilled into a continuous sweep framing languishing eyes liberally outlined and lengthened with black kohl. A small rosette and a fleur de lys are tattooed at the join of the eyebrows and numerous beauty spots are dotted over cheeks and chin.[55] A girl in an oil painting dated 1826 in the Hermitage collections displays large breasts tattooed with animal motifs and encircled with a beaded outline.[56] Dr Wills

Above. Plate 121. Dancing girl. Oil painting, Persia, early 19th century.

Left. Plate 122. Brassière. Blue silk embroidered in silver and gold. Persia, late 19th century.

Plate 123. Girl playing a drum. Detail to show cosmetics. Oil painting, Persia, 1816.

records that these cosmetic fashions continued well into the latter part of the nineteenth century:

> The face on all important occasions – as at entertainments, weddings, etc. – is usually much painted, save by young ladies in the heyday of beauty. The colour is very freely applied, the cheeks being reddled, as are a clown's and the neck smeared with white, while the eyelashes are marked round with kohl (black antimony). This is supposed to be beneficial to the eyes, and almost every woman uses it – very needlessly, as the large languishing eye of the Persian belle needs no adventitious aid. The eyebrows are widened and painted till they appear to meet, while sham moles or stars are painted on the chin and cheek – various in their way, as the patches of the eighteenth-century belles: even spangles are stuck at times on the chin or forehead. Tattooing is common among the poor and villagers, and is seen among the upper classes.

The hair, though generally hidden by the chargat, is at times exposed and plaited into innumerable little tails of greath length, while a coquettish little skull-cap of embroidery or shawl or coloured silks is worn. False hair is common. The Persian ladies' hair is very luxuriant, and never cut; it is nearly always dyed red with henna, or black with indigo to a blue-black tinge; it is naturally a glossy black.[57]

As in previous centuries all this finery was discreetly concealed when the wearer ventured out of doors. Both pictorial and written sources

Plate 124. Woman in outdoor costume. Miniature painting inscribed 'Cashan Oct. 29th 1811'.

Plate 125. Woman's face veil. White cotton with embroidered eye lattice. Persia, late 19th century.

indicated that several fashions were worn, although the *chadar* wrap combined with the *ru-band* face veil were the most usual. Sir William Ouseley, who accompanied the British diplomatic mission of 1810 to 1812, saw in South-West Persia in March 1811: 'In lanes and corners and on the flat-roofed buildings were multitudes of women, enveloped but with little attention to the graces of drapery, in dark blue cloaks after the Arabian fashion; or in white sheets their faces generally being concealed by pieces of black crepe.'[58] Gaspard Drouville, a French

Plate 126. Woman's outdoor trousers. Black serge. Isfahan, late 19th century.

cavalry officer of the Russian army, who visited Persia in 1812 to 1813 described the white *chadar* and *ru-band* and also the black horsehair mask – *picheh*, which he ascribed to the women of Kurdistan.[59] James Baillie Fraser who travelled in North East Persia in the 1820s while noting the use of different patterned fabrics for *chadars* records the use of another garment. '. . . They draw upon their legs a sort of stocking called chak-chir which takes in the trowsers like a boot and over these they wear the usual green and high-heeled slipper.'[60] Together the *chadar, ru-band* and *chak-chir* became the three inseparable garments of urban outdoor dress. A painting (Plate 124) collected by Sir William Ouseley and inscribed 'Cashan Oct. 29th 1811' charmingly depicts this costume.[61] Here the *chadar* is white with the *ru-band* pinned over it while the *chak-chir* are in the form of a pair of voluminous stocking boots which are tied at knee level. Later darker colours such as blue and black became a preferred choice for the *chadar*. The *chak-chir* also evolved from the stocking boot to a pair of voluminous trousers where each leg was in at the ankle and sewn to a flat soled slipper. The wearer would then simply tuck all her skirts into the trousers and fasten them around her waist before putting on *chadar, ru-band* and high-heeled clogs. Again Dr Wills gives an evocative description of this outdoor costume: 'The outdoor costume of the Persian women is quite another thing; enveloped in a huge blue sheet, with a yard of linen as a veil, perforated for two inches square with minute holes, the feet thrust into two huge bags of coloured stuff, a wife is perfectly unrecognisable, even by her husband, when out of doors.'[62] Two surviving pieces of outdoor costume of late nineteenth-century date in the Royal Museum of Scotland's collection supplement his description. A *ru-band* made of fine white cotton (Plate 125) is finely embroidered in cream silk with eye-lattice and borders worked in reticella cut and drawn threadwork and needleweaving.[63] Decoration was largely a matter of personal taste and means. The *chak-chir* (Plate 126) are made of a black twill weave fabric, and have voluminous legs gathered tightly at the ankle into flat-soled slippers.[64] The trousers are bias-cut, with each leg made from two lozenge-shaped pieces of fabric joined diagonally.

The nineteenth century costumes of Persia closely resembled those worn in the neighbouring country of Afghanistan. This is hardly surprising as the Herat and Balkh districts of Western Afghanistan had long been subject to Persian political and cultural influence. Visually this was expressed in costume which was described and illustrated by Europeans such as the civil and military officials of the British East India Company. Lieutenant James Rattray who served with the Second Grenadiers of the Bengal Army has left a spirited description (Plate 127) of the Persian-influenced costume of the ladies of the capital Kabul:

> . . . The lady Shukkhr Lub was a Kuzzilbaushe belle of the first water, the description of whose dress will show that of her country-women in general. Her long black hair, allowed to enshroud her whole figure was divided into a hundred strings of gilded plaits. The back of her head was covered with a golden skull-cap adorned with a row of coins of the same model. Splendid jewels, set in peculiar workmanship hung from her nose and ears. Her eyes were dyed with 'soormeh' (antimony) which, put on with a bodkin, drawn between the closed lids, gives to the organ that almond-shape so much admired. Her brows, by artificial means, assumed a crescent shape, the dye extending down either side the nose; a shawl pattern was painted between the arches. Her neck and cheeks were also dotted with models and rouge, and henna stained her hands, feet, finger-nails, and toes a deep brown colour. These women amuse themselves indoors with their pipes, embroidery and conversation. They are very fond of gossip, but their toilette is the principal object of their existence. A few read; but writing is considered highly improper, as conducive to mischief and intrigues. Their habiliments are a loose shirt of crimson, or other bright-coloured silk, or satin, braided with broad gold lace, open at the bosom, and fastened at the throat by a brooch or jewel; a chintz jacket resembling an hussar's adorned with loops and buttons, with wide sleeves pointed at the cuff, and caught by a stud at the wrist, to display the flowing shirt beneath; and trousers of rich velvet, or kimkob, edged with a massive band of gold, the joining of which is fringed out into a large tassel.[65]

Opposite. Plate 127. Afghan women indoors. Engraving from James Rattray, *The Costumes of the Various Tribes of Afghaunistan.*

His engraving and description also depict the outdoor dress:

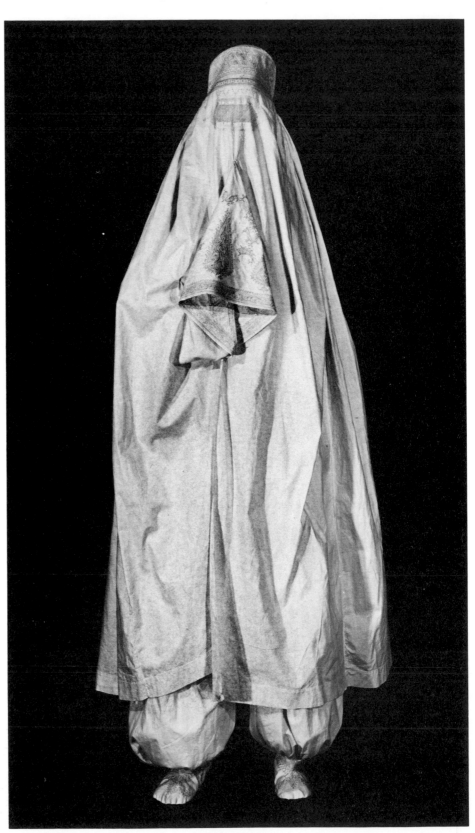

Plate 128. Woman's outdoor dress. Afghanistan, late 19th century.

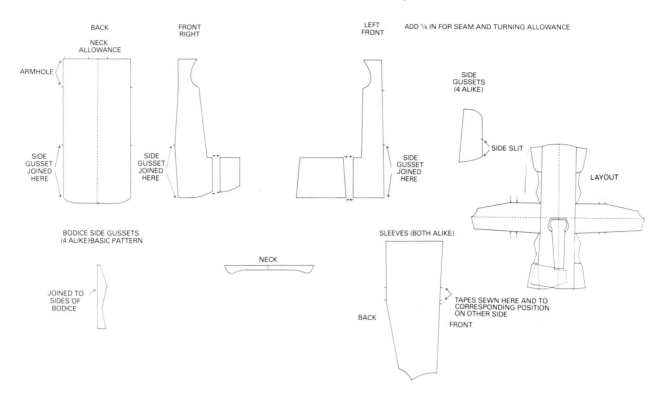

BACK

FRONT
RIGHT

LEFT
FRONT

ADD ¼ IN FOR SEAM AND TURNING ALLOWANCE

NECK
ALLOWANCE

ARMHOLE

SIDE
GUSSETS
(4 ALIKE)

SIDE SLIT

LAYOUT

SIDE
GUSSET
JOINED
HERE

SIDE
GUSSET
JOINED
HERE

SIDE
GUSSET
JOINED
HERE

BODICE SIDE GUSSETS
(4 ALIKE)BASIC PATTERN

SLEEVES (BOTH ALIKE)

NECK

JOINED TO
SIDES OF
BODICE

BACK

TAPES SEWN HERE AND TO
CORRESPONDING POSITION
ON OTHER SIDE

FRONT

Diagram 21. Woman's *chadri*. Afghanistan, late 19th century. Scale – 1:24.

. . . When out of doors, or taking horse exercise, these ladies don an immense white sheet, reaching from the top of the skull-cap to the feet; a long square veil attached by a clasp of gold or jewels to the back of the head, conceals the face, across which is an opening of net-work, to admit light and air. This dress is called a 'Boorkha'. It conceals the whole figure, all outline of which is so entirely lost, that a stranger, on first viewing a party of these shrouded beings flitting about him in the streets, might well be at a loss to guess to what class of creatures they belonged. In addition to the winding-sheet they wear long loose white boots of calico fastened by a silken garter (Dulakbund) above the knee, and turned back like a falling collar, in order to display the lining. The soles of these bag-like leggings are of shawl; and the garters 'in their glitt'ring tissues bear emblazoned Holy Memorials, acts of seal and love Recorded eminent' from the Koraun with scrolls and birds; the loose boots and veils also are embroidered in white and coloured silks.[66]

The Afghan version of outdoor dress also known as a *chadri*, while resembling the Persian original, underwent modification as a surviving example of late nineteenth-century date (Plate 128) in the Royal Museum of Scotland shows. Made of fine white cotton the *chadar* and *ru-band* are combined into one tent-like garment falling from a pillbox cap (Diagram 21), while the leg coverings have evolved into a matching pair of voluminous trousers tied at the waist and gathered at the ankles into flat-soled slippers resembling the Persian *chak-chir*.[67]

8

Conclusions

Within the necessarily restricted limits of this book it has been possible to give a sample of the range and vitality of female costume within the boundaries of the Ottoman Empire and to show that fashion was continually evolving and receptive to new influences. This naturally prompts inquiry into the survival of tradition especially in view of the constant pressure from mass-produced clothing manufactured in European styles. To a certain extent this depends on the preference of individuals for the convenience of purchasing ready-made clothes over the work involved in making them, a choice which is indeed universal. Here considerations of professional and social roles have to be taken into account. It is general, for example, in the cities of the area for European-style dress to be worn in varying degrees of current fashion, especially among those who consider themselves increasingly emancipated from the conservative social habits of traditional life. To service this ever growing market, there are boutiques selling smart clothes and fabrics, shops in the local bazaars providing cheaper versions and a brisk trade in magazines giving reports of the latest fashions from Europe copiously illustrated so that they can be copied by professional and home dressmakers.

Remarkably, however, costumes have continued to develop along traditional lines and have even been revitalised by the introduction of foreign accessories and synthetic fabrics, to produce a situation of dynamic transition. In the same way as the fashions of Turkish women in the nineteenth century evolved through such features as the addition of deep frilled collars and borders of machine-made imported laces to their undershirts, and the combination of heavy velvets of crimson and purple lavishly couched in gold with designs of floral bouquets and garlands with dress patterns using the tight-waisted bodices and long trailing bell-shaped skirts of European inspiration, so comparable parallels are to be found, for example, in the modern costumes of village and tribal women of Iraq and Persia – notably the Kurds and Qashqa'i. Paradoxically, both groups wear garment types such as jackets with tight sleeves, shaped cuffs, deep underarm openings and curved peplums – once part of the costume of Persian women of the nineteenth century – over long flowing dresses or layers of full skirts, yet they make them in modern fabrics ranging from diaphanous sequin-spattered nylon, to flocked rayon patterned with gold and silver lurex motifs to create brilliant combinations of colour and drapery beyond the resources of their predecessors. Similarly an acrylic sweater or cardigan in fuchsia pink or peacock blue improves out of all recognition when worn over one of these costumes as a replacement for the more traditional jacket, while neat stiletto-heeled court shoes or bright flower-trimmed plastic sandals complete the effect. Turkish village women continue to wear voluminous *şalvar* trousers in fabrics manufactured in colours and designs – often red, yellow or green patterned with large flowers, to suit local taste. The cut and construction, however, are reminiscent of older fashions especially among the Muslim women of Jugoslavia whose *şalvar* are made in shapes no longer current in Turkey. Where veiling habits have survived as in Persia and Afghanistan synthetic fabrics are also used so that it is not unusual to see Persians in light flowered *chadars* and Afghans whose *chadris* are made of permanently pleated artificial silks in blue, green, or even scarlet instead of white calico.

While European garments and fabrics may continue to be adopted it is likely that traditional and modern fashions will continue to evolve and exist together. It is important that this sartorially interesting situation is recorded in sufficient detail – something that is often all too sadly absent from the study of historical costume.

Notes

Chapter 2

1 Sherrard, Philip, *Constantinople, Iconography of a Sacred City* (London, 1965, pp. 17–26).

2 For a contemporary eye-witness account see Geoffrey de Villehardouin, *The Conquest of Constantinople* (London, Penguin Classics, 1963, pp. 91–93).

3 Harun-Ibn-Yahya and his description of Constantinople by A. Vasiliev in *Seminarium Kondakovianum* V, 1932. Quoted in Sherrard op. cit. 1, pp. 73–74.

4 For an edition and translation of these poems see Mavrogorado, John (ed.) *Digenes Akrites* (Oxford, 1956).

5 Procopius, *The Secret History*. Penguin Classics edition translated by G. A. Williamson (London, 1966, pp. 72–73).

6 Kritovoulos, *History of Mehmed the Conqueror*, translated by Charles E. Riggs (Princeton University Press, 1954, p. 22).

7 Vogt, A., *Le livre des ceremonies* (Paris, 1935–39, 2 vols). An account of Byzantine court ceremonies and rituals compiled by Emperor Constantine VII Porphyrogenitos 913–959. Book I written between 938 and 944 contains accounts of religious and court ceremonies including the Emperor's Coronation.

8 Many lavishly illustrated manuscripts commemorating the circumcision ceremonies of Ottoman princes have survived including the Surnâma of the circumcision festival of Mehmet son of Sultan Murat III (1583) (Topkapi Palace Museum H.1344) and the Surnâma-i Vehbi of the circumcision festival of four sons of Sultan Ahmet III (1720) (Topkapi Palace Museum A.3593).

9 For example in a miniature painting depicting the accession of Sultan Mehmet II 1451 in the Hünername of Osman, 1584.

10 For example the tombs of Sultan Süleyman the Magnificent (d. 1566), his eldest son Şehzade Mehmet (d. 1543), Sultan Abdul Hamit I (d. 1789).

11 For example Justinian's Empress Theodora (reigned 527–548). Her life and power are vividly described by Procopius op. cit. 5.

12 For a clear and detailed summary see Herrin, Judith, *Women and the Church in Byzantium* (*Bulletin of the British Association of Orientalists*, 1979–80 (New Series) Vol. 11, pp. 8–14).

13 Some notable occupants of the position of Valide Sultan were Safiye Sultan mother of Sultan Mehmet III (1595–1603), Kösem Mahpeyker Sultan, mother of Sultan Murat IV (1623–1640), Hadice Turhan Sultan, mother of Sultan Mehmet IV (1648–1687) and Pertevniyal Sultan, mother of Sultan Abdul Aziz (1861–1876).

14 For example Mihrimah Sultan daughter of Sultan Süleyman the Magnificent amassed a considerable fortune, a large part of which she devoted to religious and charitable foundations including two great mosques in Istanbul, one at the Edirne Gate and the other at Üsküdar.

15 See chapter 10, The Ottomans abroad – the Arab World, for a discussion of Coptic clothing traditions.

16 Grange-Taylor, H., *Weaving Clothes to Shape in the Ancient World; the Tunic and Toga of the Arringatore* (Textile History, 1982, vol. 13, No. 1, pp. 3–25).

17 Miniature from a manuscript of the Homilies of St. John Chrysostom (Bibliothèque Nationale, Paris, Coislin 79, fol. IV).

18 Enamel plaque from the Pala d'Oro in St. Mark's, Venice.

19 The Travels of Bertrandon de la Brocquière, A.D. 1432 and 1433 in *Early Travels in Palestine*, ed. Thomas Wright (London, 1848, pp. 338–339).

20 See two enamelled plaques depicting dancing girls in tight-fitting Persian-style clothes from a crown sent by the Emperor Constantine IX (1042–1055) to Hungary, and now in the National Museum, Budapest.

Chapter 3

1 Rudenko, Sergei I., *Frozen Tombs of Siberia – the Pazyryk Burials of Iron Age horsemen* (London, 1970); and *Frozen Tombs – The Culture and Art of the Ancient Tribes of Siberia* (British Museum, 1978).

2 Rudenko op. cit. 1, plate 63, p. 31; and British Museum op. cit. 1, cat. 20.

3 British Museum op. cit. 1, p. 95, cat. 128.

4 Rudenko op. cit. 1, pp. 91–92, figs. 32–33, and plate 152A.

5 British Museum op. cit. 1, p. 16, cat. 5, colour plate 5.

6 For example a painting of a young woman in an orange dress and a tall cylindrical headdress of figured silver brocade, c.1620. British Museum, Oriental Antiquities, 1928, 3.23.046.99.

7 Trippett, Frank (ed.) *The First Horsemen*. Time Life International, 1975, p. 22. Photograph and discussion of young woman's burial, Ukraine, c.5th–4th century B.C.

8 Trippett op. cit. 7, pp. 78–79. Woman's coat, excavated in northern Mongolia, Hsiung-nu, 2nd century B.C.

9 Trippett op. cit. 7., pp. 78–79. Woman's trousers excavated in northern Mongolia, Hsiung-nu, 2nd century B.C.

10 Hartel, Herbert and Yaldiz, Marianne. Along the silk routes, Central Asian art from the West Berlin State Museums, New York, 1982, p. 169, cat. 109, Wall painting Bezeklik, Temple 9., MIK III, 6876b, Berlin.

11 Hartel op. cit. 10, p. 158, cat. 95, Fresco painting, Khocho, Nestorian temple, MIK III 6912, Berlin.

12 Azarpay, Guitty. *Sogdian Painting – the pictorial element in oriental art.* California, 1981, p. 118, fig. 50 and colour plate 18.

13 Rudenko op. cit. 1., pp. 205–206, plate 177.

14 Herrmann, Georgina, *The Iranian Revival* (London, 1977, p. 23).

15 Herrmann op. cit. 14, p. 133.

16 Wall painting from the Jausak Palace, Samarra 836–839. Reconstructed by Ernst Herzfeld. Surviving fragments in the Museum of Turkish and Islamic Art, Istanbul.

17 Öney, Gönül. *Türk Cini Sanati – Turkish Tile Art* (Istanbul, 1976, p. 40, tile from Kubadabad c.1236).

18 *The Book of Dede Korkut*, translated by Geoffrey Lewis (Penguin Classics, London, 1974, p. 131).

Chapter 4

1 See Atil, Esin, the Art of the Book, in Atil, Esin (ed.) *Turkish Art* (Washington, 1980, pp. 139–238), for an excellent account of current research into Turkish painting.

2 Topkapı Sarayı Müzesi Library, H.2164.
3 Topkapı Sarayı Müzesi Library, H. 2143.
4 Cezar, Mustafa. *Sanatta bati 'ya açılış ve Osman Hamdi.* Türkiye iş Bankası A.Ş. Kültür Yayınları 109 (Istanbul, 1971).
5 See Belkin, Kristin Lohse, *The Costume Book, Corpus Rubenianum Ludwig Burchard,* Part XXIV (Brussels, 1980, pls. 180, 182, 214).
6 Aelst, Peter Coeck van, *Moeurs et fachons de faire les Turcz* (Antwerp, 1553); Lorch, Melchior, *Engravings of Turkish costume animals and buildings 1570–83*; Nicolay, Nicholas de, *Les navigations, peregrinations, et voyages faites en la Turquie* (Paris, 1576).
7 Ferriol, de, *Recueil de cent estampes réprésentant differentes nations du Levant tirées sur les tableaux peints d'après nature en 1707 et 1708 par les orders de m. de Ferriot, ambassadeur du roi à la Porte et gravées en 1712 et 1713 par les soins de M. le Hay* (Paris, 1714).
8 Loche, Renée and Roethlisberger, *L'opera completa di Liotard* (Milan, 1979).
9 Ribeiro, Aileen, Turquerie, *Turkish dress and English fashion in the eighteenth century* (*Connoisseur*, 1979, Vol. 201, no. 807, pp. 16–23, fig. 5).
10 Loche op. cit. 8, plate VII.
11 Hamdy Bey, S. E. Osman and Launay, Marie de, *Les costumes populaires de la Turquie en 1873, ouvrage publiée sous la patronat de la Commission Imperiale Ottomane pour l'exposition universelle de Vienne* (Constantinople, 1873).
12 Montague, Lady Mary Wortley, *The Complete Letters of Lady Mary Wortley Montague* (ed. Robert Halsband) (Oxford, 1965, Vol. 1, 1708–1720); Pardoe, Julia, *The City of the Sultan and Domestic Manners of the Turks in 1836* (London, 1837, 2 vols); White, Charles, *Three Years in Constantinople or Domestic Manners of the Turks* (London, 1844, 3 vols); Garnett, Lucy, *The Women of Turkey and Their Folklore* (London, 1890–91, 2 vols).
13 Cuinet, Vital, *La Turquie en Asie.* Geographie administrative et raisonnée de chaque province de l'Asie – Mineure (Paris, 1890–95, 4 volumes).
14 Barkan, Ömer, Edirne Askeri Kassamı'na Ait Tereke Defterleri (1545–1659) *Belgeler* 1966, Cilt III, Sayı 5–6, p. 221 and 250.
15· Haidar, Muzbah, *Arabesque* (London, 1944); Tugay, Emine Foat, *Three Centuries – Family Chronicles of Turkey and Egypt* (London, 1963); Ayşe Sultan, *Babanim Abdulhamit* (Istanbul, 1958).
16 Royal Museum of Scotland, Edinburgh, 1983, 232.
17 Tomb cover of Maria of Mangop, 1477. Collection of Putna monastery, Suceava province, Romania.
18 Royal Museum of Scotland, Edinburgh, 1980, 171.
19 Royal Museum of Scotland, Edinburgh, 1979, 160.
20 Inalcik, Halil, *The Ottoman Empire – the Classical Age 1300–1600* (London, 1973, pp. 130 and 133).
21 Topkapı Sarayı Müzesi, Library R. 989, fol. 93A.
22 See Chapter 3, for a discussion of headdresses worn in Siberia and the Ukraine.
23 Lorch op. cit. 6, engraving of Hürrem Sultan.
24 British Museum, Department of Oriental Antiquities 2502.
25 Marriage of King Louis of Naples and Sicily to Prince Yolande of Aragon, France, late 15th century, British Library, Harley MS. 4379, f. 19b.
26 Topkapı Sarayı Müzesi, Library H. 799 fol. 196A.
27 Keir collection.
28 Bodleian Library Oxford, MS Bodl. Or. 430, f. 99b.
29 Op. cit. 28, fol. 90b.
30 Royal Museum of Scotland, Edinburgh, nos. 1884. 65. 1–29. and Victoria and Albert Museum, 738, 740–744, 746, 749–750, 752–773, 1884.
31 Royal Museum of Scotland, Edinburgh, 771. 1884. D.I.
32 Royal Museum of Scotland, Edinburgh, 1884. 65. 24.
33 British Museum, Department of Oriental Antiquities. A relation of the Turckes, their Kings, Emperors or Grandsigneurs, their conquests, religion, customs, habits at Constantinople. One with initials P.M., and dated 1618 O.A. 1974, 6–17, 013; Bibliotheca Sloaniana 5258, no. 263, A book of 122 figures in miniature representing the habits of the Grand Signor's Court, O.A. 1928, 3, 23, 046.
34 Compare 1974.6–17, 013 518. 1928. 3. 23, 046. 76; both views of a Persian woman.
35 British Museum, Department of Oriental Antiquities, O.A. 1974. 6–17. 013 (46).
36 British Museum, Department of Oriental Antiquities, O.A. 1928. 3–23. 046 (101).
37 Royal Museum of Scotland, Edinburgh. 1982. 351.
38 British Museum, Department of Oriental Antiquities. O.A. 1974. 6–17. 013 (49).
39 British Museum, Department of Oriental Antiquities. O.A. 1974. 6–17. 013 (44).
40 Topkapı Sarayı Müzesi Library, H.2132, fol. 4b.
41 Topkapı Sarayı Müzesi Costume Section 2/3106.
42 Royal Museum of Scotland, Edinburgh. 1974. 162.
43 For example, Royal Museum of Scotland, Edinburgh, 1979, 294, woman's robe of purple velvet embroidered with spindling rose stems, and 1979, 295 woman's robe of red velvet embroidered with floral bouquets, both 19th century.
44 Ferriol op. cit. 7, plate 3.
45 Topkapı Sarayı Müzesi Library, H.2164. fol. 19b.
46 Topkapı Sarayı Müzesi Library, H.2164. fol. 20b.
47 Topkapı Sarayı Müzesi Library, H.2143.
48 Topkapı Sarayı Müzesi Library, H.2164. fol. 14b.
49 Montagu op. cit. 12, pp. 326–327.
50 British Museum, Department of Oriental Antiquities. O.A. 1974. 6–17 012 (1) 136f and (2) 128f.
51 British Museum op. cit. 50, 1974. 6. 17. 012. (2) 5.
52 Pardoe op. cit. 12. I, pp. 6–7.
53 Allom, Thomas, *Character and Costume in Turkey and Italy* (London, 1845, p. 18).
54 Allom op. cit. 53, p. 23.
55 Pardoe, op. cit. 12. II pp. 214–215.
56 Royal Museum of Scotland, Edinburgh, 1979, 316–322; Scarce, Jennifer M., Turkish fashion in transition. *Costume, the Journal of the Costume Society,* 1980, no. 14, pp. 144–167.
57 White op. cit. 12. III. p. 192.
58 Allom op. cit. 53.
59 White op. cit. 12. III. pp. 192–193.
60 White op. cit. 12. III, p. 193.
61 White op. cit. 12. III, pp. 193–194.
62 White op. cit. 12. III, p. 195.
63 White op. cit. 12. III, pp. 189–190.

64 Pardoe op. cit. 12. I, p. 304.
65 White op. cit. 12. III, p. 195.
66 Pardoe op. cit. 12. I, pp. 116–117.
67 Pardoe op. cit. 12. I, pp. 29–30.
68 White op. cit. 12. II, pp. 85–86.
69 White op. cit. 12. II, pp. 80–81.
70 Pardoe op. cit. 12. I, p. 33.
71 Garnett op. cit. 12. II, p. 430.
72 Hamdi op. cit. 11, pl. IV.
73 Foat Tugay op. cit. 15, p. 209.
74 Topkapı Saràyı Müzesi Costume, Section 13/768 & 769.
75 Garnett op. cit. 12, pp. 429–430.
76 Foat Tugay op. cit. 15, p. 292.
77 Topkapı Saràyı Müzesi Costume, Section 13/772.
78 Haidar op. cit. 15, pp. 37–38.
79 Royal Museum of Scotland, Edinburgh, 1982, 349.
80 Haidar op. cit. 15, p. 200.
81 Royal Museum of Scotland, Edinburgh, 1983. 351 & 347 & A.

Chapter 5

1 Pardoe, Julia, *The City of the Sultan and Domestic Manners of the Turks in 1836*, 2 vols., 1837, II, pp. 38–40.
2 Royal Museum of Scotland, Edinburgh, 1970, 991.
3 Hamdy Bey, S. E. Osman and Launay, Marie de, *Les costumes populaires de la Turquie en 1873, ouvrage publiée sous le patronat de la Commission Imperiale Ottomane pour l'exposition universelle de Vienne* (Constantinople, 1873, pl. XVI).
4 Royal Museum of Scotland, Edinburgh, 1982. 347 and 348.
5 British Museum, Department of Oriental Antiquities. O.A. 1974. 6–17–012 (2) 17.
6 Hamdy Bey op. cit. 3, pl. XVIII.
7 Pardoe op. cit. 1, II. p. 38.
8 British Museum, Department of Oriental Antiquities. O.A. 1974. 6–17–012 (2) 24.
9 British Museum, Department of Oriental Antiquities. O.A. 1974. 6–17–012 (2) 25.
10 Pardoe op. cit. 1, I, p. 242.
11 Malița, M., Bănățeanu, T., Zlotea, E. *Romania, from the thesaurus of the traditional popular costume*, Bucharest, 1977, for a good survey.
12 Carl Goebbel, *Vue de Belgrade*, watercolour c.1860. Signed and inscribed. Carl Goebbel (1824–1899) studied at the Vienna Academy and painted portraits, landscapes, scenes of everyday life and architecture.
13 Djilas, Milovan, *Land Without Justice – an Autobiography of His Youth* (London, 1958, 213).
14 Charol de Popp de Szathmary, *A town girl – Belgrade*, watercolour c.1849–85, Charol de Popp de Szathmary (1812–1887) born at Cluj and died at Bucharest, studied painting at Rome, 1832–34. Worked in Vienna and Paris. Travelled widely in the Ottoman Empire, Persia, India.
15 Broughton, J. C. H., *Travels in Albania and Other Provinces of Turkey* (2 vols, London, 1855. Vol. I, pp. 447–449).
16 British Museum, Department of Oriental Antiquities. O.A. 1974. 6–17–012 (2) 47.
17 Čulić Zorislava, *Narodne Nošnje u Bosni i Hercegovini. Zemaljski Muzej u Sarajevu* 1963, pl. XXXII.
18 Čulić op. cit. 17, pl. XXXIII.
19 Čulić op. cit. 17, pl. XXXIV.

20 Čulić op. cit. 18.
21 For an excellent discussion and collation of the evidences see Gervers, Veronika, *The Influence of Ottoman Turkish Textiles and Costumes in Eastern Europe* (Royal Ontario Museum, Toronto, 1982).
22 Nicolescu, Corina, *L'art islamique en Roumanie*, AARP (Art and Archeology Research Papers) 1979, Vol. 9, pp. 75–81.
23 Nicolescu op. cit. 22, p. 79, note 7.
24 Nicolescu, Corina, *Costumul de curte în Țările Române* (sec. XIV–XVIII) Bucharest, 1970.
25 For example the portraits of the voivodes of Wallachia Petru Cercel at the princely church of Tirgoviște (1583) and Constantine Brîncoveanu and his family (1688–1714) at Hurez monastery (1690–93).
26 See chapter 4 for a discussion of this tomb cover.
27 Tomb cover of Ieremia Movila. Collection of Sucevița Monastery, Suceava province, Romania.
28 Tomb cover of Simon Movila. Collection of Sucevița Monastery, Suceava province, Romania.
29 See Nicolescu op. cit. 24, pp. 154–155.
30 Nicolescu op. cit. 24, pp. 35–38, figs 11–14. Muzeul de artă al R. S. România, Secția de artă veche românească Inv. T. 59/10780.
31 Muzeul de artă al R. S. Romania, Secția de artă veche românească Inv. F. 222.
32 Muzeul de artă al R. S. Romania. Secția de artă veche românească. Manuscript Inv. 11.
33 Cozia monastery, Vilcea province Romania, Bolnița chapel built 1542–43 by the voivode of Wallachia Radu Paisie, Portrait of his wife Roxanda on the south wall of the nave.
34 Hurez monastery, Vilcea province, is the most important religious foundation of Constantine Brîncoveanu (1668–1714). Built between 1690 and 1693 it consists of a church with fine fresco painting, surrounded by monastic buildings.
35 Library of the Academy of the Socialist Republic of Romania, Bucharest ms. r. 3514, fol. 128b.
36 British Museum, Department of Oriental Antiquities, O.A. 1974. 6–17–012 (2) 36 and 37.
37 Mihail Töpler (1780–1820), from Toplitz in Bohemia, was trained at the Vienna Academy and worked in both Iași and Bucharest where he was much in demand for his portraits of the aristocracy.
38 Portrait of Safta Ipsilanti Muzeul de artă al R. S. România, Romanian painting section Inv. 1545.
39 Dinu Golescu travelled in Switzerland, Germany and Italy in 1824, 1825 and 1826 and wrote an account of his travels; see Dinicu Golescu, *Însemnare a călătoriii mele* (ed mircea Iorgulescu) Bucharest, Editura Minerva, 1977.
40 Muzeul de artă al R. S. România, Romanian painting section Inv. 1138. Stefan Anton Chladek (1794–1882), from Elemer village in the Banat, a region in south-west Romania, studied in Budapest and Vienna. He established himself as a professional painter in Bucharest in 1835 where he painted elegant portraits of the aristocracy, icons and religious frescoes.

Chapter 6

1 University College London, Petrie Collection. U.C. 28614B.
2 University College London, Petrie Collection, U.C. 31182 &

31183.

3 University College London, Petrie Collection, U.C. 17743.

4 Janssen, J. J., *Commodity Prices from the Ramessid Period* (Leiden, 1975, pp. 249–250).

5 Lane, Edward William, *The Manners and Customs of the Modern Egyptians* (Everyman's Library edition, 1908 (using text of 1860), pp. 33–34).

6 See Kendrick, A. F., *Catalogue of Textiles from Burying grounds in Egypt* (Victoria and Albert Museum, London, 1920. vol. I. p. 9).

7 This chronological scheme is proposed in Bourguet, Pierre du, Musée National du Louvre, *Catalogue des Etoffes Coptes I* (Paris, 1964, pp. 22–35).

8 See chapter 2 for a discussion of Theodora's costume.

9 See Seagroatt, Margaret, *Coptic Weaves, Notes on the Collection of Coptic Textiles in the City of Liverpool Museums* (City of Liverpool Museums, 1965, pp. 4–24), for a clearly described and illustrated account of the development of this tunic.

10 See Baginski, Alisa and Tidhar, Amalia, *Textiles from Egypt 4th–13th centuries C.E., L.A.* (Mayer Memorial Institute for Islamic Art, Jerusalem, 1980, pp. 14–17).

11 Royal Museum of Scotland, Edinburgh, 1893. 438.

12 Royal Museum of Scotland, Edinburgh, 1924. 328.

13 Royal Museum of Scotland, Edinburgh, 1924. 329.

14 See Grube, Ernst, *Islamic Pottery of the Eighth to the Fifteenth Century in the Keir Collection* (London, 1976, p. 145 no. 93).

15 For an excellent clear discussion of 'tiraz' fabrics see Kühnel, Ernst & Bellinger, Louise, *Catalogue of Dated Tiraz Fabrics – Umayyad, Abbasid, Fatimid* (The Textile Museum, Washington, 1952).

16 Kühnel & Bellinger op. cit. 15, p. 6, Textile Museum Washington Inv. 73, 645.

17 Kühnel & Bellinger op. cit. 15, p. 81, Textile Museum Washington Inv. 73, 199.

18 See Kühnel & Bellinger op. cit. 15, pp. 121–125, for lists of factories.

19 See Kühnel & Bellinger op. cit. 15, pp. 125–128 for names of factory supervisors.

20 Royal Museum of Scotland, Edinburgh, 1898, 482–491; 1910, 111. 371; 1911, 268; 1934, 482.

21 For example a 14th-century silk cap and a 16th-century silk embroidered linen robe, Museum of Islamic Art, Kuwait, LNS 95T and LNS 57T, three face veils of the 14th–15th century, see Eastwood, op. cit. 30, two caps, a gown and trousers, see Mayer, L. A., *Mamluk costume*, Geneva, 1952, plates XII–XIII.

22 Stillman, Yedida, New data on Islamic textiles from the Geniza. *Textile History*, vol. 10, 1979, pp. 184–195.

23 British Library, Department of Oriental Printed Books and Manuscripts, Add. 22114 & Or. 9718.

24 British Library, Department of Oriental Printed Books and Manuscripts. Add. 22114 fol. 100 v.

25 British Library, Department of Oriental Printed Books and Manuscripts, Add. 22114 fol. 32 r.

26 Museum of Islamic Art, Kuwait, LNS 17MS.

27 British Library, Department of Oriental Printed Books and Manuscripts, Or. 9718.

28 British Library, Department of Oriental Printed Books and Manuscripts, Or. 9718 fol. 49r.

29 British Library, Department of Oriental Printed Books and

Manuscripts. Or. 9718 fol. 39r.

30 Eastwood, Gillian, A medieval face-veil from Egypt. *Costume, The Journal of the Costume Society*, No. 17, 1983, pp. 33–38.

31 British Library, Department of Printed Books and Manuscripts, Or. 9718 fol. 159v.

32 Lewis, Major-General Michael, C.B.E., *John Frederick Lewis, R.A.*, Leighton-on-Sea (F. Lewis Publishers Ltd, 1978).

33 Lane op. cit. 5. pp. 30–36, men's costumes; pp. 37–53, women's costumes and accessories.

34 Lott, Emmeline, *The Governess in Egypt, Harem Life in Egypt and Constantinople* (2 vols. London, 1865).

35 Chennells, Ellen, *Recollections of an Egyptian Princess by her English Governess* (Edinburgh and London, 1893).

36 John Frederick Lewis (1805–1872), Indoor gossip, Cairo. Oil painting, 1873. Whitworth Art Gallery, Manchester.

37 Lane op. cit. 5, p. 42.

38 See chapter 4, notes 53 & 54, & plate 43.

39 Lott op. cit. 34, II, pp. 75–76.

40 Lane op. cit. 5, pp. 46–47.

41 Lott op. cit. 34, I, pp. 228–229.

42 Lott op. cit. 34, II, pp. 6–8.

43 Lott op. cit. 34, I, pp. 68–69.

44 Lott op. cit. 34, I, p. 97.

45 Chennells, op. cit. 35, p. 27.

46 Chennells, op. cit. 35, plates facing title page and p. 102.

Chapter 7

1 For a detailed account of the Gulestan Palace see Zoka, Yahya, *A Short History of the Buildings of the Royal Citadel of Tehran and a Guide to the Gulestan Palace* (Tehran, 1349).

2 Chardin, Sir John, *Travels in Persia* [ed. N. M. Penzer from the English translation of 1720] (London, 1927).

3 Porter, Sir Robert Ker, *Travels in Georgia, Persia, Armenia, Ancient Babylonia during the years 1817, 1818, 1819 and 1820* (2 vols, London, 1821–22).

4 Piemontese, Angelo, The photographic album of the Italian diplomatic mission to Persia (summer 1862). *East and West, new series*, Vol. 22, nos 3–4, Sept–Dec 1972, pp. 249–311.

5 Scarce, Jennifer M., *Isfahan in camera – 19th-century Persia through the photographs of Ernst Hoeltzer*, AARP (Art and Archaeology Research Papers) London, 1976.

6 Piemontese op. cit. 5, pp. 261–2.

7 For example the photograph his principal wife Shukuh es-Sultaneh, reproduced in Scarce, Jennifer M., *A Persian Brassière*, AARP (Art and Archaeology Research Papers) no. 7. 1975, pp. 15–21, fig. 5.

8 Sheil, Lady, *Glimpses of Life and Manners in Persia* (London, 1856); Wills, C. J. *In the Land of the Lion and Sun or Modern Persia, being Experiences of Life in Persia from 1866 to 1881* (London, 1891); Sykes, Ella, *Through Persia on a Sidesaddle* (London, 1898), and *Persia and Its People* (London, 1910).

9 National Library Vienna, Cod. A. F. 10. fol. 1. L.

10 Edinburgh University Library, Arab MS. 20 fol 42r.

11 Comparable methods of draping this headshawl may still be seen in the Persian Gulf coastal regions today where it takes the form of a piece of black nylon net wound tightly around the head.

12 Edinburgh University Library, Arab MS. 161, fol 14–101 b.

13   Royal Asiatic Society, London, MS 246. fol. 269.

14   Saltykov – Shehedrin Public Library, Leningrad.

15   British Library Department of Oriental Printed Books and Manuscripts Or. 6810 fol. 39v.

16   Clavijo, Ruy Gonzales de. *Narrative of the Embassy of Ruy Gonzales de Clavijo to the Court of Timour at Samarcand A.D. 1403–06* (London, Hakluyt Society, 1859, V. p. 89).

17   Zeno, Caterino, *Travels in Persia* (London, Hakluyt Society, 1873, p. 13).

18   Royal Museum of Scotland, Edinburgh, 1982. 721.

19   Royal Armoury Stockholm, no. 3414.

20   British Library, Department of Oriental Printed Books and Manuscripts. Or. 2265 fol. 66v.

21   Fogg Art Museum, John Goelet Gift 1958.60.

22   Bodleian Library, Oxford, MS Elliot 189.

23   British Library, Department of Oriental Printed Books and Manuscripts. Add. 27257.

24   Metropolitan Museum of Art, New York, MS 13, 228. 14.

25   Freer Gallery of Art, Washington, MS, no. 46, 12 fol. 100b.

26   D'Alessandri, Vincentio, *Narrative of the most noble Vincentio d'Alessandri* (London, Hakluyt Society, 1873, p. 217).

27   British Library, Department of Oriental Printed Books and Manuscripts. Add. 7776 fol. 79b.

28   See Marly, Diane de, King Charles II's own fashion and the theatrical origins of the English vest. *Journal of the Warburg and Courtauld Institutes*, Vol. 37, 1974, pp. 378–82.

29   These portraits are located in Petworth House, West Sussex.

30   British Museum, Department of Oriental Antiquities 1948. 10–9–059.

31   Negaristan Museum, Tehran. 77.2.8.

32   Victoria and Albert Museum, Textile Department T. 1060. 1900.

33   Royal Museum of Scotland, Edinburgh 1890. 408; Victoria and Albert Museum, Textile Department T. 962. 1889.

34   Chardin op. cit. 2, pp. 215–216.

35   Chardin op. cit. 2, pp. 216–217.

36   Chardin op. cit. 2, p. 215.

37   Fryer, John, *A New Account of East India and Persia, Being Nine Years Travels 1672–1681 by John Fryer* (London, Hakluyt Society, 1915, p. 128).

38   Chardin op. cit. 34.

39   Hanway, Jonas, *An Account of British Trade over the Caspian Sea* (London, 1753).

40   Bodleian Library, Oxford, Pers. 1.53 fol. 143V.

41   Goldsmid, Colonel Sir Frederick, *Telegraph and Travel* (London, 1874, p. 534).

42   Negaristan Museum, Tehran.

43   Wills op. cit. 8, p. 323.

44   Royal Museum of Scotland, Edinburgh, 1890, 404 & 407.

45   Sheil, op. cit. 8, pp. 132–133.

46   Victoria and Albert Museum. Paintings Department P. 56–1941.

47   Wills op. cit. 8, p. 40.

48   Wills op. cit. 8, pp. 322–324.

49   Sykes, op. cit. 8, p. 17.

50   Royal Museum of Scotland, Edinburgh, 1978. 435 & 436. Both acquired in Isfahan.

51   Negaristan Museum, Tehran.

52   op. cit. 7.

53   Royal Museum of Scotland, Edinburgh, 1890. 409.

54   Porter op. cit. 3, Vol. 1, p. 233.

55   Negaristan Museum, Tehran.

56   Published in N. N. Karpova, *Stankovaya Zhivopis Irana XVII–XIV Vekov*, Sovetskii Khudozhnik Moskva, 1973, plate 8.

57   Wills op. cit. 8, p. 323.

58   Ouseley, Sir William, *Travels in Various Countries of the East; More Particularly Persia* (London, 1819–23, Vol. 1, p. 189).

59   Drouville, Gaspard, *Voyage en Perse en 1812 et 1813* (2nd edition, Paris, 1825, Vol. 1, pp. 74–76, plates facing p. 70 & p. 218, Vol. 11, plate facing p. 183).

60   Fraser, James Baillie, *Travels and Adventures in the Persian Provinces on the Southern Banks of the Caspian Sea* (London, 1826, p. 51).

61   Bodleian Library, Oxford, Ouseley MS, 297 fol. 9.

62   Wills op. cit. 8, p. 325.

63   Royal Museum of Scotland, Edinburgh, 1930. 122.

64   Royal Museum of Scotland, Edinburgh, 1978. 433. Acquired in Isfahan.

65   Rattray, James, *The Costumes of the Various Tribes, Portraits of Ladies of Rank, Celebrated Princes and Chiefs, Views of the Principal Fortresses and Interior of the Cities and Temples of Afghaunistan* (London, 1848, p. 24).

66   Rattray op. cit. 64, p. 29.

67   Royal Museum of Scotland, Edinburgh, 1892. 104 & A.

Select Bibliography

The paucity of detailed and critical study on the subject is reflected in the material available for reference. Apart from an examination of surviving garments, information has basically to be extracted from illustrations and first-hand descriptions of costume. In compiling this bibliography, therefore, priority has been given to works which feature plenty of material for comparison, such as catalogues of exhibitions and collections, both public and private, of paintings, and textiles, and careful descriptions such as the accounts of the more reliable European travellers. Where serious studies have been written they have also been included together with some essential material for historical and cultural background. Within the bibliography references have been classified under sections corresponding to their primary use.

General Background
The Arts of Islam, Catalogue of an exhibition held at the Hayward Gallery (London, 8 April–4 July 1976).
The Fine Art Society, *Eastern Encounters, Orientalist Painters of the Nineteenth Century* (London, 1978).
Robinson, B. W., Grube, E., Meredith-Owens, G. M., and Skelton, R. W., *Islamic Paintings and the Arts of the Book* (London, 1976).
Searight, Sarah, *The British in the Middle East*, second revised edition (London, 1979).
Spuhler, Friedrich, *Islamic Carpets and Textiles in the Keir Collection* (London, 1978).
Vaczek, Louis and Buckland, Gail, *Travellers in Ancient Lands. A Portrait of the Middle East 1839–1919* (New York, 1981).
Verrier, Michelle, *The Orientalists* (London, 1979).

Basic Costume Reference Works
Dozy, R. P. A., *Dictionnaire Détaillé des Noms des Vetements chez les Arabes* (Amsterdam, 1845).
Tilke, Max, *Oriental Costumes, their Designs and Colours* (London, 1922).
Tilke, Max, *Costume Patterns and Designs* (New York, 1956).
Tilke, Max, *Folk Costumes from East Europe, Africa and Asia* (London, 1978).

The Ottoman Inheritance – Byzantium
Grange-Taylor, H., 'Weaving Clothes to Shape in the Ancient World: The Tunic and Toga of Arringatore', *Textile History*, vol. 13, no. 1 (1982), pp. 3–25.
Mango, Cyril, *Byzantium the Empire of New Rome* (London, 1980).
Runciman, Steven, *Byzantine Style and Civilization* (London, 1975).
Sherrard, Philip, *Constantinople Iconography of a Sacred City* (Oxford, 1965).
Talbot Rice, David, *Art of the Byzantine Era* (London, 1981).
Vogt, A., *Le Livre des Cérémonies*, four vols (Paris, 1935–39).

The Ottoman Inheritance – Central Asia
Azarpay, Guitty, *Sogdian Painting* (Berkeley and London, 1981).
Härtel, Herbert, and Yaldiz, Marianne, *Along the Silk Routes. Central Asian Art from the West Berlin State Museums* (New York,

Metropolitan Museum of Art, 1982).
Herrmann, Georgina, 'The Darabgird Relief – Ardashir or Shahpur? A Discussion in the Context of Early Sassanian Sculpture', *Iran*, Journal of the British Institute of Persian Studies, vol. vii (1969), pp. 63–88.
Peck, Elsie Holmes, 'The Representation of Costumes in the Reliefs of Taq-I Bustan, *Artibus Asiae*, vol. xxxi (1969), pp. 101–66.
Pope, Arthur Upham (ed.), *A Survey of Persian Art*, Vols I and IV (Oxford, 1938).
Rudenko, Sergei, *Frozen Tombs of Siberia. The Pazyryk Burials of Iron-Age Horsemen* (London, 1970).

The Ottomans at Home – Mainly Istanbul

Historical and Cultural Background
Cuinet, Vital, *La Turquie d'Asie – Geographie Administrative et Raisonnée de Chaque Province de L'Asie-Mineure* four vols (Paris, 1890–95).
Inalcik, Halil, *The Ottoman Empire, the Classical Age 1300–1600* (London, 1973).
Lewis, Raphaela, *Everyday Life in Ottoman Turkey* (London, 1971).
Mantran, R., *La Vie quotidienne à Constantinople au Temps de Soliman le Magnifique et ses Successeurs* (xvie et xviie Siècles) (Paris).
Mantran, R., *Istanbul dans la Seconde Moitié du xviie Siecle Essai d'Histoire institutionelle, economique et sociale* (Paris, 1962).
Shaw, Stanford, *History of the Ottoman Empire and Modern Turkey*, two vols (Cambridge, 1976).

General Art Studies
Atil, Esin (ed.), *Turkish Art* (Washington, Smithsonian Institution, 1980).
Petsopoulous, Ianni (ed.), *Tulips Arabesques and Turbans, Decorative Arts from the Ottoman Empire* (London, 1982).

Paintings – Studies and Catalogues
Atasoy, Nurhan, and Cağman, Filiz, *Turkish Miniature Painting* (Istanbul, 1974).
Cezar, Mustafa, *Sanatta Bati'Ya Açiliş Ve Osman Handi* (Türkiye Iş Bankasi A. Ş. Kültür Yayinlari 109, Istanbul, 1971).
Ipsiroğlu, M. S., *Painting and Culture of the Mongols* (London, 1967).
Stchoukine, Ivan, *La Peinture Turque d'après les Manuscrits illustrés* (i^{re} partie, Paris, 1966; iie partie, Paris, 1971).
Titley, Norah M., *Miniatures from Turkish Manuscripts*, catalogue and subject index of paintings in the British Library and the British Museum (London, 1981).

Textiles
Berker, Nurhayat, *Işlemeler* [Embroideries] (Topkapi Sarayi Müzesi, 6, Istanbul, 1981).
King, Donald, and Goedhuis, Michael *Imperial Ottoman Textiles* (London, 1980).
Victoria and Albert Museum, London, *Brief Guide to Turkish Woven Fabrics* (London, 1950).

Costumes
Aelst, Peter Coeck van, *Moeurs et Fachons de Faire les Turez*

(Antwerp, 1553).

Alexander, William, *Picturesque Representations of the Dress and Manners of the Turks* (London, 1814).

Allom, Thomas, *Character and Costume in Turkey and Italy* (London, 1845).

Altay, Fikret, *Kaftanlar* [Kaftans in the Topkapi Saray Museum] (Istanbul, 1979).

Arif, Pacha, *Les Anciens Costumes de l'Empire Ottoman depuis l'Origine de la Monarchie jusqu'à la Reforme du Sultan Mahmoud* (Paris, 1863).

Arnold, Janet, 'The Pattern of a Caftan Said to Have Been Worn by Selim I (1512–20) from the Topkapi Sarayi Museum', *Costume*, Journal of the Costume Society, no. 2 (1968), pp. 49–52.

Bruyn, Cornelius Le, *A Voyage to the Levant* (London, 1702).

Dalvimart, Octavian, *The Costume of Turkey* (London, 1802).

Dupré, Louis, *Voyage à Athènes et à Constantinople ou Collection de Portraits Vues et Costumes Grecs et Ottomans* (Paris, 1825).

Ferriol, de, 'Recueil de Cent Estampes Réprésentant Differentes Nations du Levant, tirées sur les Tableaux peints d'après Nature en 1707 et 1708 par les Ordres de M. de Ferriol Ambassadeur du Roi à la Porte, et gravées en 1712 et 1713 pars les soins de M. Le Hay' (Paris, 1714).

Garnett, Lucy, *The Women of Turkey and their Folklore*, two vols (London, 1890–91).

Gervers, Veronika, 'The Vanishing Cloaks of Afyon: Textile Treasures from Turkey and the Balkans', *Rotunda*, no. 6, (3) pp. 4–15.

Haidar, Muzbah, *Arabesque* (London, 1944).

Halsband, Robert, *The Complete Letters of Lady Mary Wortley Montagu*, three vols (Oxford, 1965–7).

Hamdy Bey, S-E., Osman and Launay, Marie de, *Les Costumes populaires de la Turquie en 1873, Ouvrage publiée sous le Patronat de la Commission Imperiale Ottomane pour l'Exposition universelle de Vienne* (Constantinople, 1873).

Karabacek, Josef von, 'Abendländische Künstler zu Konstantinopel im xv and xvi Jahrhundert', pp. 67–89. Der Hennin. *Wien Philosophisch-Historische Klasse Denkschriften*, 62, Band i, Abhandlung (1918).

Kurz, Otto, 'The Turkish Dresses in the Costume-Book of Rubens', in Otto Kurz, *The Decorative Arts of Europe and the Islamic East, Selected Studies*, xv (London, 1977), pp. 275–90.

Lachaise, *Costumes de l'Empire Turc* (Paris, 1821).

Lorch, Melchior, *Engravings of Turkish Costume, Animals and Buildings, 1570–83*.

Nicolay, Nicholas de, *Les Navigations, Peregrinations et Voyages faites en la Turquie* (Paris, 1576).

Öz, Tahsin, *Turkish Textiles and Velvets xiv–xvi Centuries* (Ankara, 1950).

Pardoe, Julia, *The City of the Sultan and Domestic Manners of the Turks in 1836*, two vols (London, 1837).

Penzer, N. M., *The Harem* (London, 1936).

Preziosi, Amadeo, *Stamboul Moeurs et Costumes* (Paris, 1883).

Ribeiro, Aileen, 'Turquerie, Turkish Dress and English Fashion in the Eighteenth Century', *Connoisseur*, vol. 201, no. 807 (1979), pp. 16–23.

Scarce, Jennifer M., 'Turkish Fashion in Transition', *Costume*, Journal of the Costume Society, no. 14 (1980), pp. 144–67.

Tuchelt, Klaus, *Türkische Gewänder und Osmanische Gesellschaft im Jahrhundert* (Graz, 1966).

Tugay, Emine Foat, *Three Centuries – Family Chronicles of Turkey and Egypt* (London, 1963).

White, Charles, *Three Years in Constantinople or Domestic Manners of the Turks*, three vols (London, 1844).

The Ottomans Abroad – South-East Europe

Historical and Cultural Background

Beldiceanu, N., *Le Monde Ottoman des Balkans (1402–1566) Institutions, Société, Economie* (London, 1976).

Stavrianos, S., *The Balkans Since 1453* (New York, 1958).

Sugar, P. F., *Southeastern Europe under Ottoman Rule 1354–1804* (Seattle and London, 1977).

Costumes

L'Art Albanais à travers les Siècles (Paris, Petit Palais, Decembre 1974–Février 1975).

Banateanu, T., Focsa, G., and Ionescu, E., *Folk Costumes, Woven Textiles and Embroideries of Rumania* (Bucharest, 1968).

Broughton, J. C. H., *Travels in Albania and Other Provinces of Turkey*, two vols (1855).

Čulič, Z., *Narodne Nosnje V Bosni I Hercegovini* [Costumes Nationaux de Bosnie-Herzegovine] (Sarajevo, 1963).

Drăgut, V., Florea, V., Grigorescu, D., and Mihalache, M., *Romanian Painting* (Bucharest, 1977).

Gervers, Veronika, 'The Historical Components of Regional Costume in South Eastern Europe', *Textile Museum Journal*, vol. 4, no. 2 (1975), pp. 61, 78.

Gervers, Veronika, 'A Nomadic Mantle in Europe', *Textile History*, vol. 9 (1978), pp. 9–34.

Gervers, Veronika, *The Influence of Ottoman Turkish Textiles and Costumes in Eastern Europe* (Toronto, Royal Ontario Museum, 1982).

Gervers-Molnar, Veronika, *The Hungarian Szür, an Archaic Mantle of Eurasian Origin* (Toronto, Royal Ontario Museum, 1973).

Hadzimichali, A., *Hellenic National Costumes*, two vols (Athens, Benaki Museum, 1948).

Malita, M., Bănăteanu, T., and Zlotea, E., *Romania from the Thesaurus of the Traditional Popular Costume* (Bucharest, 1977).

Nicolescu, Corina, *Costumul de Curte în Țările Române* [sec. xiv–xviii] [Le Costume de Cour dans les Pays Roumains] (Bucharest, 1970).

Nicolescu, Corina, *Istoria Costumului de Curte în Țarile Române, Secolele xiv–xviii* [The History of Romanian Court Costume 14th–18th Century] (Bucharest, 1970).

Popescu-Vîlcea, G., *Erotocritul Logofătului Petrache* (Bucharest, 1977).

Start, L. E., and Durham, E. M., *The Durham Collection of Garments and Embroideries from Albania and Yugoslavia* (Halifax, Bankfield Museum, 1939).

Vlahović, Mitar, and Radović, Bosiljka, *Popular Costumes of the xixth Century in Beograd* (Beograd, Ethnographical Museum of Beograd, 1958).

The Ottomans Abroad – the Arab World

Pharaonic and Coptic Egypt

Baginski, Alisa and Tidhar, Amalia, *Textiles from Egypt 4th–13th*

Centuries C.E. (Jerusalem, L. A. Mayer Memorial Institute for Islamic Art, 1980).

Bourguet, Pierre Du, *Les Etoffes Coptes du Musée du Louvre* (Paris, 1964).

Hall, Rosalind, 'A Mohair Dress in the Petrie Museum', *Göttinger Miszellen*, 41 (1980), pp. 51–8.

Hall, Rosalind, 'Two Linen Dresses from the Fifth Dynasty Site of Deshasheh now in the Petrie Museum of Egyptian Archaeology, University College London', *Journal of Egyptian Archaeology*, vol. 67 (1981), pp. 168–71.

Hall, Rosalind, 'Fishing-Net [ízdt] Dresses in the Petrie Museum', *Göttinger Miszellen*, 42 (1981), pp. 37–43.

Hall, Rosalind, 'Garments in the Petrie Museum of Egyptian Archaeology', *Textile History*, vol. 13, no. 1 (1982), pp. 27–45.

Kendrick, A. F., *Catalogue of Textiles from Burying-Grounds in Egypt*, three vols (London, Victoria and Albert Museum, 1920).

Thompson, Deborah, *Coptic Textiles in the Brooklyn Museum* (New York, The Brooklyn Museum, 1971).

Trilling, James, 'The Roman Heritage. Textiles from Egypt and the Eastern Mediterranean AD 300 to 600', *Textile Museum Journal*, vol. 21 (1982).

Costumes and Textiles

Ahmad, Ahmad 'Abd Al-Raziq, *La Femme au Temps des Mamlouks en Égypte* (Cairo, Institut Français d'Archeologie Orientale, 1973).

Arie, R., 'Notes sur le Costume en Égypte dans la Première Moitié du xixᵉ Siècle, *Revue des Études Islamiques*, 36 (1968), pp. 201–13.

Britton, Nancy P., *A Study of Some Early Islamic Textiles in the Museum of Fine Arts Boston* (Boston, 1938).

Chennells, Ellen, *Recollections of an Egyptian Princess by her English Governess* (Edinburgh and London, 1893).

Ettinghausen, Richard, *Arab Painting* (Geneva, 1962).

Grey, Hon. Mrs William, *Journal of a Visit to Egypt, Constantinople, the Crimea, Greece etc. in the Suite of the Prince and Princess of Wales* (London, 1869).

Kendrick, A. F., *Catalogue of Muhammadan Textiles of the Medieval Period* (London, Victoria and Albert Museum, 1924).

Kühnel, Ernst, and Bellinger, Louise, *Catalogue of Dated Tiraz Fabrics* (Washington, The Textile Museum, 1952).

Lane, Edward William, *The Manners and Customs of the Modern Egyptians* (London, 1860).

Lotti, Emmeline, *The Governess in Egypt, Harem Life in Egypt and Constantinople*, two vols (London, 1865).

Mayer, L. A., *Mamluk Costume A Survey* (Geneva, 1952).

Preziosi, Amadeo, *Le Caire Moeurs et Costumes* (Paris, 1880).

Stillman, Yedida K., 'The Importance of the Cairo Geniza Manuscripts for the History of Medieval Female Attire', *International Journal of Middle Eastern Studies*, 7 (1976), pp. 579–89.

Stillman, Yedida K., 'New Data on Islamic Textiles from the Geniza', *Textile History*, vol. 10 (1979), pp. 184–95.

Close and Distant Neighbours – Persia and Afghanistan

Historical and Cultural Background

The Cambridge History of Iran, Vol. 1, W. B. Fisher (ed.), *The Land of Iran* (Cambridge, 1968). Vol. 4, R. N. Frye (ed.), *From the Arab Invasion to the Saljuqs* (Cambridge, 1975). Vol. 5, J. A. Boyle (ed.), *The Saljuq and Mongol Periods* (Cambridge, 1968).

Piemontese, Angelo, 'The Photographic Album of the Italian Diplomatic Mission to Persia (Summer 1862)', *East and West*, new series, vol. 22, nos. 3–4 (Sept–Dec 1972), pp. 249–311.

Scarce, Jennifer M., *Isfahan in Camera – 19th Century Persia through the Photographs of Ernst Hoeltzer* (London, AARP [Art and Archaeology Research Papers], 1976).

Paintings – Studies and Catalogues

Falk, S. J., *Qajar Paintings – Persian Oil Paintings of the 18th and 19th Centuries* (London, 1972).

Gray, Basil, *Persian Painting* (Geneva, 1961).

Robinson, B. W., *A Descriptive Catalogue of the Paintings in the Bodleian Library* (Oxford, 1958).

Robinson, B. W., 'The Court Painters of Fath Ali Shah', *Eretz Israel*, 7, L.A. Memorial Volume (1963), pp. 94–105.

Robinson, B. W. *Persian Miniature Paintings from Collections in the British Isles* (London, Victoria and Albert Museum, 1967).

Robinson, B. W., *Persian Paintings in the India Office Library* (London, 1976).

Robinson, B. W., *Persian Paintings in the John Rylands Library* (London, 1980).

Stchoukine, Ivan, *La Peinture Iranienne sous les Derniers Abbasides et les Il-Khans* (Bruges, 1936).

Stchoukine, Ivan, *Les Peintures des Manuscrits Timûrides* (Paris, 1954).

Stchoukine, Ivan, *Les Peintures des Manuscrits Safavis de 1502 à 1587* (Paris, 1959).

Stchoukine, Ivan, *Les Peintures des Manuscrits de Shah Abbas I à la Fin des Safavis* (Paris, 1964).

Titley, Norah M., *Miniatures from Persian Manuscripts Catalogue and Subject Index of Paintings from Persia, India and Turkey in the British Library and the British Museum* (London, 1977).

Welch, Stuart Cary, *Wonders of the Age Masterpieces of Early Safavid Painting 1501–1576* (Harvard University, Fogg Art Museum, 1979).

Textiles

Gluck, Jay, and Hiramoto, Sumi (eds), *A Survey of Persian Handicrafts* (Tehran, 1977).

Murdoch Smith, Robert, *Persian Art* (London, 1876).

Reath, Nancy A., and Sachs, Eleanor B., *Persian Textiles and their Technique from the Sixth to the Eighteenth Centuries, including a System for General Textile Classification* (New Haven, 1937).

Pope, Arthur Upham (ed.), *A Survey of Persian Art*, Vols III and VI (Oxford, 1938).

Victoria and Albert Museum, London, *Brief Guide to Persian Woven Fabrics* (London, 1950).

Victoria and Albert Museum, London, *Brief Guide to Persian Embroideries* (London, 1950).

Wulff, Hans E., *The Traditional Crafts of Persia* (Cambridge, Massachusetts, 1966).

Costumes – Persia

Allemagne, Henry-René D', *Du Khorassan au Pays des Bakhtiaris*, four vols (Paris, 1911).

Allgrove, Joan, *The Quashqa'i of Iran* (Manchester, Whitworth Art Gallery, 1976).

Andrews, Peter and Muğul, *The Turcoman of Iran* (Kendal, Abbot Hall Art Gallery, 1971).

Andrews, Muğul and Peter, *Türkmen Needlework, Dressmaking and Embroidery among the Türkmen of Iran* (London, Central Asian Research Centre, 1976).

Binning, Robert B. M., *A Journal of Two Years Travel in Persia, Ceylon etc.*, two vols (London, 1857).

Bishop, Isabella Bird, *Journeys in Persia and Kurdistan*, two vols (London, 1891).

Chardin, Sir John, *Travels in Persia* [N. M. Penzer (ed.) from the 1720 English translation] (London, 1927).

Colliver Rice, C., *Persian Women and their Ways* (London, 1923).

Drouville, Gaspard, *Voyage en Perse en 1812 et 1813*, two vols (Paris, 1825).

Du Mans, Père Raphael, *Estat de la Perse en 1660* (Paris, 1890).

Feuvrier, Dr J., *Truis Ans à la Cour de Perse – 1889–92* (Paris, 1895).

Firouz, Iran Ala, *Silver Ornaments of the Turkoman* (Tehran, The Hamdani Foundation, 1978).

Fraser, James Baillie, *Travels and Adventures in the Persian Provinces on the Southern Banks of the Caspian Sea* (London, 1826).

Gervers, Veronika, 'Construction of Türkmen Coats', *Textile History*, vol. 14, no. 1 (1983), pp. 3–27.

Gonzales De Clavijo, Ruy, *Narrative of the Embassy of Ruy Gonzales De Clavijo to the Court of Timour at Samarcand 1403–06* (London, Hakluyt Society, 1859).

Hansen, Henny Harald, *The Kurdish Woman's Life* (Copenhagen, National Museum, 1961).

Housego, J., 'Honour Is According to Habit. Persian Dress in the Sixteenth and Seventeenth Centuries', *Apollo*, vol. 93, no. 109 (1971), pp. 204–9.

Hume-Griffith, M. E., *Behind the Veil in Persia and Turkish Arabia* (London, 1909).

Layard, Henry, *Early Adventures in Persia, Susiana and Babylonia, including a Residence among the Bakhtiyari and Other Wild Tribes before the Discovery of Nineveh*, two vols (London, 1887).

Ouseley, Sir William, *Travels in Various Countries of the East: More Particularly Persia*, three vols (London, 1819–23).

Porter, Sir Robert Ker, *Travels in Georgia, Persia, Armenia, Ancient Babylonia . . . During the Years 1817, 1818, 1819 and 1820*, two vols (London, 1821–22).

Rich, Claudius J., *Narrative of a Residence in Koordistan, and on the Site of Ancient Nineveh; with Journal of a Voyage down the Tigris to Baghdad and an Account of a Visit to Shirauz and Persepolis*, two vols (London, 1836).

Rosen, Countess Maud von, *Persian Pilgrimage* (London, 1937).

Scarce, Jennifer M., 'The Development of Women's Veils in Persia and Afghanistan', *Costume*, Journal of the Costume Society, no. 9 (1975), pp. 4–14.

Scarce, Jennifer M., *A Persian Brassière* (AARP [Art and Archaeology Research Papers], no. 7, 1975), pp. 15–21.

Scarce, Jennifer M., *Middle Eastern Costume from the Tribes and Cities of Iran and Turkey* (Edinburgh, The Royal Museum of Scotland, 1981).

Sheil, Lady, *Glimpses of Life and Manners in Persia* (London, 1856).

Stackelberg, Comte Ernest, *Scènes Paysages Moeurs et Costumes du Caucase. Dessinés d'après Nature par le Prince Grègoire gagarine et accompagnes d'un Texte explicatif par le Comte Ernest Stackelberg* (Paris, 1845).

Sykes, Ella C., *Through Persia on a Sidesaddle* (London, 1898, second edition 1901).

Sykes, Ella C., *Persia and its People* (London, 1910).

Welch, Anthony, *Shah Abbas and the Arts of Isfahan* (New York, Asia House Gallery, 11 October, 2 December, 1973; Asia Society, 1973).

Wills, C. J., *In the Land of the Lion and Sun or Modern Persia, Being Experiences of Life in Persia from 1866 to 1881* (London, 1891).

Costumes – Afghanistan

Atkinson, James E. I. C., *The Expedition into Afghanistan: Notes and Sketches Descriptive of the Country* (London, 1842).

Elphinstone, Hon. Mountstuart E. I. C., *An Account of the Kingdom of Caubul and its Dependencies in Persia, Tartary, and India, Comprising a View of the Afghaun Nation and a History of the Doorhaunee Monarchy* (London, 1815).

Hart, Captain Lockyer Willis, *Character and Costumes of Afghanistan* (London, 1843).

Rattray, James, *The Costumes of the Various Tribes, Portraits of Ladies of Rank, Celebrated Princes and Chiefs, Views of the Principal Fortresses, and Interior of the Cities and Temples of Afghaunistan* (London, 1848).